Editor
Julia Lee

Art Editor
Alexandra Bourdelon

Consultant Editor
Mark Rasmussen

Advertisement Manager
Jay Jones

Senior Sales Executive
Rachel Neave

Production
Paul Lincoln

Publisher
Clive Birch

Illustrations supplied by
Mark Rasmussen

Published by
IPC Media,
Leon House, 233
High Street,
Croydon CR9 1HZ

Distributed to the newstrade by
MarketForce, London.
Blue Fin Building,
110 Southwark Street,
London SE1 0SU
Tel: 020 7633 3300

Distributed to the book trade by
BookSource, Glasgow.
Tel: 0845 370 0067.
ipc@booksource.net
Tel 01202 665432

Printed by
Positive Images UK,
44 Wates Way, Mitcham,
Surrey

© IPC Media Ltd 2010

All Rights reserved

While every care has been taken in compiling this guide, the Publishers do not accept any responsibility for errors and omissions and their consequences.

SPECIAL FEATURES

The year in coins: market trends
Commemorative coins

RIGHT: This Charles II crown sold for £8,200 at a Dix Noonan Webb auction earlier this year

LATEST MARKET PRICES

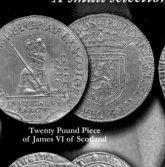

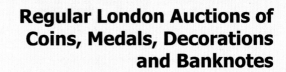

THE YEAR IN COINS

Find out what were the biggest sellers at auctions held over the last 12 months, and the current state of the British market

ABOVE: Charles I 1642 Oxford Triple Unite, sold by St James'

The last year has been another extraordinary one for British coins. The season was characterised by some challenging external conditions, such as the general election in May and economic uncertainty, yet the market position for British coins remains a firm one.

It has now been a consistently strong market for well over a decade and though some series experience temporary lows, few prices have fallen significantly and coin values have been steadily appreciating since the gloom of the 1990s.

This year has seen a decent cross-section of material which, combined with unprecedented levels of demand, has lifted coin values in general by an average of 10% or so. High quality material and the most desirable series have registered significant rises, while mainstream material in the lower grades has seen more marginal gains.

Collector-driven growth in a narrow market explains the enduring strength of the British coin market. A large influx of new buyers contributes to the increase in demand. Price levels are attractive but not spectacular compared to the highs of the 1960s and 1970s. Collectors, spurred on by the rising market, are prepared to pay more for their coins but not hugely so, and supply remains tight. These trends are therefore unlikely to change.

COINEX SALES

The season began in September with the Coinex week of sales. First was Baldwin's, which offered a broad selection of British material, including a straightforward run of late Saxon pennies. An Edward the Confessor Pax/small cross type penny mule of Lincoln sold for £1,000, well above its estimate of £600-800.

Meanwhile in Germany, Künker auction 159 contained a small good group of early to late Saxon pennies. A very pleasing Viking 'Orsnaforda' type penny in VF fetched €3,600 and an attractive VF portrait penny of Aethelberht realised €2,600.

Dix Noonan Webb's Auction 83 featured 675 middle-ranking British milled coins. The cover coin, a rare 1841 Victoria halfcrown, which was lightly marked but EF, sold for £3,700, nearly 50% above its top estimate. The sale also contained two important new finds. An unpublished variety of the extremely rare Viking 'sword/hammer' type penny of Sihtric, found in Nottinghamshire in 2005, good VF but perforated in parts, achieved the robust price of £7,500. A unique cut halfpenny of Stephen, tentatively catalogued as an issue of William Cumin as Bishop of Durham, found in Northumbria in 2009 and in unusually good metal, was fought up to £3,600.

The highlight of Spink's October sale was a new example of the extremely rare 'Benutigo' type thrymsa. It comfortably sold for an impressive £10,000 against an estimate of £4,000-5,000.

AUTUMN SALES

In November, St James's Auction 12 featured an attractive range of hammered and milled coins, together with an almost complete date-run of Commonwealth unites from a private collection. Such runs are unusual and the group sold extremely strongly; one of the highest prices was £11,500 for an almost EF 1657 unite. The star lot, however, was a Charles I 1642 Oxford triple unite, from the famous Montagu sale in 1896. In EF condition and struck on a large round flan, it is not an exceptional piece but highly desirable, and was successfully secured for £96,000 by a determined phone-bidder. This is a British record price for a currency triple unite.

The same month, Noble Numismatics offered the Cornwall collection of British hammered and milled silver crowns in Sydney. Formed mainly in the 1970s and 1980s, the group was extensive but predominantly of middling grade. An almost VF Commonwealth crown with the extremely rare date of 1649 was fought up to AUS$16,000 (£9,800) by two keen collectors, while a 1663 Crown, nicely toned and almost EF, so well above the average condition for this difficult early series, quixotically only fetched AU$5,000 (£3,000).

Spink's autumn auction contained a decent compact group of Saxon and Norman pennies. As many pieces were prettily toned and in high-grade, prices ruled consistently high. A practically as-struck Edward the Confessor expanding cross penny of London, from the Duke of Argyll collection, was £1,300. The sale also included a small parcel of hammered gold which all sold strongly. An Elizabeth I half-pound, almost EF though lightly burnished, fetched £15,000. Another popular Elizabethan 'type' coin, an eight testerns of 1600, slightly double-struck and almost VF, made £14,000. A previously unrecorded specimen of the deceptively rare Henry VI restored half-angel, though a recent find, smashed the record of £9,250 to sell for £21,000.

In December, Morton & Eden offered the balance of the Brackley Hoard of silver groats, discovered in 2005, in 87 lots. Dating from 1351-1465, they were in collectable grade, and as new hoards are rarely released to the market, it generated widespread interest. Despite much duplication, common varieties still achieved an average of £150. High prices were realised for the rare individual pieces, including an Edward IV heavy coinage groat, good VF with a detailed portrait. This achieved £1,500. The highlight of the sale was a crisply struck and extremely full Edward III Calais Treaty noble. Not rare in real terms – the current VF value is about £1,900 – the realisation price of £5,800 indicates the demand for quality early gold coins.

A fortnight later, Davisson's Auction 28 had two classic rarities from the English silver series; a Charles I 1642 Rawlins' Oxford pound and a Cromwell 1658 pattern sixpence. The Rawlins' pound, in good VF, is believed to be the finest known example. It sold for £23,500 as recently as 2009 and now realised £33,700.

The Cromwell pattern sixpence, though slightly tooled in the reverse field but in EF and also highly desirable, likewise has an impressive pedigree and fetched £6,100.

NEW YEAR SALES

The season resumed in earnest in January with the traditional run of US sales.

Gemini's sale IV achieved the remarkable price of £14,900, for an EF Alfred the Great 'Londonia' portrait penny. The market for the Anglo-Saxon series is worldwide so it is likely 'recognition factor' contributed to the realisation price.

Heritage Auction 3008 presented the best range of British material in a strong general sale of nearly 600 lots. Very high prices were realised for coins of unusual quality. A George II 1738 Half Guinea, practically as-struck, fetched $11,750 (£7,500) and an extremely fine William and Mary 1693 two guineas reached an impressive $29,900 (£18,500).

ABOVE: Edward the Confessor expanding cross type penny, sold by Spink

Most remarkably, an 1847 Victoria young head crown in mint state went for a staggering $12,650 (£7,800).

Meanwhile, Stack's sale featured a small selection of British coins. The two most valuable pieces were a lightly hair-lined but pleasing George III 1820 pattern two pounds and an extremely rare George IV 1825 uniface pattern five pounds. The former reached its top estimate at $32,200 (£20,000) and the latter fetched $34,500 (£21,500).

Nihon Coin Auction 22, held in Tokyo at the beginning of March, contained a superb selection of Victorian large milled silver. An extremely rare 1839 Victoria Pattern 'Una and the Lion' crown by William Wyon struck in silver had the added distinction of coming from the famous 1974 Douglas-Morris collection, where it had realised £3,400. It now advanced to £40,000. A similar piece struck in copper went for £33,000,

A large component of Künker's March Auction 165 was devoted to the 'Kiwi' Collection of 181 Irish coins. The most expensive lot was from the emergency issues of the Great Rebellion. A very rare Charles I 'Inchiquin' crown in VF sold for €6,500.

The *Spink Numismatic Circular* in March 2010 was a very strong issue, containing an important collection of 23 siege coins of the English civil war of Charles I, notably two Carlisle siege pieces – a 1645 three shillings and a 1645 shilling. The former, with the highly desirable Bridgewater House provenance, is extremely rare; there are possibly only 10 specimens in private hands. The group attracted widespread interest and both key pieces found an appreciative buyer.

The same month, DNW Auction 85 offered an extremely rare cross-moline type Matilda penny of

Oxford. Though chipped and creased, it fetched £4,600, and a Charles II 1662 crown, in almost EF condition but possibly cleaned, realised £4,700. The bulk of the British section comprised a deep selection of hammered silver coins in generally reasonable grade. Prices were robust, especially for high grade or prettier pieces. An almost VF silver crown of Elizabeth I with the scarce mint-mark 2 went for £9,000. Most remarkable was a fair grade specimen of an extremely rare Philip and Mary 1554 shilling, with the date below busts. This type is notoriously difficult to obtain and is always in poor condition. There are probably only half a dozen specimens in private hands. It now set the fortunate collector back by £4,900.

March also saw the launch of another auction house, TimeLine Auctions. Their inaugural sale contained a mix of British material. The highest price was £3,400 for a VF Wulfred monogram type penny. By contrast, a Mary penny – always a tough coin to find – went largely unappreciated at £1,150, perhaps on account of its poor condition.

Spink's spring sale featured a small collection of British crowns. Perhaps the pick was an almost EF James I second coinage crown from the famous Norweb collection. It was acquired by an internet bidder at £8,300. By contrast, a once-cleaned 1817 George III pattern 'Three Graces' crown by William Wyon sold for a lowly £7,500. A Charles I Pontefract shilling 1648, in good VF and struck on a full lozenge-shaped flan, realised £6,500.

An unusual feature of Heritage Auction 3009 was a parcel of 22 pieces from Curedale Hoard of 1840 – 19 Viking Cunnetti-type pennies and three Carolingian deniers of Charles the Bald. Offered as one lot with an estimate of $25,000-$30,000, the group realised $14,300 (£9,000).

At the beginning of May, Baldwin's presented a two-day sale which included two classic rarities from the pattern and proof series. The first, an FDC 1817 George III pattern 'INCORRUPTA' crown by William Wyon, realised an impressive £22,000 only to be outdone by a good EF 1817 George III pattern 'Three Graces' crown at £25,000.

St James's Auction 13 showcased a well-balanced selection from Celtic through to the 20th century,

ABOVE: Edward III Calais treaty noble, sold by Morton & Eden

ABOVE: Philip and Mary 1554 shilling, with date below bust, sold by Dix Noonan Webb

featuring some very choice pieces. An EF Henry VI pinecone-mascle issue noble achieved £8,500. An attractive Edward VI third period sovereign sold for £29,000. An EF Cromwell 1656 broad realised £20,000 and a Victoria 1860 almost uncirculated copper penny sold for £3,600. There was the usual run of sovereigns including a proof-like 1820 George III which sold for £5,000 and a Victoria 1859 'Ansell' variety, in almost mint state for £8,000.

Goldberg's Auction 59 contained high-grade English milled silver and a fine run of gold coins. There were some spectacular prices. A superb 1656 Cromwell broad sold for $60,000 (£41,400) and George II 1746 LIMA crown in almost as struck condition attained a whopping $12,500 (£8,600).

Elsewhere, Astarte in Switzerland offered 10 lots of British coins. Devoid of provenance, this tiny erratic mix contained a number of significant pieces. A slightly creased but EF Anlaf Sihtricsson triquetra/standard type penny fetched an impressive CHF19,000 (£11,300).

A few days later DNW Auction 86 featured an extremely rare Patrick Earl of Salisbury penny, one of five known examples sold for £9,000. A practically as struck William and Mary halfcrown 1689 sold for £1,850. A remarkable price was for a brilliant George II 1746 proof set. Offered individually but obviously a matching set, it sold for a combined price of £21,000!

Spink's June auction 203 offered an excellent selection of high quality British material including many significant and rare pieces. Lot one was an extremely rare Eadbald thrymsa, struck at London. An important piece – the first known gold coin in the name of an English king – attracted worldwide

interest. Discovered in Kent in 2010, it is the seventh known specimen and sold for a record price of £26,000. Prices for this fascinating Anglo-Saxon series have been subdued for years so it is encouraging to see this market strengthen again.

There was also a good quality run of hammered gold, featuring a number of rarities, many with good provenances; it offered many useful price comparisons. The star of the sale was an EF but perforated Richard III type III London angel. It realised £27,000. A good VF James I third coinage rose-ryal sold for £20,000; nearly 30% above its top estimate. In contrast, a badly clipped and almost VF light coinage quarter-noble of Henry IV, a deceptively rare denomination, was sold for a reasonable £2,300, and an unusually good example of a Henry VII tentative issue groat, good VF and on a very full flan, was well-priced at £1,300.

The final sale of the season, Heritage Auction 3010, held in Boston in August, had a small group of British coins in all metals. A Charles I 1644 OXON triple unite apparently removed from a mount fetched a huge $103,500 (£66,300) and an EF William III 1701 'fine work' five guineas sold well at $32,200 (£21,000). In contrast, a William IV proof 1831 crown with light surface scuffing realised a relatively conservative $13,800 (£8,800).

A good run of Victorian copper and silver coins in high grade attracted commensurate prices. An uncirculated 1856 Victoria penny sold for $2,990 (£1,900). The strong demand in the US for the 'perfect coin' is clearly illustrated by the huge price of $9,775 (£6,300) attained for an 1870 Victoria florin, compared to a UK average of about £1,000.

DEALERS' LISTS

A pleasing feature of the 2009-10 season has been the material available from dealers' price lists.

The highlight of Mark Rasmussen's winter list was an unusual group of proof/trial coins struck in gold, comprising 1935 proof crown, 1927 specimen halfcrown, 1922 proof florin and 1924 specimen sixpence. They were sold with the same coins in silver for more than £80,000. His next list offered a Henry VI London rosette-annulet issue quarter-noble, one of only two examples known. Priced at £4,250, it attracted multiple orders.

ABOVE: Wulfred monogram type penny, sold by TimeLine

Roddy Richardson's New Year List 2010 featured a number of very good coins, for example an Elizabeth I crown with the scarce mint-mark 2, on offer at £15,500. It also included one of the finest known Charles II first hammered issue halfcrowns at £25,000. His summer list 2010 contained the Lockett Henry VIII third coinage testoon. It had a slight striking crack but was VF with an unusually strong portrait and priced at £11,500. Also on offer was a Charles I Silver Shrewsbury Pound 1642, from the Murdoch collection, at £32,500.

Baldwin's winter list was rich with British material, the highlights being an exceedingly rare 1661 Charles II pattern crown in gold and an extremely rare 1818 George III pattern crown. They were respectively priced at £85,000 and £25,000. Their summer list offered two important gold rarities – a Charles I Oxford 1643 triple unite at £89,000 and an 1813 George III pattern guinea by Thomas Wyon at £20,000.

CELTIC

The Celtic market is generally subdued as it does not attract the high-ranking collector like the later

series. A number of collections have been sold and not been replaced by new buyers. However any rarities and gold staters of high quality continue to achieve good prices. The highest price this year was for an extremely rare 'Sego' type gold stater, which sold for £3,200 in DNW Auction 85 in March. Silver and copper denominations are generally popular only in high grade and, like gold, seem undervalued compared to other areas.

HAMMMERED GOLD

British hammered gold continues to be one of the most valuable sectors of the worldwide coin

ABOVE: Henry VI Calais muled noble of annulet/rosette-mascle issues, sold by Morton & Eden

market. This success is drawing out material as there has been a reasonable quantity of good hammered gold on offer this year.

Demand significantly outstrips supply, driving prices steadily upwards. Specifically, the larger denominations in high grade attract the most attention and achieve the headline prices. A spectacular James I third coinage spur-ryal ran far beyond its estimate of $60,000 to realise $82,500 (£54,000). As a result, the prices of ordinary type coins in the more 'accessible' middle grades have risen, and in some cases disproportionately so.

However as a general rule, good hammered gold is still neither expensive nor rare in historic terms. Hammered gold prices have advanced considerably from their lows of the mid 1990s but are still below the levels reached in the 1960s and 1970s booms.

A market success-story has been the resurgence

ABOVE: Catuvellauni 'Sego' type gold stater, sold by Dix Noonan Webb

Solid Wood Case Premium

Pure wood case containing 3 wooden trays with recess to enable easy removal from case. Several different combinations of red inserts, which are compatible with the standard Lindner coin boxes, are available.

Item 2493-1 Wood Case & 3 trays, 1 each 48, 25 & 20 compartments

Price £53.40

Item 2493-1

Südafrika
Krugerrand
1 oz Fine Gold
1974

REBECK L Coin Holders

Self adhesive coin holders with extra space for writing on. Can be used in landscape or portrait format. Overall size of each coin holder 50mm x 70mm. Packet of 25, available in the following sizes
17.5 mm, 20.0 mm
22.5 mm, 25.0 mm
27.5 mm, 30.0 mm
32.5 mm, 35.0 mm
37.5 mm, 39.5 mm

Price £3.20

REBECK L Coin Holder Storage Cases

Specially made for the Rebeck L coin holders these solid wood boxes, fitted with brass latches, have a detachable lid making scrolling through.

Small box to hold 80-100 coin holders, overall size 295mm x 60mm x 80mm Single compartment with 1 fixed and 1 movable wooden wedge.**Ref RCB1**   **£8.30**

Large box to hold 400-500 coin holders, overall size 235mm x 300mm x 80mm Five compartments supplied with 1 fixed and 5 movable wooden wedges.
Ref RCB2   **£18.80**

of the noble. Their prices were beginning to look inexpensive, but interest has been rekindled. The series has now been significantly re-rated and prices are on the increase for the high-grade pieces. A crisp Edward III Post-Treaty Calais noble fetched £5,200 in Spink's June sale. By contrast, an Edward III Treaty Calais noble in superb condition offered by Heritage in January fetched a very substantial $25,300 (£15,700). The price differential reflects the strong investor base in the US.

The highest price was attained in Morton & Eden's June sale for an extremely rare Henry VI Calais muled noble of annulet/rosette-mascle issues. This is one of only two known specimens. It sold for £28,000.

HAMMERED SILVER

Hammered silver is universally popular, encompassing a broad selection of reigns and types; it appeals to a variety of tastes and budgets.

Prices for good Saxon and Norman pennies have been steadily rising since the late 1990s. Attractive and sound examples, even in the more common types, and strong portrait type coins have registered significant increases in value. Mint-type combinations are widely collected, with the more rare mints generating the most interest. This strengthening appears to be purely collector-driven as opposed to speculative.

A highlight was a previously unrecorded Henry I type VIII penny of Gloucester, in exceptionally fine condition and with an unusually strong portrait, which went for £8,000 in Spink's November auction. A very similar coin, from the London mint and reportedly from the same European source, realised £7,200 in September 2007.

The later hammered series is very competitive. It

ABOVE: Henry I type VIII penny of Gloucester, sold by Spink

attracts many specialist collectors who will collect varieties within their area of interest. Many collectors are seeking to form a collection using a single example in good grade from across the entire range of series. Consequently the values for basic 'type' coins, particularly in exceptional condition, rather than varieties, are continuing to rise and remain firm.

Common but attractive groats in VF or better from the medieval series are now selling at around the £200 mark. Demand is still significant for the more uncommon varieties. A pair of Henry VI unmarked issue groats from the Brackley Hoard, the first slightly double-struck but a strong VF and the second, an honest VF, made £1,100 and £1,200 respectively.

Portrait coins of the Tudors and Stuarts, particularly shillings and sixpences, remain a popular area and highly desirable in high grade. In DNW Auction 85, an exceptionally crisp Elizabeth I third issue sixpence 1564, a relatively common coin, was bid up to £1,050.

Despite the considerable volume of Charles I material which has come on to the market in recent years, prices continue to be robust. An unrecorded Charles I 1643 Rawlins' pound in good VF sold for a solid CHF48,000 (£31,000) at Astarte.

MILLED GOLD

Milled gold has been significantly re-rated in recent years and continues to go from strength to strength. A combination of good material and a strong demand has meant prices have built on the gains made last year.

The best individual result was for a magnificent James II 1688 five guineas which was knocked down in Goldberg's Auction 59 for the princely sum of $92,500 (£63,700).

In common with the rest of the British series, good milled gold still does not look expensive particularly when seen alongside hammered gold equivalents or compared to its last market high of the late 1970s.

This year, there has been a distinct shortage of high grade material prior to George III.

A feature has been the number of George IV 1826 proof five pieces and Victoria 1839 'Una and Lion' £5 pieces being offered for sale. Not great

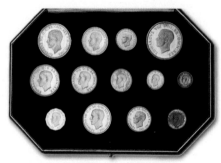

ABOVE: Edward VIII 1937 proof set, sold by Mark Rasmussen

ABOVE: Charles II 1662 crown, sold by Dix Noonan Webb

rarities but aesthetically pleasing, examples sold for approximately £18,500 and £35,000 in Heritage's August sale.

By far the strongest sector continues to be the sovereign series. High bullion prices and plenty of rare and high quality material have generated demand. Key dates and rare varieties are commanding the highest premiums. An 1843 Victoria sovereign, with narrow shield, in almost EF, realised £7,800 in St James's Auction 13 and a rare George V 1917 (London) sovereign, 'about mint state', realised a very substantial £8,500.

The major event of the year was the sale by private treaty of a full Edward VIII 1937 proof set from gold £5 to farthing for £1.35 million by British dealer Mark Rasmussen. This is a world-record price for anything British.

MILLED SILVER

More UK numismatists collect milled silver than any other series. Quality is high on the agenda so EF+ coins, especially with attractive toning, are very desirable. There has been very little material available with demand again overtaking supply.

There are now very few large collections in private hands, especially pre-George III, so the high grade coins that have been sold over the last decade are now spread very thinly.

Currency pieces performed strongly: a proof-like 1658 Cromwell crown fetched a handsome $19,000 (£12,000) in Goldberg's Auction 59 and an EF Charles II 1662 crown was knocked down for £8,200 in DNW Auction 86. The Swiss auction house Astarte Coins and Fine Art sold a mint example of a Charles II 1663 halfcrown for CHF 11,500 (£7,500).

The later milled series (post-George III) is equally buoyant; condition is critical and coins can easily be over-graded. Uncirculated currency pieces command a considerable premium over EF examples and have been scarce in the last twelve months. Rare dates continue to climb in value, especially for the popular denominations.

There have been a number of sales offering proof and pattern coins. Despite the more specialised market, demand is high. An FDC Victoria 1847 'Gothic' crown achieved a remarkable £6,900 at the Nihon Coin Auction and St James's Auction 13 sold a 1951 matt proof set which was split and sold as individual lots; it cumulatively achieved a hammer price of £13,700.

COPPER AND BRONZE

Early copper and tin coins in extremely fine condition have always been very difficult to obtain, so exceptionally lustrous pieces command high prices and by comparison to the gold and silver coins they appear undervalued. Baldwin's Auction 65 offered a William III 1695 farthing, extremely fine and with considerable lustre, which was knocked down at £1,400.

With the exception of the bronze penny market, the values for copper and tin are disproportionately low as the market is biased towards the precious metals and the larger denominations.

The later coinage, from George III to the present, continues to be strong with record prices, particularly the bronze pennies. A considerable number of new varieties have been discovered over the years especially in the Victorian series; many of which are beautifully presented in the special edition of *The Bronze Penny, 1860-1901* by

Coins at Auction

Bonhams incorporating Glendinings has been selling coins and medals at auction since the turn of the last century. Recent results have reflected the current buoyancy of the market, with high prices being achieved for quality items.

ABOVE: William III 1695 farthing, sold by Baldwin's

ABOVE: Edward IV 'Doubles coinage' halfgroat of Drogheda, sold by Spink

Michael Gouby. Publications such as this can only stimulate the market.

The highest price was £19,000, for a fair Victoria 1863 penny, with the rare slender 3, in London Coin Auctions' sale 126 in September.

SCOTTISH

Scottish coins are a very attractive series; they are aesthetically appealing and differ considerably from their English counterparts. There has been a reasonable offering of material and the market remains as buoyant as ever.

ABOVE: James VI 1581 third coinage sixteen shillings, sold by Dix Noonan Webb

The best group was the collection belonging to Roderick Macpherson sold in DNW Auction 83. A rare David I sterling of Roxburgh sold for £1,150. A pretty EF Robert II groat of Edinburgh with B behind bust realised £2,200. A 1553 Mary Queen of Scots first period portrait testoon, a very rare and desirable type fetched £4,500. Also in the sale was an extremely rare James VI 1581 third coinage sixteen shillings, in VF+ with an impeccable pedigree, which sold for £5,200.

Baldwin's winter list contained a modest selection of Scottish gold, including a very rare William II 1701 gold pistole, with a retail price of £15,000.

IRISH

Last year, the Irish series had been very quiet due to an extreme shortage of material. But since the sale of the 'Kiwi collection' by Künker in March all fears of a drop-off have receded.

The collection was a well-balanced representative group, ranging from Ring money to modern Irish coinage, and gave a good picture of market values. A small run of Hiberno-Norse pennies attracted strong prices, notably a rare Phase 3 penny, EF and attractively toned, which realised €1,300. In the medieval series, a slightly chipped but pleasing VF Edward IV Dublin 'crown' coinage groat fetched €3,800. Good Tudor portrait type coins and the emergency issues of Charles I and the Great Rebellion performed well. A good example of an Elizabeth I 'fine coinage' 1561 shilling, almost EF aside from a minor dig on the forehead, was carried up to €2,400. A Charles I 'Dublin' (1649) crown, though weakly struck, sold for a reasonable €5,000 and in the early milled, a pretty EF Charles II St Patrick's coinage farthing realised €5,500.

An exciting addition to the Irish hammered series was an apparently unique Edward IV 'Doubles' coinage halfgroat of Drogheda which was offered in Spink Auction 202. It sold for £4,200.

In the pre-decimal coinage, the highlight was an Irish Republic 1938 pattern penny, which featured in Baldwin's summer list with an asking price of £50,000.

ANGLO-GALLIC

It has been another quiet year for Anglo-Gallic because there have been no significant offerings.

There were a few exceptions. At Spink's June auction a good VF but weakly struck Edward III leopard d'or, fourth issue, sold for £10,000, and an extremely rare Edward the Black Prince pavillion d'or, first issue of Limoges, sold for £8,000.

C⊕incraft

An open letter to Dealers

When a dealer sold us some coins a while ago I asked him why we were not doing more business together, his answer was, that he didn't want to bother us. Hell, we want to be bothered, especially when it comes to business. You will find that Claire, Ian, Barry and myself (Richard) are easy to talk to and we are always interested in buying material. On large lots or collections we are even willing to put up the money for you.

We now have 18 full time and 3 part time staff and we need material to offer our collectors. As the busiest coin firm in the United Kingdom, we now send out 30 different catalogues a year, we need material. Single pieces, hoards, accumulations and of course collections. We buy British and world coins, British and world banknotes, ancient coins and antiquities, medallions, bulk coins and banknotes, in fact almost anything.

Please give us a call and join the many satisfied dealers who do business with Coincraft everyday. We will say yes or no, without messing you around. When we agree a price, we will write you a cheque on the spot. We need you and will treat you right, if you haven't tried us, please do. You will find dealing with Coincraft easy, pleasurable and I hope, profitable.

Richard Lobel
Founder of Coincraft

Call in person at either of our two shops at 44 & 45 Great Russell Street, just across from the British Museum. Open Monday to Friday 9.30 to 5.00 and Saturday from 10.00 till 2.30.

Friendly, personal service and an interesting display of coins, banknotes, medallions, ancient coins and antiquities, to tempt and delight you.

Buy by post through Britain's only coin newspaper, The Phoenix, published every three weeks. It contains 24 tabloid sized pages of special offers and rare items, many not available anywhere else.

You can't buy a subscription, but you can get a complimentary copy free, just for the asking.

On the Internet Our website, www.coincraft.com is available 24 hours a day. There are many interesting features including a comprehensive numismatic glossary.

Keep looking, more is being added every day.

44 & 45 Great Russell Street, London WC1B 3LU

Nice people to do business with

Tel 020-7636-1188 or 020-7637-8785

Fax 020-7323-2860 or 020-7637-7635

Web www.coincraft.com
Email info@coincraft.com

We always need to buy Coincraft needs to buy: single items to entire collections, dealers inventories, hoards, accumulations, you name it and we will make you an offer. Over 90% of our offers are accepted. Sell where the dealers sell.

Find out why collectors say; Coincraft, nice people to do business with.

COINING IT

Richard West looks at the rise of coins issued to mark special occasions by the Royal Mint

ABOVE: The 1977 crown for the Queen's Silver Jubilee

Most homes have a Churchill Crown tucked away somewhere; back in 1965 the idea of a special coin was novel. They had been produced only on a few occasions: the Silver Jubilee of King George V in 1935, the Festival of Britain in 1951 and the Coronation in 1953.

Today, special coins turn up in loose change, though people might still keep them without really realising why they are special.

Even after the Churchill crown, issues came at lengthy intervals, marking Britain's entry to the European Economic Community in 1973, the Queen's Silver Jubilee in 1977, the Royal Wedding in 1981, and the Commonwealth Games in 1986.

This began to increase in 1989 with two £2 coins, for the Bill of Rights and Claim of Right, and a sovereign that marked the 500th anniversary of the gold sovereign. The following year a £5 coin celebrated the 90th birthday of the Queen Mother. Then in 1992 came a 50p piece to mark the United Kingdom's Presidency of the Council of Ministers and the Single European Market.

But the policy changed in 1993, after Roger Holmes became Deputy Master of the Royal Mint. Writing at the end of his nine-year term he said: 'I believe that we, and other mints overseas, have demonstrated in recent years that the public wants commemorative coins marking a greater diversity of anniversaries and events than was the previous practice.'

The Royal Mint argues that it is responding to the demand to celebrate the history of our nation and at the same time, marking current events of importance.

Is the Royal Mint pushing demand or responding to it? Sales remain buoyant, which suggests the current policy is appreciated. In fact, interest has increased, reflecting a greater interest in history.

Nevertheless, while some mints adopt a fairly aggressive policy, the Royal Mint prefers to be more conservative.

HOW THE THEMES ARE CHOSEN

The process of choosing which events to celebrate in a particular year begins two years earlier.

Departments of the Royal Mint are asked to offer ideas. Separate research is undertaken by the Royal Mint, and there are be discussions with Royal Mail, which also be marks major anniversaries with stamp issues.

The Royal Mint Advisory Committee is consulted, as are a number of Royal Mint customers on both the ideas already being considered and new ideas.

By the spring (18 months before the coins' issue date), the ideas will have been distilled into a 'shortlist'. This will be discussed with focus groups. From these discussions, and using the criteria of commercial viability, historical integrity and national importance, the list will be reduced to three or four themes.

A committee, including some members of the Advisory Committee, makes the final selection. Its recommendations are forwarded to the Chancellor of the Exchequer for approval, and then to the Queen.

FINDING THE DESIGNS

With the choice approved, a brief is prepared for the chosen designers. Designers are often selected for their expertise in specific areas, such as portraiture, and their ability to produce a plaster model. Usually, three or four artists are invited to submit ideas, plus a member of the Royal Mint's own Engraving Department.

A brief is drawn up, which provides the designers with technical information, a timetable, and an explanation of what is required. This often covers what approach to use. For example, in the case of the coin for Florence Nightingale, whether to use a portrait or focus on her work.

ABOVE: The crown to mark the Millennium

Preparing the first ideas takes about six to eight weeks. Each designer is asked to submit two possible designs, although most prepare more. All the designs are considered by the Advisory Committee, which will select two or three for further development.

After any requested amendments have been made, the Committee reaches its final decision; the selected design is forwarded for approval by both the Treasury and the Queen.

A NEW PHASE BEGINS

Although the new Deputy Master did not influence the coins for 1993, the year saw a crown issued to mark the 40th anniversary of the Coronation. This was followed in 1994 by a 50p piece to mark the 50th anniversary of D-Day, and a £2 coin to celebrate the tercentenary of the Bank of England.

The £2 denomination was also used in 1995 for coins to mark the 50th anniversary of the end of the Second World War and the founding of the United Nations.

Two coins appeared in 1996: a crown for the 70th birthday of the Queen, and a £2 European Football Championship coin.

The Golden Wedding in 1997 was, naturally, commemorated – by a £5 coin. For the first time, the coin featured the portrait of a royal consort. After a photo sitting for the Queen and Prince Philip, the obverse was created by Philip Nathan, using the portrait, while the heraldic reverse was designed by Leslie Durbin. The Queen and Prince Philip visited the Royal Mint on May 9 to witness the striking of special gold versions of the crown.

The year also marked the tenth anniversary of the Britannia gold bullion coin, so a new reverse design was commissioned from Nathan.

For 1998 there were three special coins. The 25th anniversary of the entry of the United Kingdom into the European Economic Community and Britain's Presidency of the EU was marked by a 50p coin, while a crown celebrated the 50th birthday of the Prince of Wales in November. Another 50p marked the 50th anniversary of the National Health Service. These used a new portrait of the Queen that had been created by Ian Rank-Broadley.

ABOVE: The gold £5 which marked the Queen Mother's 90th birthday in 1990

ABOVE: The 50p piece to mark the United Kingdom's Presidency of the Council of Ministers and the completion of the Single European Market

ABOVE: The crown which marked the Golden Wedding, in sterling silver, in 1997

The first two were subject to the usual limited invitation competition, but even so, for the EEC coin, the Committee considered

ABOVE: The crown for the centenary of Queen Victoria's death

ABOVE: The 2002 Golden Jubilee reverse

160 drawings. A design by John Mills, which was modelled by Robert Elderton, was selected.

For the Prince of Wales coin, the choice was a design by the painter Michael Noakes, also modelled by Robert Elderton. Three artists were invited to submit ideas for the NHS coin, with David Cornell being selected.

A further three coins appeared in 1999, as a memorial to Diana, Princess of Wales; for the Rugby World Cup and to mark the new Millennium. For the memorial, a design by David Cornell was selected. Medallist Ron Dutton created the Rugby World Cup design, an innovation for the Royal Mint, as the silver piedfort version had the central feature of the reverse design reproduced as a hologram.

THE NEW MILLENNIUM

To mark the new Millennium, a crown featured a map of the United Kingdom, with the hands of a clock pivoted on Greenwich and pointing to 12 o'clock positioned between the years 1999 and 2000. The coin was released in both 1999 and 2000, appropriately dated on the obverse. The design was by stamp designer Jeffery Matthews, who had been runner-up in the competition to design the £2 circulating coin.

The year 2000 saw the 150th anniversary of the Public Libraries Act, for which the 50p coin was designed by Mary Milner Dickens; her design shows the façade of a classical library building and the pages of a book. The year also marked the centenary of the birth of the Queen Mother, celebrated by a crown designed by Ian Rank-Broadley featuring a portrait of the Queen Mother with cheering crowds in the background.

For 2001 two commemorative coins were made: a crown for the centenary of the death of Queen Victoria, and a £2 to celebrate the first long-distance wireless transmission by Guglielmo Marconi. The submitted Marconi designs went into a competition where readers of the *Radio Times* voted on the final choice. It was a close-run decision, but the preferred design was by a member of the Royal Mint Engraving Department, Robert Evans.

A more limited competition continued for the coins for 2002, to mark the Commonwealth Games and for the Golden Jubilee.

In 2003, the Advisory Committee decided to find artists who had not previously been involved in coin and medal design, and upped the number of coins to three. Tom Phillips designed a 50th anniversary of the Coronation crown which had a new portrait of the Queen on the obverse, and a stylised rendering of 'God Save The Queen' on the reverse, a complete departure from normal royal coin celebrations. The other two were a £2 coin for the 50th anniversary of the discovery by Francis Crick and James Watson of DNA and a 50p coin for the centenary of the Women's Social and Political Union.

There were again three commemorative coins in 2004. First was a £2 coin for the 200th anniversary of the first locomotive, built by Richard Trevithick, then a 50p coin for the 50th anniversary of the first four-minute mile, run by Roger Bannister.

The third coin of the year was the crown for the centenary of the Entente Cordiale between Britain and France; it was suggested to the artists that they might use the symbolic figures of La Semeuse and Britannia. The chosen design was by David Gentleman, an accomplished stamp designer,

LEFT: Britannia and La Semeuse, the sower, on the 50p celebrating the Entente Cordiale in 2004

COIN & MEDAL FAIRS LTD

Organisers of the London Coin Fair and Midland Coin Fair

THE LONDON COIN FAIR

**HOLIDAY INN
LONDON, BLOOMSBURY
Coram Street, WC1N 1HT**

Fair dates:
6th November 2010, 5th February 2011,
4th June 2011, 5th November 2011

THE MIDLAND COIN FAIR

**NATIONAL MOTORCYCLE MUSEUM
BICKENHILL, BIRMINGHAM, B92 0EJ**
Opposite the NEC on the M42/A45 junction

Fair dates:
2010: 14th November, 12th December
2011: 9th January, 13th February, 13th March,
10th April, 8th May, 12 June, 10th July,
14th August, 11th September, 9th October,
13th November, 11th December

*For more information please contact: Lu Veissid
Hobsley House, Frodesley, Shrewsbury SY5 7HD
Tel: 01694 731781*

www.coinfairs.co.uk

ABOVE: The 2005 end of World War II coin shows St Paul's amid searchlights

ABOVE: The 2006 £2 showing Isambard Kingdom Brunel in his trademark hat

150th anniversary of the Victoria Cross. Again, they looked at different aspects, one the award itself and the other acts of heroism.

The Diamond Wedding of the Queen and Prince Philip in 2007, like the Golden Wedding, adopted a joint portrait by Ian Rank-Broadley for the obverse, and a depiction of the Rose Window at Westminster Abbey. There were three other coins that year: a 50p piece to mark the centenary of Scouting, the £2 coin for the bicentenary of the Abolition of Slavery and another £2 coin marking the 300th anniversary of the Act of Union between England and Scotland.

UP TO THE OLYMPICS

In the run-up to the London Olympic Games in 2012, the centenary of the 1908 Games in London was marked by a £2 coin in 2008. In the same year, the Prince of Wales celebrated his 60th birthday, and Ian Rank-Broadley designed a crown coin. A crown was also issued for the 450th anniversary of the accession of Queen Elizabeth I.

In 2009 a crown marked the reign of King Henry VIII, with a portrait by John Bergdahl based on the famous painting by Holbein. The year also saw a £2 coin for the bicentenary of the birth of Charles Darwin, and a 50p coin for the 250th anniversary of the Royal Botanic Gardens at Kew.

The commemorative coins in 2010 have included a 50p design, a crown by David Cornell to mark the 350th anniversary of the restoration of the monarchy, and a £2 to mark the centenary of the death of Florence Nightingale.

Now, the attention turns to the exciting and ambitious programme that is builds up to the Olympic Games.

whose design gave equal weight to the two national figures. So well appreciated was the design that the French Mint also adopted it.

The 200th anniversary of the Battle of Trafalgar fell in 2005, and was celebrated with two crown coins, the first marking the death of Nelson, and the second the battle itself. Two different groups of artists were commissioned in each case. Other commemorations for the year were a £2 coin for the 400th anniversary of the Gunpowder Plot and a 50p coin for the 250th anniversary of the publication of Samuel Johnson's *Dictionary of the English Language*, focusing on the meanings of the words 'Fifty' and 'Pence'.

Finally in 2005 there was a £2 coin to mark the 60th anniversary of the end of the Second World War, the reverse design showing St Paul's Cathedral surrounded by searchlights.

Among the special coins for 2006 was a crown for the 80th birthday of the Queen. One of the designs submitted immediately found favour with the Committee, a trumpet fanfare by Polish-born Danuta Solowiej-Wedderburn. The year also continued the practice of having two coins celebrating one event, with two £2 coins marked the 200th anniversary of the birth of Isambard Kingdom Brunel: one focuses on the man and his character, the second on his achievements with a depiction of the roof of Paddington Station. Finally two 50p coins marked the

ABOVE: The joint portrait for the 2007 crown, to mark the Diamond Wedding anniversary

ABOVE: The pagoda at Kew on the coin that marks its 250th anniversary in 2009

ABOVE: A suffragette on the coin marking the Women's Social and Political Union's 100th anniversary

TIPS FOR COLLECTING

If you are new to the hobby, here is some advice to get you started and put you in touch with the experts

HOW MUCH IS IT WORTH?

There was a time when newcomers to coin collecting would ask the question 'What is it?'

Nowadays, the most common question dealers hear is 'What is it worth?'

The aim of *British Coins Market Values* is to try to place a value on all the coins in the British Isles, in other words England, Wales, Scotland and Ireland, the Channel Islands as well as the Anglo-Gallic series and British banknotes.

This is a difficult task because many items do not turn up in auctions or lists every year, even though they are not really rare.

However, we can estimate a figure so that you can have an idea of what you will have to pay.

HOW TO SELL AT AUCTION

Potential sellers have considerable choice when it comes to auction houses.

In London alone there are several: Spink & Son Ltd, A H Baldwin & Sons Ltd, St. James's Auctions, Dix Noonan Webb, Morton & Eden and Bonhams.

There are also smaller companies up and down the country, such as Croydon Coin Auctions and London Coins.

The best approach for the seller is to compare the auction houses' catalogues and if possible attend the auctions so that you can see how well they are conducted.

Talk over your collection with the specialist, for you may have specific cataloguing requirements and you may find that one of the firms will look after your needs better than the others.

A well-known coin requires little expertise and will probably sell at a certain price in most auctions.

However, if you require cataloguing of a specialist collection of a more academic nature, for example early medieval coinages, then you need to know what a company is capable of before you discuss a job rate.

You should remember that, while it is not complicated to sell by auction, and a good auction house will guide you through the process, you may have to wait three or four months from the time you consign the coins to the auctioneers before you receive any money.

There are times when items at auction manage to achieve very high prices, and other times when, for some reason, they fail to reach even a modest reserve.

Finally, auctioneers will usually charge you at least 10% of the knock-down price, and will charge the buyer a premium of up to 17.5% plus VAT.

HOW TO TRADE WITH DEALERS

The British coin market is very much dependent upon and benefits from the support of a strong network of dealers, with their professional numismatic expertise and long experience of the business. Fortunately, the needs of the collector, at any level, are eminently well served by them.

Most offer a large and varied stock of coins for sale at marked prices. All dealers will provide advice and guidance on any aspect of collecting or disposal free of charge. When selling to a dealer, it is true that they generally prefer to obtain fresh material.

A proportion of the dealers also offer to sell on a commission basis. The retail prices are discussed in advance, allowing the collector a degree of control and a far more active role in the dispersal of their collection. Hence, the dealer offers a valuable and unique personal service and it is this relationship which has been responsible for helping to form some of our greatest numismatic collections.

BULLION COINS

Bullion coins can be priced by looking at the price of gold, which is fixed twice daily by a group of leading banks. Most newspapers carry

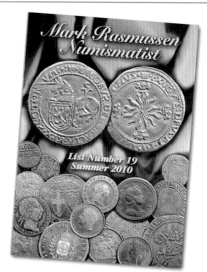

this information in their financial pages.

Anyone can buy bullion coins, such as sovereigns or Krugerrands, and they are not subject to VAT.

Normally, when you sell a bullion coin you expect the coin dealer to make a few pounds profit on each coin.

For mounted or damaged coins do not expect more than their intrinsic value.

HOW TO COLLECT COINS

You should obviously purchase your coins from a reputable dealer or auction house.

You can be sure of some protection if you choose a member of the British Numismatic Trade Association or the International Association of Professional Numismatists.

Membership lists, detailing their main interests, can be obtained from the respective secretaries:

☐ Mrs Rosemary Cooke, PO Box 2, Rye, East Sussex TN31 7WE.
Tel/Fax: 01797 229988. E-mail: bnta@lineone.net
☐ Jean-Luc Van Der Schueren, 14 Rue de la Bourse, B 1000 Brussels, Belgium.
Tel: +32 2 513 3400. Fax: +32 2 513 2528.

However, many are not members of either organisation, and it does not mean that they are not honest and professional. The best approach is simply to find one who will unconditionally guarantee that the coins you buy from him are genuine and accurately graded.

As a general rule, you should only buy coins in the best condition available, normally considered to be Extremely Fine or better. This applies particularly to the milled (post-1600) series, which is more commercial and therefore there is more emphasis on condition.

Hammered coins should be clear, legible and struck in good metal, with Very Fine being perfectly acceptable. One can obtain specimens in higher grade but they are much more difficult to get than their milled counterparts.

Collectors should be prepared that in some series and in the case of great rarities, they might have to make do with a coin that is only Fine or even Poor.

It very much depends on factors such as type, reign and rarity and of course affordability, so be realistic.

It is worth taking out subscriptions with auction houses so that you regularly receive their catalogues, because this is an excellent way to keep up with current market prices and trends, as well as the collections that are being offered. Arguably just as important are dealers' fixed price lists, where coins can be chosen and purchased at leisure by mail order or alternatively from the Internet.

The most famous list is *Spink's Numismatic Circular*, first published in 1892 and still going strong with 6 issues a year.

It is more than a price list, being an important forum for numismatic debate, the reporting of new finds and other useful information (annual subscription £20 in the UK).

A good cross section of other dealers, who produce excellent retail lists, either for mail order or online, in alphabetical order, follows.
☐ A H Baldwin & Sons, 11 Adelphi Terrace, London WC2N 6BJ. Hammered and milled.
☐ Lloyd Bennett, PO Box 2, Monmouth, Gwent NP25 3YR. Hammered, milled, tokens.
☐ Dorset Coin Company, 193 Ashley Road, Parkstone, Poole, Dorset BH14 9DL.
All coins and banknotes.
☐ Format, Unit K, Burlington Court 2nd Floor, 18 Lower Temple Street, Birmingham B2 4JD.
All British.
☐ K B Coins, 50 Lingfield Road, Martins Wood, Stevenage, Hertfordshire SG1 5SL.
Hammered, milled.
☐ Knightsbridge Coins, 43 Duke Street, St James, London SW1Y 6DD. Hammered, milled.
☐ Timothy Millet, PO Box 20851, London SE22 0YN. Medallions.
☐ Simon Monks, Suite 313, St Loyes House, 20 St Loyes Street, Bedford MK40 1ZL. Medallions, tokens, hammered, milled.
☐ Peter Morris, PO Box 223, Bromley, Kent BR1 4EQ. Hammered, milled, tokens.
☐ Spink & Son, 69 Southampton Row,

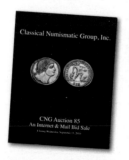

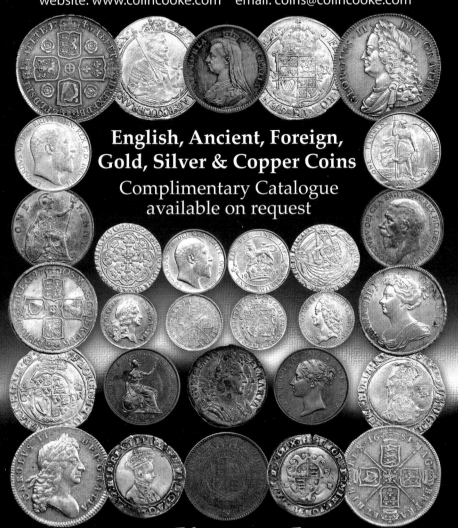

Bloomsbury London WC1B 4ET. Hammered, milled, tokens, medallions.

☐ S R Porter, 18 Trinity Road, Headington Quarry, Oxford OX3 8QL. Hammered and milled.

☐ Studio Coins, 16 Kilham Lane, Winchester, Hampshire S022 5PT. Hammered.

☐ Mark Rasmussen, PO Box 42, Betchworth, Surrey RH3 7YR. Hammered, milled, medallions, tokens.

☐ Roderick Richardson, The Old Granary Antiques Centre, King's Staithe Lane, King's Lynn, Norfolk PE30 1LZ. Hammered and milled.

☐ Chris Rudd, PO Box 222, Aylsham, Norfolk NR11 6TY. Celtic.

☐ Mike Vosper, PO Box 32, Hockwold, Brandon IP26 4HX. Ancient, Celtic, hammered.

☐ Classical Numismatics Group (Seaby Coins), 14 Old Bond Street, London W1X 4JL. Hammered, some milled.

☐ Simmons Gallery, PO Box 104, Leytonstone, London E11 1ND. Medallions, tokens.

SOCIETIES

Consider joining your local numismatic society, of which there are over 50 across the UK. To find if there is one near you, get in touch with the present Secretary of British Association of Numismatic Societies, Phyllis Stoddart.
Tel: 0208 980 5672.
www.coinclubs.freeserve.co.uk

BANS organises annual congresses and seminars, and it is a good idea for the serious collector to consider attending these. Details are published in the numismatic press or available via their website.

Collectors who wish to go further can apply for membership of the British Numismatic Society. The Society holds ten meetings each year at the Warburg Institute, Woburn Square, London, WC1H 0AB, in addition to out-of-town lecture days. As a member, you receive a copy of the *British Numismatic Journal*, which has details of current research, articles and book reviews.

The current Secretary of the BNS is Peter Preston-Morely, c/o The Warburg Institute.
E-mail: secretary@britnumsoc.org

COIN FAIRS

Whilst it is important to visit museums to see coins, it is worth remembering that there is often a fine array on show at coin fairs around the country, and most dealers do not mind showing coins to would-be collectors, even if they cannot afford to buy them on the spot.

The UK's premier international numismatic show, the BNTA Coinex show, is held in late September every year. For more information call the BNTA Secretary, Rosemary Cooke.
Tel: 01797 229988. E-mail: bnta@lineone.net

Mike and Lu Veissid run the London Coin Fairs at the Holiday Inn, Bloomsbury, London. They take place in February, June and November. For all enquiries contact Mike Veissid.
Tel: 01964 731781.

The Croydon team of Davidson and Monk organise regular shows at the Jury's Hotel, Russell Street, London. Tel: 0208 656 4583.
www.lindamonkfairs.co.uk

The monthly Midland Coin and Stamp Fairs are on the second Sunday of every month at the National Motorcycle Museum in Birmingham. For further details, contact Mike Veissid.
Tel: 01694 731781. www.midlandcoinfair.co.uk

The Harrogate Coin Show has recently been revived. The venue for this popular spring event is the Old Swan Hotel, Harrogate. Contact Simon Monks. Tel: 01234 270260.

There are also biannual coin and stamp fairs at York racecourse in January and July coordinated by Kate Puleston and Chris Rainey. Tel: 01793 513431 or 0208 946 4489.
www.stampshows.co.uk

STORING YOUR COINS

Here are some helpful hints, along with some of the best accessories on the market, to help you keep your collection in good condition

ABOVE: One of Peter Nichols' handmade wooden cabinets

S tore coins carefully, as a collection which is carelessly or inadequately housed can suffer irreparable damage.

Water vapour causes corrosion and therefore coins should not be stored in damp attics or spare bedrooms but, where possible, in evenly heated warm rooms.

One must be careful only to pick up coins by the edges, as sweaty fingerprints contain corrosive salt.

WOODEN CABINETS

A collection carefully laid out in a wooden cabinet looks very impressive.

Unfortunately, custom-built wooden cabinets are not cheap.

Their main advantages are the choice of tray and hole sizes but also, more importantly, they are manufactured from untreated well-matured wood, ideally mahogany, which has historically proven to be the perfect material for the long-term storage of coins.

Makers of wooden cabinets include Peter Nichols of St Leonards-on-Sea, East Sussex. Tel: 01424 436682 www.coincabinets.com Another is Rob Davis in Woodville, Derbyshire. Tel: 01332 740828 (evenings).

If you cannot afford a new cabinet, then a second-hand one may be the answer.

These can sometimes be purchased at coin auctions or from dealers but it can be hard to find

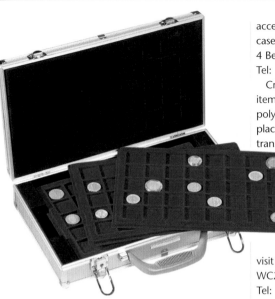

ABOVE: Attaché cases are available from the Duncannon Partnership

accessories, including presentation and carrying cases, is available from the Duncannon Partnership, 4 Beaufort Road, Reigate, Surrey RH2 9DJ. Tel: 01737 244222. www.duncannon.co.uk

Crystalair Compression packs immobilise items between two layers of clear, inert, polyurethane film that moulds to the object placed between it. They are perfect for storing and transporting valuable and delicate items that also need to be viewed.

For details contact Lane Packaging, Headley Park 8, Headley Road East, Woodley, Reading, Berkshire RG5 4SA. Tel: 0118 944 2425. www.lanepackaging.com

In central London, the best place to visit is Vera Trinder, 38 Bedford Street, London WC2E 9EU, which keeps a good stock. Tel: 0207 257 9940. www.veratrinder.co.uk

one with tray hole sizes to suit your coins.

Do-it-yourself cabinet-makers should be careful not to use new wood, which will contain corrosive moisture.

ALBUMS, PLASTIC CASES AND CARRYING CASES

There are many of these on the market, some both handsome and inexpensive.

There are also attractive Italian and German-made carrying cases for collectors. These can be obtained from a number of dealers such as Lodge Hill Collectors Accessories. Tel: 01694 731439. www.lodge-hill.co.uk

Coin albums, where the coins are contained in cards with crystal-clear film windows, claim to prevent oxidisation. The cards slide into pages in the album, which is a convenient method of storage, especially for new collectors.

Lindner Publications, Unit 3A, Hayle Industrial Park, Hayle, Cornwall TR27 5JR, supplies useful coin and collecting boxes, as well as albums. Tel: 01736 751910. Fax: 01736 751911. www.prinz.co.uk

An extended range of Lighthouse coin

ENVELOPES

Transparent plastic envelopes are very useful for exhibitions, but not recommended for long-term storage purposes.

They tend to make the coins 'sweat' which, can lead to corrosion.

Manila envelopes are much more suitable

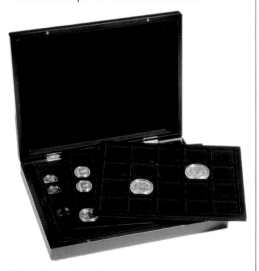

ABOVE: Another type of attaché case

ABOVE: Lindner supply coin albums

a dirty gold coin. But it is vital that gold coins are not rubbed in any way.

SILVER COINS

Silver coins will discolour easily, and are susceptible to damp or chemicals in the atmosphere. Gentle brushing with a soft, non-nylon, bristle brush will clear loose dirt. If the dirt is deep and greasy, a dip in ammonia and careful drying on cotton wool should work. There is no need to clean a coin that has a darkish tone.

COPPER AND BRONZE COINS

There is no safe method of cleaning copper or bronze coins without harming them. Use only a non-nylon, pure bristle brush to deal with dirt.

There is no way of curing verdigris (green spots) or bronze disease (blackish spots) permanently, so do not buy pieces with these problems, unless they are very inexpensive.

Remember that looking after your coins could make you money in the future!

since the paper is dry. Most collectors use them with a cardboard box, a simple, unobtrusive and inexpensive method of coin storage.

The best article on coin and medal storage is by L R Green, who is Higher Conservation Officer at the Department of Coins and Medals at the British Museum. It appeared in the May 1991 issue of *Spink's Numismatic Circular*.

CLEANING COINS

Every week, coin dealers examine coins that someone has unwittingly ruined by cleaning.

Never clean coins unless they are very dirty or corroded. 'Dirt' does not mean oxide, which on silver coins can give a pleasing bluish tone favoured by collectors.

Do not clean extremely corroded coins found in the ground, because if they are important, they will be handed over to a museum conservationist.

GOLD COINS

Gold should cause collectors few problems, since it is subject to corrosion only in extreme conditions such as a long spell in the sea.

A bath in methylated spirits will usually improve

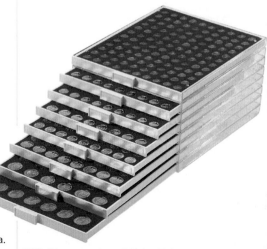

ABOVE: Coin cases are also available from Lindner

READING MATERIAL

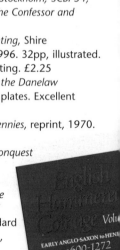

Our directory of suggested books has a range of essential and specialist titles for all aspects of the hobby

> **We have included the prices you can expect to pay, but some of the books are long out of print and can only be obtained secondhand, indicated by SH**

☐ Allen, M, *The Durham Mint*, British Numismatic Society Special Publication number 4, 2003. 222pp, 12 plates. £45

☐ Bateson, J D, *Coinage in Scotland*, 1997. 175pp, well illustrated. The most up-to-date narrative account of Scottish coins in print. £25

☐ Bateson, J D, *Scottish Coins*, Shire Publications number 189, 1987. 32pp, illustrated. A useful little introduction to the subject. The Shire publications are always good value. £2.95

☐ Besly, E, *Coins and Medals of the English Civil War*, 1990. 121pp, beautifully illustrated. SH

☐ Besly, E, *Loose Change, a Guide to Common Coins and Medals*, 1997. 57pp, £6.95

☐ Blunt, C E, Stewart, B H I H, Lyon, C S S, *Coinage in 10th Century England*, 1989. 372pp, 27 plates. £50

☐ Buck, I, *Medieval English Groats*, 2000. 66pp, illustrated. £15

☐ Bull, M, *The Half-Crowns of Charles I 1625-1649*, Volume 1-5, 2009. Highly detailed and illustrative analysis of the series. £85

☐ Byatt, D, *Promises to Pay: The First Three Hundred Years of Bank of England Notes*, 1994. 246pp, beautifully illustrated. SH

☐ British Academy, publisher, *Sylloge of Coins of the British Isles*. 50 volumes, many still in print

☐ Brooke, G C, *English Coins*, reprinted 1966. 300pp, 72 plates. An important one-volume guide to English coinage. SH

☐ Carroll, J and Parsons, D N, *Anglo-Saxon Mint Names, volume 1: Axbridge-Hythe*, 2007. £25

☐ Challis, C, *A New History of the Royal Mint*, 1992. 806pp, 70 figures and maps. £95

☐ Coincraft, publisher, *Standard Catalogue of English and UK Coins*, 1999. 741pp, fully illustrated. £19.50

☐ Coincraft, publisher, *Standard Catalogue of the Coins of Scotland, Ireland, Channel Islands and Isle of Man*, 1999. 439pp, illustrated. £34.50

☐ Colman, F, *Royal Cabinet Stockholm, SCBI 54, Anglo-Saxon Coins, Edward the Confessor and Harold II*. £60

☐ Cooper, D, *Coins and Minting*, Shire Publications number 106, 1996. 32pp, illustrated. An excellent account of minting. £2.25

☐ Dolley, M, *Viking Coins in the Danelaw and Dublin*, 1965. 32pp, 16 plates. Excellent introductory handbook. SH

☐ Dolley, M, *Anglo-Saxon Pennies*, reprint, 1970. 32pp, 16 plates. SH

☐ Dolley, M, *The Norman Conquest and English Coinage*, 1966. 40pp, illustrated. SH

☐ Dowle, A, and Finn, P, *The Guide Book to the Coinage of Ireland*, 1969. The first standard catalogue of Irish, still useful, good bibliography. SH

☐ Dyer, G P, editor, *Royal Sovereign 1489-1989*, 1989. 99pp, fully illustrated. £30

☐ Elias, E R D, *The Anglo-Gallic*

Coins, 1984. 262pp, fully illustrated. Essential for collectors of this series. £30

☐ Freeman, A, *The Moneyer and Mint in the Reign of Edward the Confessor 1042-1066*. Two parts, 1985. £40. A complete survey of the coinage of the reign.

☐ Frey, A R, *Dictionary of Numismatic Names*, reprinted 1973. 405pp. The best numismatic dictionary; search for a secondhand copy. SH

☐ Giodarno, J S, *Portraits of a Prince: Coins, Medals and Banknotes of Edward VIII*, 2009. 704pp, fully illustrated, values in US$. £49.50

☐ Grinsell, L V, *The History and Coinage of the Bristol Mint*, 1986. 60pp, illustrated. £5

☐ Grüber, H A, *Handbook of the Coins of Great Britain and Ireland*, revised edition, 1970. 272pp, 64 plates. A superb book. SH

☐ Hobbs, R, *British Iron Age Coins in the British Museum*, 1996. 246pp, 137 plates. Invaluable. Lists over 4,500 pieces. £40

☐ Holmes, R, *Scottish Coins, a History of Small Change in Scotland*, 1998. An invaluable guide to historic small change. 112pp, illustrated. £5.99

☐ Holmes, N M McQ, SCBI 58, *Scottish Coins in the Museums of Scotland*, Part 1, 1526-1603, 2006. 58pp, 99 plates. £55

☐ de Jersey, P, *Celtic Coinage in Britain*, Shire Publications, 1996. 56pp, illustrated. £4.99

☐ Linecar, H W A, *British Coin Designs and Designers*, 1977. 146pp, fully illustrated. SH

☐ Linecar, H W A, *The Crown Pieces of Great Britain and the Commonwealth of Nations*, 1969. 102pp, fully illustrated. The only book dealing solely with all British crowns. SH

☐ Linecar, H W A, editor, *The Milled Coinage of England 1662-1946*, reprinted 1976. 146pp, illustrated. Useful volume with degrees of rarity. SH

☐ Linecar, H W A, and Stone, A G, *English Proof and Pattern Crown-Size Pieces, 1658-1960*, 1968. 116pp, fully illustrated. SH

☐ Manville, H E, and Robertson, T J, *Encyclopedia of British Numismatics, volume 1: British Numismatic Auction Catalogues from 1710 to the Present*, 1986. 420pp, illustrated. £40

☐ Manville, H E, *Encyclopedia of British Numismatics, volume 2.1: Numismatic Guide to British and Irish Periodicals, 1731-1991*, 1993. 570pp, illustrated. £60

☐ Manville, H E, *Encyclopedia of British Numismatics, volume 2.2: Numismatic Guide to British and Irish Periodicals, 1836-1995*, 1997. 634pp, 31 illustrations. An important reference. £60

☐ Manville, H E, *Encyclopedia of British Numismatics volume 2.3: Numismatic Guide to British and Irish Printed Books, 1600-2004*, 2005. 291pp. £60

☐ Manville, H E, *Encyclopaedia of British Numismatics volume 2.4: Biographical Dictionary of British Numismatics*, Spink, 2009. 358pp. £60

☐ Manville, H E, *Tokens of the Industrial Revolution: Foreign Silver Coins Countermarked for Use in Great Britain, c1787-1828*. 308pp, 50 plates. A highly important work. £40

☐ Marsh, M A, *The Gold Sovereign*, Jubilee edition, 2002. 136pp. £16.95

☐ Marsh, M A, *The Gold Half-Sovereign*, 2nd edition, 2004. 119pp, 54 plates. £18.50

☐ Martin, S F, *The Hibernia Coinage of William Wood, 1722-1724*, 2007. 492pp, illustrated. £60

☐ Mass, J P, *The J P Mass Collection: English Short Cross Coins, 1180-1247*, 2001. 2,200 specimens from the author's collection. £50

☐ McCammon, A L T, *Currencies of the Anglo-Norman Isles*, 1984. 2 volumes, 358pp, fully illustrated. Essential for students and collectors.

☐ Mucha, M, *Hermitage Museum, St Petersburg, Part IV: English, Irish and Scottish Coins, 1066-1485*, 2005. 23 plates. £40

☐ North, J J, *English Hammered Coins, volume 1: Early Anglo-Saxon to Henry III, cAD600-1272*, 1994. 320pp, 20 plates. Essential. A great reference for collectors. £45

☐ North, J J, *English Hammered Coins, volume 2: Edward I-Charles II, 1272-1662*, 1993. 224pp, 11 plates. Essential. A great reference for collectors. £45

☐ North, J J, and Preston-Morley, P J, *The John G Brooker Collection: Coins of Charles I*, 1984. £25

☐ O'Sullivan, W, *The Earliest Irish Coinage*, 1981. 47pp, 4 plates. Hiberno-Norse coinage. SH

ENGLISH PATTERN TRIAL AND PROOF COINS IN GOLD

1547 - 1968
WILSON AND MARK RASMUSSEN

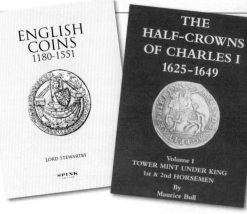

☐ O'Sullivan, W, *The Earliest Anglo-Irish Coinage*, 1964. 88pp, 10 plates. Deals with coinage from 1185-1216. SH. Reprint available at £5

☐ Peck, C W, *English Copper, Tin and Bronze Coins in the British Museum*, 1558-1958, 1960. 648pp, 50 plates. Essential. The seminal work on the subject. SH

☐ Pudill, R, and Eyre, C, *The Tribes and Coins of Celtic Britain*, 2005. 81pp, fully illustrated, price list included. £15

☐ Rayner, P A, *English Silver Coins since 1649*, 1992. 254pp, illustrated, 3rd edition. Essential. 3,000 coins listed, 400 illustrated. Deals with varieties, rarities, patterns and proofs and mintage figures. £25

☐ Robinson, B, *Silver Pennies and Linden Towels: The Story of the Royal Maundy*, 1992. 274pp, 118 illustrations. A very important work on the subject, entertaining. £29.95

☐ Spink, publisher, *Standard Catalogue of British Coins*, 2006. 42nd edition. Fully illustrated. Still the first point of reference for collectors. £25

☐ Spink, publisher, *Coins of Scotland, Ireland and the Islands*, 2003. 2nd edition. Illustrated. An important addition to one's library. £25

☐ Stewart, I H, *The Scottish Coinage*, 1967. 2nd edition. 215pp, 22 plates. Long out of print, but still essential for the serious collector. SH

☐ Stewartby, Lord, *English Coins 1180-1551*, 2009. 624 pp, illustrated. An indispensable overview of English medieval coins. £45

☐ Sutherland, C H V, *English Coinage, 600-1900*, 1973. 232pp, 108 plates. Beautifully written and the best narrative account of coinage. SH

☐ Thompson, J D A, *Inventory of British Coin Hoards*, AD 600-1500, 1956. 165pp, 24 plates. SH

☐ Van Arsdell, R D, *Celtic Coinage of Britain*, 1989. 584pp, 54 plates. A pioneering, controversial work; important for the images alone. SH

☐ Williams, J, *Money, A History*, 1997. 256pp, fully illustrated. Accompanies the British Museum's HSBC Money Gallery. £25

☐ Wilson, A and Rasmussen, M, *English Pattern Trial and Proof Coins in Gold*, 1547-1968, 2000. 537pp, illustrated. Covers a fascinating series. £85

☐ Withers, P and B, *British Coin Weights*, 1993. A corpus of the coin-weights made for use in England, Scotland and Ireland. 366pp, illustrated.

For the serious student. £95

☐ Withers, P and B, *Farthings and Halfpennies, Edward I & II*, 2005. 60pp, illustrated. Helpful series guide. £12

☐ Withers, P and B, *Farthings and Halfpennies, Edward III & Richard II*, 2002. 56 pp, illustrated. £12

☐ Withers, P and B, *Halfpennies and Farthings, Henry IV, V & VI*, 2003. 68pp, illustrated. £12

☐ Withers, P and B, *Halfpennies and Farthings, Edward IV-Henry VII*, 2004. 56pp, illustrated. £12

☐ Withers, P and B, *Small Silver, Henry VIII-the Commonwealth*, 2004. 56pp, illustrated. £12

☐ Withers, P and B, *Irish Small Silver, John-Edward VI*, 2004. 56pp, illustrated. £12

☐ Withers, P and B, *The Galata Guide to the Pennies of Edward I & Edward II and the Coins of the Mint Berwick-upon-Tweed*, 2006. 64pp, fully illustrated. £20

☐ Woodhead, P, *The Herbert Schneider Collection of English Gold Coins, Part 1: Henry III-Elizabeth I*, 1996. 466pp, 83 plates. A great catalogue of the best collection in private hands. £60

☐ Woodhead, P, *The Herbert Schneider Collection of English Gold Coins, Part 2: 1603-20th Century*, 2002. 58 plates. Essential, describes and illustrates 674 coins. £60

☐ Wren, C R, *The Voided Long Cross Coinage, 1247-1279*, 1993. 80pp, illustrated. £12

☐ Wren, C R, *The Short Cross Coinage 1180-1247*, 1992. 90pp, illustrated. Very good guide to identification with excellent drawings. £12

For these and other publications, contact the Spink Book Department. Tel: 0207 563 4046. E-mail: books@spink.com

MUSEUM COLLECTIONS

Here is a round-up of the best places to see coins on display in the UK

ABOVE: The Appledore Hoard of 11th century pennies, now on display in the British Museum

LONDON, THE BRITISH MUSEUM

The Department of Coins and Medals at the British Museum boasts the country's premier numismatic collection, a selection of which is on permanent display including the unique Anglo-Saxon gold penny of King Offa in the Money Gallery.

The collection also contains many significant hoards such as the Alton hoard of Celtic gold staters and the Appledore hoard of 11th century pennies. The latest acquisition is the 'Vale of York Hoard'. This remarkable and exciting find is expected to provide a valuable insight into the Viking world.

The museum has two or three temporary exhibitions a year. View the website for details.

Collectors can enjoy access to the museum's coin cabinets by special appointment.

The Keeper of Coins is Philip Attwood, British Museum, Great Russell Street, London WC1B 3DG.
☐ Tel: 0207 323 8607.
☐ www.britishmuseum.org
☐ E-mail: coins@thebritishmuseum.ac.uk

EDINBURGH, NATIONAL MUSEUMS OF SCOTLAND

The Museum of Scotland has the most important collection of Scottish coins in the country.

Highlights include one of the two known specimens of the Henry and Mary Ryal of 1565, acquired in 2002. A selection of coins is on display alongside other exhibits throughout the museum.

The National Museum of Scotland, Chambers Street, Edinburgh EH1 1JF.
□ www.nms.ac.uk

GLASGOW, HUNTERIAN MUSEUM

The Hunterian Museum has an extensive collection of Roman, Anglo-Saxon and medieval British coins. Currently the museum is displaying coins from the collection of eminent Scot and royal physician, Dr William Hunter.

The museum has around 1,500 Roman gold coins, and is currently displaying a selection as well as one of the four known David II nobles and the unique portrait penny of Eadwig.

The Senior Curator of Coins and Medals is Dr Donal Bateson, Hunterian Museum, University of Glasgow, Glasgow G12 8QQ.
□ Tel: 0141 330 4221.
□ www.hunterian.gla.ac.uk

CARDIFF, NATIONAL MUSEUM AND GALLERY

The integral theme of the extensive collection is the numismatic history of Wales.

The museum possesses two important hoards, the Bridgend hoard of Roman coins, part of which is on display in the Archaeology gallery, and the Tregwynt hoard of Civil War coins.

Visitors are welcome by appointment.

The Assistant Keeper in charge of coins is Edward Besly, Department of Archaeology and Numismatics, National Museum and Gallery, Cathays Park, Cardiff CF10 3NP.
□ Tel: 029 2057 3291.
□ www.museumwales.ac.uk

BIRMINGHAM, MUSEUM AND ART GALLERY

Birmingham Museum has one of the largest regional collections in England, with important Celtic, Saxon, Norman and medieval coins. Some items can be viewed online but visits are by appointment only.

The Curator of Antiquities and Numismatics is

Dr David Symons, Birmingham Museum and Art Gallery, Chamberlain Square, Birmingham B3 3DH.
□ Tel: 0121 303 4622.
□ www.bmag.org.uk

CAMBRIDGE, THE FITZWILLIAM MUSEUM

The Department of Coins and Medals has an internationally important numismatic collection, a selection of which is on permanent display.

Coins on display include an outstanding selection of medieval gold coins, including the gold leopard of Edward III, which set a record price for a British coin in 2006, and a gold penny of Henry III.

A major strength is the museum's Saxon and Norman coins, with many pieces from the Christopher Blunt and William Conte collections.

A significant recent acquisition is the impressive collection of early Anglo-Saxon and Continental thrymsas and sceattas belonging to Professor de Wit. Some 481 specimens make it one of the most comprehensive groups of coins of this period.

Certain items from the collection can be viewed on the Department's website.

Visitors are welcome by appointment.

The Keeper of Coins and Medals is Dr Mark Blackburn, Fitzwilliam Museum, Trumpington Street, Cambridge CB2 1RB.
□ Tel: 01223 332917.
□ www.fitzmuseum.cam.ac.uk/dept/coins

OXFORD, THE ASHMOLEAN MUSEUM

The museum's Heberden Coin Room contains a wide-ranging collection of Roman, Celtic and medieval coins.

Highlights include a magnificent 1645 'Oxford crown' of Charles I and a selection of Anglo-Saxon gold thrymsas from the Crondall Hoard of 1828.

Since the museum re-opened in late 2009, the Coin Room now has a major new Money Gallery where many of the coins and related numismatic items are on show in a superb thematic exhibition.

The Keeper of the Heberden Coin Room is Chris Howgego, Ashmolean Museum, Beaumont Street, Oxford OX1 2PH.
□ Tel: 01865 278058.
□ www.ashmolean.org/departments/heberdencoinroom/

YORK, YORKSHIRE MUSEUM

The museum is strong on Roman coinage, Northumbrian stycas, English hammered silver coins and trade tokens.

Hoards such as the 4th century Heslington hoard and single finds from Yorkshire are well represented, as well as Roman, Viking and medieval artefacts.

The Curator of Access-Archaeology is Andrew Morrison, Yorkshire Museum, Museum Gardens, York YO1 7FR.

☐ Tel: 01904 687620.
☐ www.yorkshiremuseum.org.uk

BELFAST, ULSTER MUSEUM

The museum houses the best collection of banknotes in Ireland.

The museum re-opened in October 2009. A representative array of coins is now incorporated into a narrative exhibition of Irish history since 1550 to recent times.

The main collection is accessible by arrangement.

For all enquiries please contact Trevor Parkhill, Keeper of History, Ulster Museum, Botanic Gardens, Belfast BT9 5AB.

☐ Tel: 028 9039 5160.
☐ www.ulstermuseum.org.uk/the-collections/history/coins-and-medals

DUBLIN, NATIONAL MUSEUM OF IRELAND

The museum has a permanent exhibition of items relating to Irish numismatic history. Some highlights are seven of the eleven known specimens of the exceedingly rare Ormonde gold pistoles.

The Curator of Coins is Michael Kenny, Keeper of the Art & Industrial Division, National Museum of Ireland, Collins Barracks, Benburb Street, Dublin 7, Ireland.

☐ Tel: +353 1677 7444.
☐ www.museum.ie

OTHER IMPORTANT UK MUSEUMS

Other museums with good collections of British coins:

☐ Blackburn Museum & Art Gallery, Museum Street, Blackburn, Lancashire BB1 7AJ. Tel: 01254 667130

City Museum, Queen's Road, Bristol BS8 1RL. Tel: 01179 223571.

☐ Royal Albert Memorial Museum, Queen Street, Exeter, Devon EX4 3RX. Tel: 01392 665858.

Manx Museum, Douglas, Isle of Man IM1 3LY. Tel: 01624 648000.

☐ The Leeds Museum Resource Centre, Moorfield Road, Yeadon, Leeds, West Yorkshire LS19 7BN. Tel: 01132 146526.

☐ Manchester Museum, The University of Manchester, Oxford Road, Manchester M13 9PL. Tel: 0161 275 2634.

☐ Reading Museum, Blagrave Street, Reading, Berkshire RG1 1QH. Tel: 0118 939 9800.

ABOVE: The unique Anglo-Saxon gold penny of Coenwulf (reigned 796-821), on display at the British Museum

COUNTERFEIT COINS

Forgeries have always been a problem. Here is some advice on the most commonly counterfeited coins

ABOVE: 'Fantasy' Celtic stater

There have been forgeries since the earliest days of coin production, so, of course, new forgeries appear on the scene every year. There is always someone willing to try to deceive the collector and the dealer.

However, nowadays few forgers end up making much money.

As a result of the diligence and ongoing monitoring of the situation by the British Numismatic Trade Association and the International Association of Professional Numismatists, the trade is now more informed about the latest forgeries before they have had a chance to be a serious menace.

ABOVE: Dennington Edward III noble

It has recently come to light that there are forgeries of British coins on the market, allegedly emanating from China. They include forgeries of modern British silver and copper coins in lower grades, including common coins. Two or more identical coins show the same defects, or purported 'damage', revealing them as fakes. It seems that the counterfeiters sell on the internet, picking up clients in various countries who are then set up as distributors.

At the moment there

ABOVE: Ceolwulf penny forgery

is not a comprehensive list available. Examples reported are: George III Halfcrowns, 1763 'Northumberland' Shilling, the rare 1816 Bank Token Three Shillings, George V 'wreath' Crowns and Victoria 'old head' Halfcrowns. There is also a convincing 1826 penny, with a die-axis deviation to 7mm off-centre and a weight of 18.04g instead of 18.8g; a 1854 penny with a die-axis deviation to 3mm off-centre, weighing 19.02g instead of 18.8.g and an Isle of Man 1813 penny with a die-axis deviation to 3mm off-centre, weight 19.11g instead of 20.3g-20.6g.

They can easily deceive as they appear to have signs of circulation and are toned, and are therefore not easily detectable.

Two hammered gold coins, apparently from the same source, have also been deemed forgeries. They are a Edward VI third period half-sovereign and an Elizabeth I angel.

ABOVE: A new forgery, of the 1826 penny

As always, collectors should buy with caution and from reputable dealers.

Forgeries were last a matter of major concern in the late 1960s and early 1970s. A considerable number of forged 1887 £5 and £2 pieces, early sovereigns and some silver pieces, in particular the 'Gothic' crown, thought to be manufactured in Beirut, came on to the market.

Also in the early 1970s, the Dennington forgeries could have made a serious impact on the English hammered gold market, but luckily they were detected early on. Fortunately, only a few of these are still in circulation.

In the late 1970s a crop of forgeries of Ancient British coins came to light, causing a panic in academic and trade circles.

This caused a lack of confidence in the trade and it took a number of years for the confidence to return.

A spate of copies of Anglo-Saxon coins from the West Country were being sold as replicas in the early 1990s, but they are still deceptive in the wrong hands.

Bob Forrest compiled a list of them and it was published in the IAPN *Bulletin of Forgeries* in 1995-96, volume 20, number 2.

ABOVE: A copy of an Apollo Ambiani stater

THE DIFFERENT TYPES OF FORGERY

Forgeries can be divided into two main groups: contemporary forgeries which are intended to be used as face-value money and forgeries which are intended to deceive collectors.

The following five methods of reproduction have been used for coins which attempt to deceive collectors:

☐ Electrotyping. These could deceive an expert.
☐ Casting. Old casts are easily recognisable, as they have marks made by air bubbles on the surface, and showing a generally 'fuzzy' effect. Modern cast copies are much more of a problem. They are produced by sophisticated pressure-casting', which can be extremely difficult to distinguish from the originals.
☐ The fabrication of false dies. With hammered coins, counter-feits are not difficult for an expert to detect. However, the sophisticated die-production techniques used in Beirut have resulted in good forgeries of modern gold and silver coins.

☐ The use of genuine dies put to illegal use, such as re-striking.
☐ Alteration of a genuine coin, most commonly a George V penny. The 1933 is extremely rare, so other years are often altered to provide the rarer date.

COUNTERFEIT COIN CLUB

There is a Counterfeit Coin Club that produces a small quarterly journal. For membership details write to its President: Ken Peters, 8 Kings Road, Biggin Hill, Kent TN16 3XU.
E-mail: kenvoy@hotmail.co.uk

DENNINGTON FORGERIES

A man called Anthony Dennington was tried at the Central Criminal Court and found guilty of six charges of 'causing persons to pay money by falsely pretending that they were buying genuine antique coins'.

A small number of these pieces are still in the trade, and since they have deceived some collectors and dealers, we have recorded them here, as they appeared in the International Bureau for the Suppression of Counterfeit Coins Bulletin in August 1976.

These copies are generally very good and you must beware of them. The following points may be useful guidelines:

☐ The coins are usually slightly 'shiny' in appearance, and the edges are not good, because they have been filed down and polished.
☐ They are usually very 'hard' to touch, whereas there is a certain amount of 'spring' in the genuine articles.
☐ They usually, but not always, feel slightly thick. They do not quite feel like an electrotype but are certainly thicker than normal.
☐ Although the Mary Fine sovereign reproduction is heavier, at 16.1986g, these pieces are usually lighter in weight than the originals.

ABOVE: A Dennington Mary Fine sovereign of 1553

MODERN COINS

As far as forgeries of modern coins are concerned, the most worrying aspect has been the enormous increase in well-produced forgeries in the last 25 years.

They are so well produced that it is often impossible for the naked eye to detect the difference, and it has therefore become the job of the scientist and metallurgist.

Many of these pieces have deceived dealers and collectors, but they do not seem to have caused a crisis of confidence.

ABOVE: A forged 1832 sovereign

This increase in the number of modern counterfeits has been due to the massive rise in

coin values since the 1960s.

The vast majority of these forgeries emanate from the Middle East, where it is not illegal to produce counterfeits of other countries' coins. But the coin trade is alert and reports are circulated quickly whenever a new forgery is spotted.

But with the profits available to the forger, no one should be complacent. At the time of writing, it only takes about £950 worth of gold to make an 1887-dated five pound piece of correct composition, valued approximately at £1650.

Detecting forgeries requires specialist knowledge, so we can only point out to you which coins are commonly counterfeited. In the catalogue section of British Coins Market Values, we have placed F beside a number of coins which have been counterfeited and which frequently turn up.

However, you should watch out for sovereigns, in particular, of which there are forgeries of every

ABOVE: A copy of an Una and Lion 1839 five pounds

ABOVE: A forged 1820 £5

DENNINGTON FORGERIES STILL IN THE TRADE

- ☐ Henry III gold penny
- ☐ Edward III Treaty period noble
- ☐ Edward III Treaty period noble with saltire before King's name
- ☐ Henry IV heavy coinage noble
- ☐ Henry V noble, Class C, mullet at King's sword arm
- ☐ Henry VI mule noble
- ☐ Henry VI noble, annulet issue, London
- ☐ Edward IV royal, Norwich
- ☐ Edward IV royal, York
- ☐ Elizabeth I angel
- ☐ Mary Fine sovereign 1553
- ☐ James I unite, mintmark mullet
- ☐ James I rose royal, third coinage, mint mark lis
- ☐ James I third coinage laurel
- ☐ Commonwealth unite 1651
- ☐ Commonwealth half-unite 1651
- ☐ Charles II touch piece

ABOVE: A copy of a 1847 Gothic Crown, edge UNDECIMO

date from 1900 to 1932 and even recent dates such as 1957 and 1976.

Pieces you should be particularly careful about, especially if they are being offered below the normal catalogue value, are listed in the box.

Most modern forgeries of, for example, Gothic crowns, are offered at prices that are 10% or 20% below the current market price.

The moral is: if something looks too good to be true, it probably is!

ABOVE: A forged 1913 sovereign

OTHER SAFEGUARDS

The best protection against purchasing forgeries is to buy your coins from a reputable dealer or auctioneer who is a member of the BNTA or the IAPN, or one who will unconditionally guarantee that all his coins are genuine.

Legal tender coins, which include £5 and £2 pieces, sovereigns, half sovereigns and crowns, are protected by the Forgery and Counterfeiting

ABOVE: A counterfeit 1822 sovereign

COMMONLY FORGED COINS

- ☐ 1738, 1739 two guineas
- ☐ 1793, 1798 guineas, there could also be other dates
- ☐ 1820 pattern five pounds
- ☐ 1820 pattern two pounds
- ☐ 1839 five pounds, plain edge variety
- ☐ 1887 five pounds
- ☐ 1887 two pounds, many forgeries in circulation
- ☐ 1893 five pounds, two pounds
- ☐ 1902 five pounds, two pounds
- ☐ 1911 five pounds, two pounds
- ☐ 1817, 1819 (altered date), 1822, 1825, 1827, 1832, 1887, 1889, 1892, 1892M, 1908C, 1913C sovereigns; 1900-1932 inclusive, plus 1957
- ☐ 1959, 1963, 1966, 1967, 1974, 1976
- ☐ 1847 Gothic crowns
- ☐ 1905 halfcrowns

Act. Contact the police if you believe this Act may have been contravened.

If your dealer is unhelpful over a non-legal tender item which you have purchased, and which you think has been falsely described, you can take legal action under the Trades Description Act 1968. This is a long and difficult process. Contact your local Trading Standards Office or Consumer Protection department.

LITERATURE ON FORGERY

The back issues of *Spink's Numismatic Circular* and *Seaby's Coin & Medal Bulletin* are useful sources of information on the forgeries that have been recorded over the years.

The ISBCC also produced a series of forgery bulletins, mainly on modern coins, which can now only be found secondhand.

The most useful work on hammered coins is by L A Lawrence in the *British Numismatic Journal* back in 1905!

ABOVE: A forged 1827 sovereign

ABOVE: A copy of a Mary ryal

RECENT FORGERIES

- ☐ George III halfcrowns
- ☐ George III 1763 'Northumberland' shilling
- ☐ George III 1816 Bank Token three shillings
- ☐ George V 'wreath' crowns
- ☐ Victoria 'old head' halfcrowns
- ☐ Edward VI third period half-sovereign
- ☐ Elizabeth I angel

Lighthouse ®

VOLTERRA coin etuis for QUADRUM coin capsules

Our high-quality **VOLTERRA** coin etuis are now also available for storing **QUADRUM** coin capsules. Choose between 7 different designs for precise fitting and representative presentation of 1 to 6 **QUADRUM** coin capsules.

[NEW]

	Overall size	Ref. No.	Price
1 x *QUADRUM*	80 x 80 mm (3 $^1/_4$ x 3 $^1/_4$")	339 043	£ 11.50
1 x *QUADRUM*	95 x 95 mm (3 $^3/_4$ x 3 $^3/_4$")	339 047	£ 15.95
2 x *QUADRUM*	148 x 93 mm (5 $^5/_6$ x 3 $^2/_3$")	339 048	£ 17.15
3 x *QUADRUM*	193 x 93 mm (7 $^3/_5$ x 3 $^2/_3$")	339 049	£ 18.25
4 x *QUADRUM*	260 x 93 mm (10 $^1/_5$ x 3 $^2/_3$")	339 050	£ 20.55
5 x *QUADRUM*	310 x 93 mm (12 $^1/_5$ x 3 $^2/_3$")	339 051	£ 22.95
6 x *QUADRUM*	193 x 150 mm (7 $^3/_5$ x 6")	339 052	£ 22.95

Digital coin scales

The practical pocket size makes our digital coin scale ideal for use on the move as well.
- LCD display. • Foldaway.
- Battery operated 2 x 3 V AAA.
- Overall size: 80 x 120 mm (3 $^1/_4$ x 4 $^3/_4$")

0.01 - 50 g
Measuring tolerance +/- 0.02 g
Ref. No. 303 863   **£ 48.50**

0.1 - 500 g
Measuring tolerance +/- 0.2 g
Ref. No. 326 729   **£ 43.50**

VARIO currency album

The VARIO currency albums consists of:

- **VARIO** binder with sturdy 4-ring mechanism.
- 10 clear **VARIO** pages for bank notes up to 190 x 80 mm   (7 $^1/_2$ x 3 $^1/_4$").
- 11 sort interleaves **VARIO**.
- Banknotes can be viewed from both sides.

Hunter green	Ref. No. 304 979	**£25.50**
Burgundy	Ref. No. 315 579	

COIN GRADING

The basics of grading and details of the different conditions

It is important that newcomers to collecting should get to know the different grades of condition before buying or selling coins.

The system of grading most commonly used in Britain recognises the following main classes in descending order of quality: Brilliant Uncirculated (B Unc, BU), Uncirculated (Unc), Extremely Fine (EF), Very Fine (VF), Fine (F), Fair, Poor.

Beginners often get confused when they first encounter these grades.

The word 'fine' implies a coin of high quality, yet this grade is near the bottom of the scale. Fine is, in fact, about the lowest grade acceptable to most collectors of modern coinage in Britain.

But, to some extent, the grade 'is in the eye of the beholder', and there are always likely to be differences of opinion as to the exact grade of a coin.

Some collectors and dealers have tried to make the existing scale of definitions more exact by adding letters such as N (Nearly), G (Good, meaning slightly better than the grade), A (About or Almost) and so on. In cases where a coin wears more on one side than the other, two grades are shown, the first for the obverse, the second for the reverse such as: GVF/EF.

Any major faults not apparent from the use of a particular grade are often described separately. These include dents and noticeable scratches, discoloration, areas of corrosion, edge knocks and holes.

SPECIAL TERMS
Full mint lustre
There are two schools of thought on the use of the terms Brilliant Uncirculated and Uncirculated. The former is often considered to be the most useful and descriptive term for coins of copper, bronze, nickel-brass or other base metals, which display what is known as 'full mint lustre'.

When this term is being used it is often necessary to employ the grade Uncirculated to describe coins which have never been circulated but have lost the original lustre of a newly minted coin.

However, some dealers and collectors tend to classify as Uncirculated all coins which have not circulated, whether they are brilliant or toned, and do not use the term Brilliant Uncirculated.

Fleur de coin
Sometimes FDC (fleur de coin) is used to define top-grade coins, but it really only applies to pieces in perfect mint state with no flaws or surface scratches.

With modern methods of minting, slight damage to the surface is inevitable, except in the case of proofs, and therefore Brilliant Uncirculated or Uncirculated best describe the highest grade of modern coins.

The word 'proof' should not be used to denote a coin's condition. Proofs are pieces struck on specially prepared blanks from highly polished dies and usually have a mirror-like finish.

Fair and Poor
Fair is applied to very worn coins which still have the main parts of the design distinguished and Poor denotes a grade in which the design and rim are worn almost flat and few details are discernible.

AMERICAN GRADING
The American grading system is quite different to the British one. It purports to be a lot more accurate, but is actually much more prone, in our opinion, to be abused, and we prefer the English dealers' more conservative methods of grading.

American dealers use many more terms, ranging from Mint State to About Good. The latter could be described as 'very heavily worn, with portions of lettering, date and legend worn smooth. The date may be partially legible'. In Britain we would simply say 'Poor'.

There is also a numerical method of describing coins, often used in the States. For example, an MS-65 coin would be Mint State and a 65 would mean 'an above average Uncirculated coin which may be brilliant or lightly toned but has some surface marks'.

The MS system seemed to be acceptable at first but there are two schools of thought in the United States and you will quite frequently see coins graded in the more traditional manner in sale catalogues.

GRADING EXAMPLES

It would be impossible to show every coin in different grades. We show instead representative examples from three different periods in the British series, to illustrate the middle range of coin conditions.

Each coin is shown in Extremely Fine, Very Fine and Fine conditions.

Extremely Fine
This describes coins which have been put into circulation, but have received only the minimum amount of damage since. There may be a few slight marks or minute scratches in the field, which is the flat area around the main design, but otherwise the coin should show very little sign of having been in circulation.

Very Fine
Coins in very fine condition show some amount of wear on the raised surfaces, but all other detail is still very clear. Here, all three coins have had a little wear which can be seen in the details of the hair and face. However, they are still in attractive condition from the collector's viewpoint.

Fine
In this grade coins show noticeable wear on the raised parts of the design; most other details should still be clear.

GRADES OF COIN

EXTREMELY FINE (EF)

VERY FINE (VF)

FINE (F)

ABBREVIATIONS & TERMS

These are the abbreviations and terms used in the price guide section

* Asterisks against some dates indicate that no firm prices were available at the time of going to press
2mm The P of PENNY is 2mm from the trident on some 1895 pennies. Otherwise, the gap is 1mm
AE numismatic symbol for copper or copper alloys
Arabic 1 or Roman I varieties of the 1 in 1887
arcs decorative border of arcs which vary in number
B on William III coins, minted at Bristol
BB beaded border
BBITANNIAR lettering error
Bank of England issued overstruck Spanish dollars for currency use in Britain 1804-1811
black farthings 1897-1918, artificially darkened to avoid confusion with half sovereigns
brilit lettering error
B Unc, BU Brilliant Uncirculated condition
BV bullion value
C on milled gold coins, minted at Ottawa, Canada
C on William III coins, minted at Chester
close colon colon close to DEF
crosslet 4 having upper and lower serifs on the horizontal bar of the 4 (compare plain 4)
cu-ni cupro-nickel
debased in 1920 the silver fineness in British coins was debased from .925 to .500
'Dorrien and Magens' issue of shillings by a group of bankers, which were suppressed on the day of issue

ABOVE: E.I.C. initials

DRITANNIAR lettering error
E minted at Exeter on William III coins
E, E* on Queen Anne coins, minted at Edinburgh
Edin Edinburgh
EEC European Economic Community
EF over price column Extremely Fine condition

ABOVE: English shilling, 1937-46

E.I.C. East India Co, supplier of metal
Eleph, eleph & castle elephant or elephant and castle provenance mark, below the bust. Taken from the badge of the African ('Guinea') Company, which imported the metal for the coins
Eng English shilling. In 1937, English and Scottish versions of the shilling were introduced. English designs have lion standing on a crown between 1937-1951 and three leopards on a shield between 1953-66
exergue segment below main design, usually containing the date
Ext extremely
F face value only
F over price column Fine condition
F forgeries exist of these pieces. In some cases the forgeries are complete fakes. In others where a particular date is rare, the date of a common coin has been altered. Be very cautious when buying any of these coins
Fair rather worn condition
fantasies non-currency items, often just produced for the benefit of collectors
far colon colon further from DEF than in close colon variety
FDC fleur de coin. A term used to describe coins in perfect mint condition, with no flaws, scratches or other marks
fillet hair band
flan blank for a coin or medal
GEOE lettering error
Gothic Victorian coins featuring Gothic-style portrait and lettering
guinea-head die used for obverse of guinea

ABOVE: Victoria Gothic florin

ABOVE: The Jubilee Head was introduced in 1887 to mark Victoria's Golden Jubilee

ABOVE: KN mintmark

H mintmark of The Mint, Birmingham

hd head

hp, harp for example early, ordinary varieties of the Irish harp on reverse

hearts motif in top right-hand corner of Hanoverian shield on reverse

im initial mark

inc incised, sunk in

inv inverted

JH Jubilee Head

KN mintmark of the Kings Norton Metal Company

L.C.W. Initials of Leonard Charles Wyon, engraver

ABOVE: 'Military' guinea, reverse

LIMA coins bearing this word were struck from bullion captured from vessels carrying South American treasure, which may have come from Lima, Peru

low horizon on normal coins the horizon meets the point where Britannia's left leg crosses behind the right. On this variety the horizon is lower

LVIII etc regnal year in Roman numerals on the edge

matt type of proof without a mirror-like finish

M on gold coins minted at Melbourne, Australia

'military' popular name for the 1813 guinea struck for the payment of troops fighting in the Napoleonic Wars

mm mintmark

mod eff modified effigy of George V

mule coin struck from wrongly paired dies

N on William III coins, minted at Norwich

obv obverse, usually the 'head' side of a coin

OH Old Head

OT ornamental trident

P on gold coins, minted at Perth, Australia

pattern trial piece not issued for currency

piedfort a coin which has been specially struck on a thicker than normal blank. In France, where the term originates, the kings seem to have issued them as presentation pieces from the 12th century onwards. In Britain, medieval and Tudor examples are known, and their issue has been reintroduced by the Royal Mint, starting with the twenty pence piedfort of 1982

plain on silver coins, no provenance marks in angles between shields on reverse

plain 4 with upper serif only to horizontal bar of 4

plumes symbol denoting

ABOVE: Plumes provenance mark

Welsh mines as the source of the metal

proof coin specially struck from highly polished dies. Usually has a mirror-like surface

prov a provenance mark on a coin, such as a rose, plume or elephant, which indicates the supplier of the bullion from which the coin was struck

PT plain trident

raised in relief, not incuse

RB round beads in border

rev reverse, 'tail' side of coin

r & p roses and plumes

rose symbol denoting west of England mines as the source of the metal

PRITANNIAR lettering error

QVARTO fourth regnal year, on edge

QVINTO fifth regnal year, on edge

rsd raised

S on gold coins minted at Sydney, Australia

SA on gold coins mined at Pretoria, South Africa

Scot Scottish shilling. In 1937, English and Scottish versions of the shilling were introduced. Scottish designs has a lion seated on crown, holding a sword and sceptre between 1937-51 and a lion rampant on a shield between 1953-66

SS C South Sea Company, the source of the metal

SECUNDO second regnal year, on edge

SEPTIMO seventh regnal year, on edge

'spade' the spade-like shape of the shield on George III gold coins

TB toothed beads in border

TERTIO third regnal year, on edge

trnctn base of head or bust where the neck or shoulders terminate

Unc Uncirculated condition

var variety

VF above price column Very Fine condition

VIGO struck from bullion captured in Vigo Bay, Spain

VIP 'very important person'. The so-called VIP crowns were the true proofs for the years of issue. Probably most of the limited number struck would have been presented to high-ranking officials

ABOVE: 1723 halfcrown with W.C.C. initials

W.C.C. Welsh Copper Company, indicating the supplier of the metal

wire type figure of value in thin wire-like script

W.W., ww initials of William Wyon, engraver

xxri lettering error

y, Y on William III coins minted in York

YH Young Head

MARKET PRICES

CELTIC COINAGE

The early British series is the hardest to price, as the market has developed considerably since the publication of R D Van Arsdell's *Celtic Coinage of Britain* in 1989, an essential book for collectors.

A number of forgeries of this series exist, some of relatively recent production, and numerous items from undeclared hoards are also on the market. It is therefore essential to buy from a reputable dealer.

We are very grateful for the help of Robert Van Arsdell who produced the synopsis of the material we have used.

We have kept this very basic, and linked it for easy reference with *The Coinage of Ancient Britain* by R P Mack, third edition, London 1975 (now out of print), and with the *British Museum Catalogue of British Iron Age Coins* by R Hobbs, where possible.

In the listings, Mack types are indicated by 'M' and BMC types by 'B'. The V numbers relate to the Van Arsdell catalogue. The existence of forgeries is indicated by F.

The map on the right shows the distribution of the tribes in Britain based on the map in *The Coinage of Ancient Britain*, by R P Mack, published by Spink and B A Seaby Ltd.

KEY TO TOWNS:
1. Calleva Atrebatum (Silchester)
2. Verulamium (St Albans)
3. Camulodunum (Colchester)

■ GOLD STATERS WITHOUT LEGENDS

AMBIANI	F	VF
Large flan type M1, 3, V10, 12	£1100	£4000
Defaced die type M5, 7, V30, 33	£500	£1600
Abstract type M26, 30, V44, 46	£300	£875
Gallic War type M27, a, V50, 52 F	£175	£350

Gallo-Belgic Stater

SUESSIONES		
Abstract type M34a, V85	£400	£1200

VE MONOGRAM		
M82, a, b, V87 F	£395	£1100

WESTERHAM	F	VF
M28, 29, V200, 202, B1-24	£250	£575

Chute Gold Stater

CHUTE		
M32, V1205, B35-76 F	£175	£375

CLACTON		
Type I M47, V1458, B137-144	£375	£1250
Type II M46, a, V30, 1455, B145-179	£350	£1200

CORIELTAUVI		
Scyphate type M-, V-, B3187-93	£275	£650

CORIELTAUVI (N E COAST TYPE)		
Type I M50-M51a, V800, B182-191	£225	£525
Type II M52-57, S27, V804	£210	£500

NORFOLK	F	VF
Wolf type M49, a, b, V610, B212-278	£275	£650

CORIELTAUVI		
South Ferriby Kite & Domino type, M449-450a, V811, B3146-3186	£275	£675

Corieltauvi (South Ferriby) Stater

WHADDON CHASE		
M133-138, V1470-1478, B279-350 F	£250	£625
Middle, Late Whaddon Chase V1485-1509	£300	£725

WONERSH		
M147, 148, V1522, B351-56	£385	£1050

WEALD		
M84, 229, V144, 150, B2466-68	£900	£2500

ICENI		
Freckenham Type I M397-399, 403b, V620, B3384-95	£325	£850
Freckenham Type II M401, 2, 3a, 3c, V626, B3396-3419	£350	£875
Snettisham Type M-, V-, B3353-83	£500	£1350

ATREBATIC		
M58-61, V210-216, B445-76	£275	£575

SAVERNAKE FOREST		
M62, V1526, B359-64	£275	£625

DOBUNNIC		
M374, V1005, B2937-40	£500	£1375

Iceni Stater

■ GOLD QUARTER STATERS WITHOUT LEGENDS

AMBIANI		
Large flan type M2, 4, V15, 20 F	£350	£875

	F	VF
Defaced die type M6, 8, V35, 37	£275	£625

GEOMETRIC		
M37, 39, 41, 41A, 42, V65, 146, 69, 67	£90	£200

SUSSEX		
M40, 43-45, V143, 1225-1229	£85	£185

VE MONOGRAM		
M83, V87 F	£135	£350

ATREBATIC		
M63-6, 69-75, V220-256, B478-546	£130	£350

KENTISH		
Caesar's Trophy type V145	£125	£300

■ GOLD STATERS WITH LEGENDS

COMMIUS		
M92, V350, B724-730	£400	£1100

TINCOMARUS		
M93, 93, V362, 363, B761-74	£525	£1450

VERICA		
Equestrian type M121, V500, B1143-58	£325	£775
Vine leaf type M125, V520, B1159-76	£385	£950

EPATICCUS		
M262, V575, B2021-23	£1100	£3250

DUBNOVELLANUS		
In Kent M283, V176, B2492-98	£375	£1100
In Essex M275, V1650, B2425-40	£385	£950

EPPILLUS		
In Kent M300-1, V430, B1125-28	£1750	£5250

ADDEDOMAROS		
M226, 7, V1605, B2390-94 F	£250	£700
Three types		

TASCIOVANUS		
Bucranium M149, V1680, B1591-1607 F	£400	£1150
Equestrian M154-7, V1730-1736, B1608-13	£375	£925

TASCIO/RICON		
M184, V1780, B1625-36	£825	£2000

SEGO		
M194, V1845, B1625-27	£2000	£5750

ANDOCO		
M197, V1860, B2011-14	£750	£1850

Tasciovanus 'Celtic Warrior' Stater

Cunobeline Stater

CUNOBELINE	F	VF
Two horses M201,V1910, B1769-71	£900	£2000
Corn ear M203 etc V2010, V1772-1835 F	£275	£650

ANTED of the Dobunni		
M385-6,V1062-1066, B3023-27 F	£525	£1400

EISU		
M388,V1105, B3039-42 F	£650	£1750

INAM		
M390,V1140, B3056 F		ext. rare

CATTI		
M391,V1130, B3057-60 F	£575	£1600

COMUX		
M392,V1092, B3061-63 F	£1100	£3250

CORIO		
M393,V1035, B3064-3133	£600	£1650

BODVOC		
M395,V1052, B3135-42 F	£950	£2500

Volisios Dumnocoveros Stater

VEP CORF		
M549-460,V940, 930, B3296-3300 F	£425	£975

DUMNOC TIGIR SENO		
M461,V972, B3330-36	£725	£1875

VOLISIOS DUMNOCOVEROS	F	VF
M463,V978, B3330-36	£450	£1200

Cunobeline Quarter Stater

■ GOLD QUARTER STATERS WITH LEGENDS

TINCOMARUS		
Abstract type M95,V365	£175	£425
Medusa head type M97,V387, B811-24	£225	£525
Tablet type M101-4,V387-390, B825-79	£135	£300

EPPILLUS		
Calleva M107,V407, B986-1015	£145	£325

VERICA		
Horse type M111-114,V465-468, B1143-46	£135	£300

TASCIOVANUS		
Horse type M152-3,V1690, 1692, B1641-1650	£125	£275

CUNOBELINE			
Various types, B1836-55	from	£175	£385

■ SILVER COINS WITHOUT LEGENDS

DUROTRIGES		
Silver Stater M317,V1235, B2525-2731 F	£45	£125
Geometric type M319,V1242, B2734-79	£30	£90
Starfish type M320,V1270, B2780-81	£65	£200

DOBUNNIC		
Face M374a, b, 5, 6, 8,V1020, B2950-3000	£35	£110
Abstract M378a-384d,V1042, B3012-22	£30	£85

CORIELTAUVI		
Boar type M405a,V855, B3194-3250	£60	£200
South Ferriby M410 etc,V875	£45	£125

ICENI		
Boar type M407-9,V655-659, B3440-3511	£30	£100
Wreath type M414, 5, 440,V679, 675, B3763-74	£35	£110
Face type M412-413e,V665, B3536-55	£75	£375

QUEEN BOUDICA	F	VF
Face type M413, 413D, V790, 792,		
B3556-3759	£50	£175

COMMIUS		
Head left M446b, V355, 357, B731-58	£45	£160

■ SILVER COINS WITH LEGENDS

EPPILLUS		
Calleva type M108, V415, B1016-1115	£50	£165

EPATICCUS		
Eagle type M263, V580, B2024-2289	£40	£125
Victory type M263a, V581, B2294-2328	£35	£120

VERICA		
Lim type M123, V505, B1332-59	£50	£165

CARATACUS		
Eagle Type M265, V593,		
B2376-2384 F	£135	£395

TASCIOVANUS		
Equestrian M158, V1745, B1667-68	£80	£295
VER type M161, V1699, B1670-73	£80	£295

CUNOBELINE		
Equestrian M216-8, 6, V1951		
1983, 2047, B1862	£80	£275
Bust right M236, VA2055, B1871-73	£75	£250

Anted, silver Unit

ANTED of the Dobunni		
M387, V1082, B3032-38	£40	£125

EISU		
M389, V1110, B3043-55	£40	£120

BODVOC		
M396, V1057, B3143-45 F	£125	£400

ANTED of the Dobunni		
M419-421, V710, 711, 715		
B3791-4009	£30	£75

ECEN		
M424, V730, B4033-4215	£25	£65

EDNAM		
M423, 425b, V740, 734, B4219-4281	£30	£65

ECE	F	VF
M425a, 426, 7, 8, V761, 764, 762,		
766, B4348-4538	£25	£60

AESU		
M432, V775, B4558-72	£50	£125

PRASUTAGUS		
King of the Iceni (husband of Boudica)		
B4577-4580	£675	£1850

ESUP ASU		
M4566, VA924, B3272	£70	£225

VEP CORF		
M460b, 464, V394, 950, B3277-3382,		
B3305-3314	£50	£110

DUMNOC TIGIR SENO		
M462, V974, 980, B3339	£165	£550

VOLISIOS DUMNOCOVEROS	£185	£575

ALE SCA		
M469, V996	£125	£375

■ BRONZE, BASE METAL COINS WITHOUT LEGENDS

POTIN		
Experimental type M22a, V104	£30	£80
Class I M9-22, V122-131	£25	£70
Class II M23-25, V136-139	£25	£70
Thurrock Types V1402-1442	£35	£90

ARMORICAN		
Billon stater	£40	£145
Billon quarter stater	£50	£175

DUROTRIGES		
Bronze stater M318, V1290	£20	£50
Cast type M332-370,		
V1322-1370	£35	£110

NORTH THAMES		
M273, 274, 281,		
V1646, 1615, 1669	£35	£110

NORTH KENT		
M295, 296, V154	£60	£225

■ BRONZE COINS WITH LEGENDS

DUBNOVELLANUS in Essex		
M277, 8, V1665, 1667	£50	£190

TASCIOVANUS		
Head, beard M168, 9, V1707	£40	£140

VERLAMIO	F	VF
M172,V1808	£40	£135
Head,VER M177,V1816	£45	£165
Boar,VER M179,V1713	£45	£165
Equestrian M190,V1892	£65	£250
Centaur M192,V1882	£75	£300

ANDOCOV	F	VF
M200,V1871	£50	£185

CUNOBELINE	F	VF
Victory,TASC M221,V1971	£35	£135
Victory, CUN M22, a,V1973	£40	£150
Winged animal, M225,V2081	£40	£150
Head, beard, M226, 9,V2131, 2085	£35	£150

	F	VF
Panel, sphinx, M230,V1977	£40	£150
Winged beast, M231,V1979	£40	£150
Centaur, M242,V2089	£30	£130
Sow, M243,V2091	£30	£130
Warrior, M244,V2093	£30	£125
Boar,TASC, M245,V1983	£40	£160
Bull,TASC M246,V2095	£30	£140
Metal worker, M248,V2097	£40	£160
Pegasus, M249,V2099	£30	£130
Horse, CAMV, M250,V2101	£40	£150
Jupiter, horse, M251,V2103	£45	£160
Janus head, M252,V2105	£45	£160
Jupiter, lion, M253,V1207	£35	£145
Sphinx, fig, M260, a,V2109	£35	£145

HAMMERED GOLD 1344-1662

Prices in this section are approximately what collectors can expect to pay for the commonest types of the coins listed. For most other types prices will range upwards from these amounts.

Precise valuations cannot be given since they vary from dealer to dealer and have to be determined by a number of factors such as a coin's condition, which is of prime importance in deciding its value.

For more detailed information, look at *English Hammered Coins, Volumes 1 and 2,* by J J North (Spink, 1994, 1992).

Serious collectors should also obtain *The Herbert Schneider Collection, Volume 1: English Gold Coins 1257-1603* (Spink, 1996) and *Volume 2: English Coins 1603-20th Century* (Spink, 2002).

■ THE PLANTAGENET KINGS

HENRY III 1216-1272	F	VF

Gold penny
One sold for £159,500 (including buyer's premium) at a Spink auction in 1996

Edward III Treaty Quarter-noble

EDWARD III 1327-77

Third coinage

		F	VF
Double-florins or Double Leopards		ext. rare	
Florins or leopards		ext. rare	
Half-florins or helms		ext. rare	
Nobles	from	£1500	£5500
Half-nobles	from	£1750	£6000
Quarter-nobles	from	£475	£1100

Fourth coinage
Pre-treaty period with France (before 1315)
With French title

	F	VF
Nobles	£800	£1800
Half-nobles	£525	£1300
Quarter-nobles	£275	£650

Transitional treaty period, 1361
Aquitaine title added

	F	VF
Nobles	£800	£2750
Half-nobles	£475	£1250
Quarter-nobles	£275	£600

Edward III Transitional Treaty Half-noble

Treaty period 1361-9
Omits FRANC

	F	VF
Nobles, London	£700	£1950
Nobles, Calais (C in centre of reverse)	£750	£1850
Half-nobles, London	£525	£1250
Half-nobles, Calais	£775	£1875
Quarter-nobles, London	£250	£550
Quarter-nobles, Calais	£265	£625

Post-treaty period 1369-77
French title resumed

	F	VF
Nobles, London	£825	£1950
Nobles, Calais (flag at stern or C in centre)	£800	£2250
Half-nobles, London	£1450	£3950
Half-nobles, Calais	£1250	£3250

There are many other issues and varieties in this reign. These prices relate to the commoner pieces.

Richard II Calais Noble

RICHARD II 1377-99

	F	VF
Nobles, London	£950	£2350
Nobles, Calais (flag at stern)	£975	£2450
Half-nobles, London	£1425	£3650
Half-nobles, Calais (flag at stern)	£1500	£4750
Quarter-nobles, London	£525	£1000

There are many different varieties and different styles of lettering.

Henry VI annulet London Noble

Henry IV heavy coinage London Noble

HENRY IV 1399-1413	**F**	**VF**
Heavy coinage		
Nobles (120g) London	£6750	£18000
Nobles, Calais (flag at stern)	£7250	£19500
Half-nobles, London	£5000	*
Half-nobles, Calais	£5500	*
Quarter-nobles, London	£1250	£3250
Quarter-nobles, Calais	£1350	£4000
Light coinage		
Nobles (108g)	£1600	£5250
Half-nobles	£2250	£6500
Quarter-nobles	£700	£1750

HENRY VI 1422-61		**F**	**VF**
Annulet issue, 1422-27			
Nobles, London		£725	£1925
Nobles, Calais (flag at stern)		£825	£2250
Nobles, York		£1250	£3250
Half-nobles, London		£650	£1500
Half-nobles, Calais		£975	£3000
Half-nobles, York		£1100	£3250
Quarter-nobles, London		£275	£575
Quarter-nobles, Calais		£300	£675
Quarter-nobles, York		£375	£875
Rosette-mascle issue 1427-30			
Nobles, London		£1500	£4250
Nobles, Calais		£1650	£4850
Half-nobles, London		£2000	£5750
Half-nobles, Calais		£2250	£6750
Quarter-nobles, London		£750	£2000
Quarter-nobles, Calais		£950	£2500

Henry V Noble

HENRY V 1413-22			
Nobles, many varieties	from	£850	£2150
Half-nobles		£850	£2500
Quarter-nobles		£375	£775

This reign sees an increase in the use of privy marks to differentiate issues.

Henry VI rosette-mascle Calais Noble

Pinecone-mascle issue 1430-4	**F**	**VF**
Nobles, London	£1450	£4000
Half-nobles, London	£2500	£7000
Quarter-nobles	£900	£2500
Leaf-mascle issue 1434-5		
Nobles, London	£3000	£8500
Half-nobles, London	£2750	£7250
Quarter-nobles	£950	£2750

Leaf-trefoil issue 1435-8	F	VF
Nobles	£3000	£8500
Half-nobles	£2750	£7750
Quarter-noble	£900	£2750

Trefoil issue 1438-43		
Nobles	£2500	£7500

Henry VI Pinecone-mascle Noble

Leaf-pellet issue 1445-54		
Nobles	£3000	£8500

Cross pellet issue 1454-60		
Nobles	£3500	£10000

EDWARD IV 1st reign 1461-70
Heavy coinage 1461-65		
Nobles (108g)	£4000	£12500
Quarter-noble		ext. rare

Light coinage 1464-70		
Ryals or rose-nobles (120g) London	£750	£1850
Flemish copy	£500	£1250

Edward IV Light coinage Norwich Ryal

	F	VF
Ryals, Bristol (B in waves)	£950	£2750
Ryals, Coventry (C in waves)	£1950	£4750
Ryals, Norwich (N in waves)	£2000	£5500
Ryals, York (E in waves)	£900	£2500
Half-ryals, London	£650	£1800
Half-ryals, Bristol (B in waves)	£1300	£3850
Half-ryals, Coventry (C in waves)	£4500	£11500
Half-ryals, Norwich (N in waves)	£3750	£9500
Half-ryals, York (E in waves)	£775	£1950
Quarter-ryals	£450	£950
Angels	£6500	*

HENRY VI restored 1470-71
Angels, London	£1400	£3750
Angels, Bristol (B in waves)	£2250	£6500
Half-angels, London	£4000	*
Half-angels, Bristol (B in waves)	£4750	*

EDWARD IV 2nd reign 1471-83
Angels, London	£700	£1750
Angels, Bristol (B in waves)	£2250	£5500
Half-angels, some varieties	£650	£1750

EDWARD IV or V 1483
im halved sun and rose		
Angels	£4000	£10500
Half-angels	£4500	*

RICHARD III 1483-85
Angels, reading EDWARD, im boar's head on obverse, halved sun and rose on reverse	£6250	£17500
Angels, reading RICHARD or RICAD	£3500	£8500
Half-angels	£5500	*

Edward IV second reign Angel

■ **THE TUDOR MONARCHS**

HENRY VII 1485-1509
		F	VF
Sovereigns of 20 shillings (all extremely rare)	from	£25000	£58500
Ryals		£20000	£65000
Angels, varieties, different ims	from	£725	£1750
Half-angels		£675	£1650

Henry VIII first coinage Angel, im portcullis

	F	VF
Angels	£725	£1850
Half-angels	£700	£1700
Quarter-angels	£625	£1500
Crowns, HENRIC 8, London	£650	£1700
Crowns, Southwark	£700	£1750
Crowns, Bristol	£700	£1750
Halfcrowns, London	£600	£1250
Halfcrowns, Southwark	£600	£1250
Halfcrowns, Bristol	£725	£1900

EDWARD VI 1547-53
Posthumous coinage in the name of Henry VIII, 1547-51

	F	VF
Sovereigns, London	£7250	£19000
Sovereigns, Bristol	£8250	£24000
Half-sovereigns, London	£900	£2250
Half-sovereigns, Southwark	£900	£2250
Crowns, London	£700	£1650
Crowns, Southwark	£800	£1950
Halfcrowns, London	£650	£1450
Halfcrowns, Southwark	£650	£1450

Henry VIII Third coinage type I Sovereign

HENRY VIII 1509-47		F	VF
First coinage 1509-26			
Sovereigns of 20 shillings im			
crowned portcullis only		£9000	£26500
Angels (6s 8d)	from	£750	£1750
Half-angels		£600	£1450

Second coinage 1526-44			
Sovereigns of 22s 6d, various ims		£7500	£21500
Angels (7s 6d)	from	£850	£2500
Half-angels im lis		£950	£2850
George-nobles im rose		£8750	£25000
Half-George-noble		£8000	*
Crowns of the rose im rose		£6500	*
Crowns of the double rose			
HK (Henry and Katherine			
of Aragon)		£750	£1750
HA (Henry and Anne Boleyn)		£1850	£4500
HI (Henry and Jane Seymour)		£800	£2000
HR (HENRICUS REX)		£725	£1850
Halfcrowns of the double-rose			
HK		£600	£1500
HI		£800	£2150
HR		£900	£2350

Third coinage 1544-47			
Sovereigns of 20s, London	from	£5750	£14500
Sovereigns of 20s, Southwark		£5250	£13500
Sovereigns of 20s, Bristol	from	£7000	£19500
Half-sovereigns, London		£1000	£2950
Half-sovereigns, Southwark		£1000	£2950
Half-sovereigns, Bristol		£2250	£5500

Coinage in Edward's own name
First period 1547-49

		F	VF
Half-sovereigns, Tower,			
reads EDWARD 6		£2150	£7000

Edward VI second period Sovereign im arrow

	F	VF
Half-sovereigns, Southwark	£1950	£6000
Crown	£3500	*
Halfcrowns	£2750	*

Second period 1549-50

	F	VF
Sovereigns	£5500	£15000
Half-sovereign, uncrowned bust, London	£3850	*
Half-sovereigns, SCUTUM on obverse	£1575	£4600
Half-sovereigns, Durham House MDXLVII	£5750	*
Half-sovereigns, crowned bust, London	£1650	£4750
Half-sovereigns, half-length bust, Durham House	£6500	*
Crowns, uncrowned bust	£1500	£5000
Crowns, crowned bust	£1400	£4500
Halfcrowns, uncrowned bust	£1400	£4250
Halfcrowns, crowned bust	£1375	£3850

Mary 1553 Sovereign

PHILIP AND MARY 1554-8	F	VF
Angels, im lis	£4500	£13500
Half-angels	£8500	*

Elizabeth I sixth issue Ryal

Edward VI third period Sovereign im tun

Third period 1550-53

'Fine' sovereigns of 30s,	F	VF
king enthroned	£28500	£65500
Sovereigns of 20s, half length figure	£3750	£10000
Half-sovereigns, similar to last	£1800	£4850
Crowns, similar but SCUTUM on reverse	£1500	£4250
Halfcrowns, similar	£1650	£4500
Angels	£8750	£25000
Half-angels		ext. rare

MARY 1553-4

Sovereigns, different dates, some undated,		
im pomegranate or half rose	£5500	£14750
Ryals, dated MDLIII (1553)	£17500	£65000
Angels, im pomegranate	£1900	£5250
Half-angels	£3250	£8000

ELIZABETH I 1558-1603
Hammered issues

'Fine' Sovereigns of 30s,	F	VF
different issues from	£5000	£13750
Ryals	£13500	£32500
Angels, different issues	£900	£2650
Half-angels	£750	£2150
Quarter-angels	£750	£2000

Elizabeth I second issue Quarter-angel

	F	VF		F	VF
Pounds of 20s, different ims	from £2750	£7500	Britain crowns	£300	£625
Half-pounds, different issues	£1750	£4500	Halfcrowns	£225	£500
Crowns	£1350	£3000	Thistle crowns, varieties	£250	£600
Halfcrowns	£900	£2250			

Elizabeth I sixth issue Crown

Milled issues

	F	VF
Half-pounds, one issue but different marks	£3000	£8000
Crowns	£2350	£6500
Halfcrowns	£3250	£8500

■ **THE STUART KINGS**

James I third coinage Rose-ryal

James I, third coinage Spur-ryal

James I third coinage Laurel

JAMES I 1603-25
First coinage 1603-4

	F	VF
Sovereigns of 20s, two busts	£2500	£7500
Half-sovereigns	£3750	£11500
Crowns	£2500	£6000
Halfcrowns	£850	£2500

Second coinage 1604-19

	F	VF
Rose-ryals of 30s	£3000	£7500
Spur-ryals of 15s	£6000	£15000
Angels	£1000	£3000
Half-angels	£2500	£7000
Unites, different busts	£750	£1500
Double crowns	£425	£1100

Third coinage 1619-25

	F	VF
Rose-ryals, varieties	£3000	£7750
Spur-ryals	£5250	£13750
Angels	£1650	£4850
Laurels, different busts	£700	£1550
Half-laurels	£485	£975
Quarter-laurels	£275	£600

CHARLES I 1625-49
Tower mint 1625-42
Initial marks: lis, cross-calvary, negro's head, castle, anchor, heart, plume, rose, harp, portcullis, bell, crown, tun, triangle, star, triangle-in-circle.

Charles I Tower mint Unite, im heart

	F	VF
Angels, varieties	£3000	£7000
Angels, pierced as touchpieces	£925	£2650
Unites	£700	£1700
Double-crowns	£450	£1000
Crowns	£275	£550

Charles I Tower mint Double-crown, im heart

Tower mint under Parliament 1642-9
Ims: (P), (R), eye, sun, sceptre

Unites, varieties	£1250	£2950
Double-crowns	£700	£1750
Crowns	£375	£750

Briot's milled issues 1631-2
Ims: anemone and B, daisy and B, B

Angels	£5000	£13700
Unites	£3750	£9000
Double-crowns	£2500	£5750
Crowns	£3500	£9000

Coins of provincial mints
Bristol 1645

Unites	£25000	£70000
Half-unites		ext. rare

Chester 1644

Unites	£30000	£80000

Exeter 1643-44

Unites	£30000	£80000

Oxford 1642-46

Triple unites,	from	£12000	£27500
Unites	from	£2250	£7000
Half-unites	from	£1750	£4500

Truro 1642-43		F	VF
Half-unites			ext. rare
Shrewsbury 1644			
Triple unites and unites			ext. rare
Worcester 1643-44			
Unites		£32500	£85000

Charles I 1643 Oxford Triple unite

Siege pieces 1645-49
Pontefract 1648-49

Unites F		
		ext. rare

Commonwealth 1651 Unite

COMMONWEALTH 1649-60

Unites im sun	£2250	£4500
im anchor	£7000	£16500
Double-crowns im sun	£1350	£3000
im anchor	£4750	£10500
Crowns, im sun	£975	£2250
im anchor	£3000	£7500

Commonwealth 1650 Crown

CHARLES II 1660-85
Hammered Coinage 1660-62

Charles II hammered coinage Unite

		F	VF
Unites, two issues	from	£1750	£4500
Double-crowns		£1250	£3250
Crowns		£1500	£3750

HAMMERED SILVER

In this section, coins are mainly valued in Fine or Very Fine condition.

However, pennies of the early Plantagenets, where higher-grade coins are seldom available, are valued in Fair or Fine condition.

Again it should be noted that prices are for the commonest types only, and are the amounts collectors can expect to pay, rather than dealers' buying prices.

Prices for the Saxon and Norman series are based on common mint towns. Rarer mints command higher premiums.

Descriptions such as 'cross/moneyer's name' indicate that a cross appears on the obverse and the moneyer's name on the reverse. For more details see *Standard Catalogue of British Coins* (Spink, annual), and *English Hammered Coins, volumes 1 and 2* by J J North, Spink (1991, 1994).

■ ANGLO-SAXON SCEATS AND STYCAS

Examples of Sceats

EARLY PERIOD c600-750		**F**	**VF**
Silver Sceats	from	£80	£195
Large numbers of types and varieties.			

NORTHUMBRIAN KINGS c737-867			
Silver Sceats c737-796 from		£100	£295
Copper Stycas c 810-867 from		£20	£55

Struck for many kings. Numerous moneyers and different varieties. The copper Styca is the commonest coin in the Anglo-Saxon series.

ARCHBISHOPS OF YORK c732-900			
Silver Sceats	from	£65	£185
Copper Stycas	from	£20	£55

■ KINGS OF KENT

	F	**VF**
HEABERHT c764		
Pennies monogram/cross		ext. rare
One moneyer (Eoba).		
ECGBERHT c765-780		
Pennies monogram/cross	£1100	£4250
Two moneyers (Babba and Udd).		
EADBERHT PRAEN 797-798		
Pennies EADBERHT REX/moneyer	£1300	£4400
Three moneyers.		
CUTHRED 789-807		
Pennies non-portrait, various designs from	£750	£2400
Bust right	£900	£2500
Different moneyers and varieties.		
BALDRED c825		
Pennies bust right	£1300	£3850
Cross/cross	£785	£2250
Different types and moneyers.		
ANONYMOUS		
Pennies bust right	£875	£2750
Different types and moneyers.		

■ ARCHBISHOPS OF CANTERBURY

		F	**VF**
JAENBERHT 766-792			
Pennies various types			
non-portrait	from	£1100	£3750
AETHELHEARD 793-805			
Pennies various types			
non-portrait	from	£925	£3250
WULFRED 805-832			
Pennies various groups			
portrait types	from	£775	£2850
CEOLNOTH 833-870			
Pennies various groups, portrait types from		£685	£2000
AETHELRED			
Pennies various types,			
portrait, non portrait		£2300	£7600
PLEGMUND 890-914			
Pennies various types non-portrait from		£725	£2000

Offa portrait Penny

■ KINGS OF MERCIA

		F	VF
OFFA 757-796			
Pennies non-portrait	from	£650	£1500
Portrait	from	£1250	£4250
CYNETHRYTH (wife of Offa)			
Pennies portrait		£2850	£9250
Non-portrait		£1500	£4850
COENWULF 796-821			
Pennies various types,			
portrait, non-portrait	from	£625	£1500

Coenwulf portrait Penny

	F	VF
CEOLWULF 821-823		
Pennies various types, portrait	£950	£3750
BEORNWULF 823-825		
Pennies various types, portrait	£925	£3500
LUCIDA 825-827		
Pennies two types, portrait F	£3000	£9750
WIGLAF 827-829, 830-840		
Pennies two groups, portrait, non-portrait	£2300	£6850
BERHTWULF 840-852		
Pennies two groups, portrait, non-portrait	£1000	£3600
BURGRED 852-874		
Pennies one type portrait, five variants	£275	£575
CEOLWULF II 874-c 877		
Pennies two types portrait	£1400	£4250

■ KINGS OF EAST ANGLIA

	F	VF
BEONNA c758		
Silver Sceat	£800	£2500
AETHELBERHT died 794		
Pennies, portrait type F		ext. rare
EADWALD c796		
Pennies, non-portrait types	£950	£3450
AETHELSTAN I c850		
Pennies various types,		
portrait, non-portrait	£475	£1400

	F	VF
AETHELWEARD c 850		
Pennies, non-portrait types	£625	£1750
EADMUND 855-870		
Pennies, non-portrait types	£400	£950

■ VIKING INVADERS 878-954

		F	VF
ALFRED			
Imitations of Alfred Pennies			
and Halfpennies	from	£525	£1450
Many different types, portrait and non-portrait.			

Danish East Anglia, c885-954

	F	VF
AETHELSTAN II 878-890/1		
Pennies cross/moneyer	£1350	£3650
OSWALD		
Pennies A/cross	£1450	£4500
ST EADMUND		
Pennies memorial coinage,		
various legends	£185	£400
Many moneyers.		
Halfpennies	£475	£1450
Many moneyers.		

St Eadmund memorial Penny

	F	VF
ST MARTIN OF LINCOLN c917		
Pennies sword/cross	£2350	£7750
AETHELRED I c870		
Pennies temple/cross	£1750	£5400
York		
SIEVERT-SIEFRED-CNUT c897		
Crosslet/small cross	£185	£425
Many different groups and varieties.		
Halfpennies	£525	£1350
Many different groups and varieties.		
EARL SIHTRIC unknown		
Pennies non-portrait	£2400	£7000
REGNALD c 910		
Pennies various types, some blundered	£1800	£6000
SIHTRIC I 921-926/7		
Pennies sword/cross	£2000	£7250

ANLAF GUTHFRITHSSON 939-941		F	VF
Pennies raven/cross		£2000	£6250
Cross/cross		£1850	£5750
Flower/cross		£2250	£7250

OLAF SIHTRICSSON 941-944, 948-952

	F	VF
Pennies various types	£1850	£5750

SIHTRIC II c941-943

	F	VF
Pennies shield/standard	£1900	£6250

REGNALD II c941-943

	F	VF
Pennies cross/cross	£1900	£6250
Shield/standard	£2000	£7250

ERIC BLOODAXE 948, 952-954

	F	VF
Pennies cross/moneyer	£3100	£9500
Sword/cross	£3400	£10750

ST PETER OF YORK c905-925

		F	VF
Pennies various types	from	£325	£800
Halfpennies, various types	from	£675	£1750

■ KINGS OF WESSEX

BEORHTRIC 786-802

Two types, non-portrait	ext. rare

ECGBERHT 802-839

	F	VF
Pennies four groups, portrait, non-portrait	£1250	£4000
Mints of Canterbury, London, Rochester, Winchester		

AETHELWULF 839-858

	F	VF
Pennies four phases, portrait, non-portrait	£525	£1650
from mints of Canterbury, Rochester		

AETHELBERHT 858-866

	F	VF
Pennies two types portrait from	£525	£1650
Many moneyers.		

AETHELRED I 865-871

	F	VF
Pennies portrait types from	£600	£1750
Many moneyers.		

ALFRED THE GREAT 871-899

	F	VF
Pennies portrait in style of Aethelred I	£725	£2250
Four other portrait types, commonest		
has the London monogram reverse	£1850	£5250
Halfpennies	£625	£1700
Pennies non-portrait types from	£500	£1100
Many different styles of lettering.		
Halfpennies	£500	£1100

Alfred the Great Halfpenny, London monogram on reverse

EDWARD THE ELDER 899-924	F	VF
Non-portrait types		
Pennies cross/moneyer's name in two lines	£275	£625
Halfpennies cross/moneyer's		
name in two lines	£850	£2400

Edward the Elder, non-portrait Penny

Portrait types	F	VF
Pennies bust/moneyer's name	£925	£3250
Many types, varieties and moneyers.		
Pennies design has buildings,		
floral designs and others	£1650	£5750
Many types, varieties and moneyers.		

■ KINGS OF ALL ENGLAND

AETHELSTAN 924-39

	F	VF
Non-portrait types		
Pennies cross/moneyer's name in two lines	£375	£800
Cross/cross	£325	£900
Portrait types		
Pennies bust/moneyer's name in two lines	£875	£3400
Bust/small cross	£775	£3000
Many other issues, some featuring buildings. There are also		
different mints and moneyer's names.		

EADMUND 939-46

	F	VF
Non-portrait types		
Pennies cross or rosette/moneyer's		
name in two lines	£325	£775
Halfpennies, cross or rosette/moneyer's		
name in two lines	£825	£2400
Portrait types		
Pennies crowned bust/small cross	£825	£2850
Helmeted bust/cross crosslet	£975	£3500
Many other issues and varieties; also different mint names and		
moneyers.		

EADRED 946-55

	F	VF
Non-portrait types		
Pennies cross/moneyer's name in two lines	£285	£650
Halfpennies cross/moneyer's		
name in two lines	£675	£1850
Pennies rosette/moneyer's name	£375	£875
Portrait types		
Pennies crowned bust/small cross	£775	£2650
Many variations and mint names and moneyers.		

HOWEL DDA King of Wales, died c948		F	VF
Pennies small cross/moneyer's name in two lines (Gillys)			ext. rare

EADWIG 955-59
Non-portrait types

		F	VF
Pennies cross/moneyer's name	from	£500	£1650
Many variations, some rare.			
Halfpennies, non portrait types cross/moneyer's name		£1050	£3250

Portrait types

Pennies bust/cross from		£3400	£10500

EADGAR 959-75
Non-portrait types

Pennies cross/moneyer's name	from	£265	£500
Cross/cross from		£265	£525
Rosette/rosette from		£285	£685
Halfpennies	from	£900	£2750

Eadgar, non portrait Penny

Portrait types

Pennies pre-reform, bust right		£950	£3250
Halfpennies, diademed bust/London monogram		£775	£2650
Pennies reform (c972), bust left		£950	£3000
Many other varieties.			

EDWARD THE MARTYR 975-78
Portrait types

Pennies bust left/small cross		£1100	£3400
Many different mints and moneyers.			

AETHELRED II 978-1016

Aethelred II last small cross type Penny

		F	VF
Pennies first small cross type from	from	£700	£2250
First hand type from	from	£190	£425
Second hand type from	from	£180	£400
Benediction hand type	from	£925	£3250

		F	VF
CRUX type from	from	£145	£300

Aethelred II CRUX type Penny

Aethelred II long cross type Penny

Long cross type		£160	£325
Helmet type		£155	£350
Agnus Dei type		£5400	*
Other issues and varieties, many mints and moneyers.			

CNUT 1016-35

Pennies quatrefoil type	from	£140	£285

Cnut quatrefoil type Penny

Pointed helmet type	from	£130	£265

Cnut pointed helmet type Penny

Short cross type	from	£115	£250
Jewel cross type	from	£500	£1450
Other types, and many different mints and moneyers.			

HAROLD I 1035-40

Pennies jewel cross type	from	£325	£775
Long cross type with trefoils	from	£315	£725
Long cross type with fleurs-de-lis		£315	£725
Many different mint names and moneyers.			

HARTHACNUT 1035-42	F	VF
Pennies jewel cross type, bust left	£1250	£3650
Bust right	£1100	£3400
Arm and sceptre type	£875	£2850
Different mint names and moneyers.		
Pennies Scandinavian types struck at Lund	£285	£650

EDWARD THE CONFESSOR 1042-66		
Pennies PACX type	£275	£650
Radiate crown/small cross type	£140	£300
Trefoil quadrilateral type	£150	£325
Small flan type	£120	£260
Expanding cross type	£145	£365

Edward the Confessor transitional pyramids type Penny

Pointed helmet type	£145	£375
Sovereign/eagles type	£160	£425
Hammer cross type	£140	£350

Edward the Confessor hammer cross type Penny

Bust facing/small cross type	£140	£315
Pyramids type	£145	£350
Transitional pyramids type	£1400	£3850

Other issues, including a unique gold penny; many different mints and moneyers.

Harold II Pax type Penny, bust left, without sceptre

HAROLD II 1066

Pennies Pax type, crowned head left,		
with sceptre	£775	£2000
without sceptre	£850	£2250

	F	VF
Pennies Pax type crowned head right,		
with sceptre	£1750	£5650

■ THE NORMAN KINGS

WILLIAM I 1066-87

		F	VF
Pennies profile left/cross fleury type	from	£385	£950
Bonnet type	from	£280	£625
Canopy type	from	£425	£1100
Two sceptres type	from	£340	£850
Two stars type	from	£285	£585
Sword type	from	£365	£950

William I profile/cross fleury type Penny

Profile right/cross and			
trefoils type	from	£485	£1350
PAXS type	from	£265	£550

WILLIAM II 1087-1100

William II cross voided type Penny

		F	VF
Pennies profile right type	from	£765	£2000
Cross in quatrefoil type	from	£700	£1750
Cross voided type	from	£700	£1750
Cross pattée over fleury type	from	£750	£1850
Cross fleury and piles type	from	£850	£2250

Henry I large bust/cross and annulets type Penny

HENRY I 1100-1135

		F	VF
Pennies annulets type	from	£550	£1450
Profile/cross fleury type	from	£385	£1050
PAXS type	from	£360	£950
Annulets and piles type	from	£385	£1050
Voided cross and fleurs type	from	£850	£2400
Pointing bust and stars type	from	£1650	£5250
Facing bust/quatrefoil and piles type	from	£375	£975
Large profile/cross and annulets type	from	£1750	£5650
Facing bust/cross in quatrefoil type	from	£800	£2100
Full bust/cross fleury type		£285	£700
Double inscription type		£625	£1650
Small profile/cross and annulets type		£525	£1400
Star in lozenge fleury type		£500	£1300
Pellets in quatrefoil type		£280	£685
Quadrilateral on cross fleury type		£215	£475
Halfpennies		£1850	£5750

STEPHEN 1135-54

		F	VF
Pennies cross moline (Watford) type	from	£275	£725

Stephen 'Watford' Penny

	F	VF
Similar, reads PERERIC	£725	£1850
Voided cross and mullets type	£325	£765
Cross and piles type	£425	£1100
Cross pommée (Awbridge) type	£315	£765

There are also a number of irregular issues produced during the civil war, all of which are very rare. These include several extremely rare and attractive pieces bearing the names of Empress Matilda and barons, such as Eustace Fitzjohn and Robert de Stuteville.

■ THE PLANTAGENET KINGS

HENRY II 1154-89

Henry II cross and crosslets (Tealby) Penny

	F	VF
Pennies cross and crosslets ('Tealby' coinage)	£130	£325

The issue is classified by bust variants into six groups, struck at 32 mints.

	F	VF
Pennies short cross	£80	£185

The 'short cross' coinage was introduced in 1180 and continued through successive reigns until Henry III brought about a change in 1247. HENRICVS REX appears on all these coins but they can be classified into reigns by the styles of the busts and lettering. CR Wren's guide *The Short Cross Coinage 1180-1247* is the best book to identify coins of this series.

RICHARD I 1189-99

	F	VF
Pennies short cross	£85	£215

JOHN 1189-1216

	F	VF
Pennies short cross	£80	£185

John short cross Penny

HENRY III 1216-72

	F	VF
Pennies short cross	£35	£90
Long cross no sceptre	£30	£70
Long cross with sceptre	£30	£70

Henry III, long cross Penny with sceptre

The 'long cross' pennies, first introduced in 1247, are divided into two groups: those with sceptre and those without. They also fall into five basic classes, with many varieties. CR Wren's *The Voided Long Cross Coinage, 1247-79* is the best guide to identification.

Edward I, 1st coinage, long cross Penny

EDWARD I 1272-1307   **F**   **VF**
1st coinage 1272-78

		F	VF
Long cross pennies	from	£30	£85

Similar in style to those of Henry III but with more realistic beard.

New coinage 1278-1307

		F	VF
Groats		£2650	£6850
Pennies, various classes, mints	from	£20	£55
Halfpennies	from	£35	£90
Farthings	from	£25	£80

Edward I Farthing London

The best guide to this era of coinage is *Edwardian English Silver Coins 1278-1351* (Sylloge of Coins of the British Isles no39).

EDWARD II 1307-27

		F	VF
Pennies, various classes, mints	from	£30	£65
Halfpennies	from	£50	£130
Farthing	from	£35	£95

EDWARD III 1327-77
1st and 2nd coinages 1327-43
Pennies (only 1st coinage)

	F	VF
various types and mints	£210	£550
Halfpennies, different types and mints	£25	£70
Farthings	£35	£80

3rd coinage 1344-51, florin coinage

	F	VF
Pennies, various types and mints	£25	£95
Halfpennies	£25	£70
Farthings	£30	£80

Edward III, post-treaty Groat

4th coinage 1351-77

		F	VF
Groats, many types and mints	from	£65	£190
Halfgroats		£40	£130
Pennies		£25	£85
Halfpennies, different types		£30	£110
Farthings, a few types		£110	£325

RICHARD II 1377-99   **F**   **VF**

		F	VF
Groats, four types	from	£485	£1600

Richard II Groat

	F	VF
Halfgroats	£325	£900
Pennies, various types, London	£200	£575
York	£75	£225
Durham	£135	£425
Halfpennies, three main types	£35	£95
Farthings, some varieties	£120	£375

HENRY IV 1399-1413

		F	VF
Groats, varieties	from	£2400	£6500
Halfgroats		£725	£2100
Pennies		£385	£1050
Halfpennies		£225	£625
Farthings		£725	£2100

Henry V Groat

HENRY V 1413-22

	F	VF
Groats, varieties	£185	£525
Halfgroats	£140	£385
Pennies	£45	£145
Halfpennies	£30	£120
Farthings	£250	£800

HENRY VI 1422-61
Annulet issue 1422-1427

	F	VF
Groats	£55	£145
Halfgroats	£35	£120
Pennies	£30	£100
Halfpennies	£25	£65
Farthings	£100	£285

Rosette-mascle issue 1427-1430

	F	VF
Groats	£60	£175
Halfgroats	£40	£125

	F	VF
Pennies	£40	£120
Halfpennies	£25	£75
Farthings	£150	£400

Pinecone-mascle issue 1430-1434
	F	VF
Groats	£55	£145
Halfgroats	£45	£135
Pennies	£40	£125
Halfpennies	£25	£70
Farthings	£150	£425

Leaf-mascle issue 1434-1435
	F	VF
Groats	£165	£475
Halfgroats	£120	£350
Pennies	£85	£210
Halfpennies	£35	£90

Leaf-trefoil issue 1435-1438
	F	VF
Groats	£85	£240
Halfgroats	£85	£210
Pennies	£70	£210
Halfpennies	£30	£70
Farthings	£140	£385

Trefoil issue 1438-1443
	F	VF
Groats	£85	£265
Halfgroats	£160	£485
Halfpennies	£30	£85

Trefoil-pellet issue 1443-1445
	F	VF
Groats	£175	£525

Henry VI, leaf-mascle issue Groat

Leaf-pellet issue 1445-1454
	F	VF
Groats	£75	£220
Halfgroats	£80	£225
Pennies	£55	£145
Halfpennies	£25	£70
Farthings	£150	£425

Unmarked issue 1445-1454
	F	VF
Groats	£550	£1650
Halfgroats	£365	£925

Cross-pellet issue 1454-1460
	F	VF
Groats	£150	£350
Halfgroats	£275	£750

	F	VF
Pennies	£50	£145
Halfpennies	£35	£85
Farthings	£250	£600

Lis-pellet issue 1454-1460
	F	VF
Groats	£265	£775

There are many different varieties, initial marks and mints in this reign. These prices are for commonest prices in each issue.

EDWARD IV 1st Reign 1461-1470
Heavy coinage 1461-4
	F	VF
Groats, many classes, all London	£165	£485
Halfgroats, many classes, all London	£250	£650
Pennies, different classes, London, York and Durham	£135	£385
Halfpennies, different classes, all London	£45	£130
Farthings, London	£210	£675

Edward IV light coinage Groat

Light coinage 1464-70
		F	VF
Groats, many different issues, varieties, ims and mints	from	£55	£165
Halfgroats, ditto		£50	£150
Pennies, ditto		£35	£95
Halfpennies, ditto		£30	£85
Farthings, two issues		£285	£825

Henry VI (restored) Groat London

HENRY VI restored 1470-71
		F	VF
Groats, different mints, different ims	from	£185	£525
Halfgroats	from	£265	£700
Pennies	from	£250	£650
Halfpennies	from	£165	£400

EDWARD IV 2nd reign 1471-83

	F	VF
Groats, different varieties, mints	£65	£175
Halfgroats	£45	£140
Pennies	£35	£110
Halfpennies	£30	£90

EDWARD IV or V 1483

im halved sun and rose

	F	VF
Groats	£1100	£3400
Pennies	£1200	£3650
Halfpennies	£285	£750

Richard III Groat London

RICHARD III 1483-85

	F	VF
Groats, reading EDWARD, initial mark boar's head on obverse, halved sun and rose on reverse	£1850	£5250
Groats, reading Ricard, London and York mints, various combinations of ims	£675	£1850
Halfgroats	£875	£2750
Pennies, York and Durham	£300	£800
London mint		unique
Halfpennies	£250	£725
Farthing	£1250	£3650

PERKIN WARBECK, PRETENDER

	F	VF
Groat, 1494	£1350	£3400

■ THE TUDOR MONARCHS

HENRY VII 1485-1509
Facing bust issues

Henry VII open crown type Groat London

	F	VF
Groats, all London		
Open crown without arches	£120	£350
Crown with two arches unjewelled	£95	£250
Crown with two jewelled arches	£70	£180
Similar but only one arch jewelled	£70	£180
Similar but tall thin lettering	£75	£190
Similar but single arch, tall thin lettering	£80	£225
Halfgroats, London		
Open crown without arches, tressure unbroken	£275	£700
Double arched crown	£45	£135
Unarched crown	£40	£100
Some varieties and different ims.		
Halfgroats, Canterbury		
Open crown, without arches	£40	£120
Double arched crown	£35	£120
Some varieties and different ims.		
Halfgroats, York		
Double arched crown	£40	£125
Unarched crown with tressure broken	£40	£120
Double arched crown with keys at side of bust	£35	£110
Many varieties and different ims.		
Pennies, facing bust type		
London	£160	£475
Canterbury, open crown	£250	£525
Canterbury, arched crown	£65	£165
Durham, Bishop Sherwood, S on breast	£65	£165
York	£40	£120
Many varieties and ims.		
Pennies, 'sovereign enthroned' type		
London, many varieties	£40	£120
Durham, many varieties	£35	£100
York, many varieties	£35	£100
Halfpennies, London		
Open crown	£40	£135
Arched crown	£30	£90
Crown with lower arch	£25	£75
Some varieties and ims.		
Halfpennies, Canterbury		
Open crown	£70	£175
Arched crown	£60	£125
Halfpennies, York		
Arched crown and key below bust	£65	£150
Farthings, all London	£350	£900

Profile issues

	F	VF
Testoons im lis, three different legends	£11500	£23000
Groats, all London		
Tentative issue, double band to crown	£250	£700

Henry VII regular issue Groat

	F	VF
Regular issue, triple band to crown	£135	£375
Some varieties and ims.		
Halfgroats		
London	£125	£350
London, no numeral after king's name	£300	£900
Canterbury	£80	£250
York, two keys below shield	£75	£225
York, XB by shield	£250	£700

HENRY VIII 1509-47
First coinage 1509-26 with portrait of Henry VII

	F	VF
Groats, London	£150	£400
Tournai	£750	£2500
Tournai, without portrait	£2250	*
Halfgroats, London	£125	£375
Canterbury, varieties	£70	£200
York, varieties	£70	£200
Tournai	£875	£2350
Pennies, 'sovereign enthroned' type, London	£50	£150
Canterbury, varieties	£70	£200
Durham, varieties	£40	£110
Halfpennies, facing bust type, London	£30	£70
Canterbury	£60	£175
Farthings, portcullis type, London	£250	£675

Henry VIII second coinage Groat York

Second coinage 1526-44 with young portrait of Henry VIII

	F	VF
Groats, London, varieties, ims	£125	£350
Irish title, HIB REX	£300	£950
York, varieties, ims	£145	£385
Halfgroats, London, varieties, ims	£65	£200
Canterbury, varieties, ims	£60	£165
York, varieties, ims	£60	£165

	F	VF
Pennies 'sovereign enthroned' type		
London, varieties, ims	£35	£120
Canterbury, varieties, ims	£75	£225
Durham	£35	£110
York	£200	£600
Halfpennies, facing bust type		
London, varieties, ims	£25	£80
Canterbury	£35	£100
York, varieties, ims	£75	£225
Farthings, portcullis type	£300	£750

Third coinage 1544-47 and posthumous issues 1547-51 with old bearded portrait

	F	VF
Testoons or shillings		
London, Tower mint, varieties, ims	£900	£3650
Southwark, varieties, ims	£850	£3250
Bristol, varieties, ims	£950	£3750
Groats, six different busts, varieties, ims		
London, Tower mint	£125	£450
Southwark	£125	£475
Bristol	£135	£525
Canterbury	£125	£450
York	£120	£450
London, Durham House	£250	£675

Henry VIII third coinage Groat

Halfgroats, only one style of bust, except York which has two, varieties, ims

	F	VF
London, Tower mint	£85	£250
Southwark	£75	£225
Bristol	£90	£300
Canterbury	£70	£225
York	£80	£240
London, Durham House	£425	£1100

Henry VIII third coinage Halfgroat Bristol

Henry VIII posthumous coinage Halfgroat Canterbury

	F	VF
Pennies, facing bust, varieties, ims		
London, Tower mint	£40	£135
Southwark	£50	£150
London, Durham House	£425	£975
Bristol	£70	£200
Canterbury	£50	£150
York	£50	£150
Halfpennies, facing bust varieties, ims		
London, Tower mint	£45	£125
Bristol	£85	£250
Canterbury	£60	£150
York	£50	£135

EDWARD VI 1547-53
First period 1547-49

	F	
Shillings, London, Durham House,		
im bow, patterns?		ext. rare
Groats, London, Tower, im arrow	£950	£3000
London, Southwark, im E, none	£950	£3000
Halfgroats, London, Tower, im arrow	£525	£1450
London, Southwark, im arrow, E	£450	£1250
Canterbury, im none	£425	£1100
Pennies, London, Tower, im	£400	£1100
London, Southwark, im E	£425	£1250
Bristol, im none	£400	£1150
Halfpennies, London, Tower im uncertain	£400	£1250
Bristol, im none	£475	£1375

Edward VI second period Shilling

Second period 1549-50

	F	VF
Shillings, London,		
Tower various ims	£200	£700
Bristol, im TC	£775	£2650
Canterbury, im T or t	£175	£700
London (Durham House),		
im bow, varieties	£175	£750

Third period 1550-53

	F	VF
Base silver (similar to issues of second period)		
Shillings, London, Tower, im lis, lion, rose	£150	£650
Pennies, London, Tower, im escallop	£65	£180
York, im mullet	£60	£175
Halfpennies, London, Tower	£175	£600
Fine silver issue		
Crown 1551 im Y, 1551-53 im tun	£875	£2500

Edward VI 1551 Crown

	F	VF
Halfcrown, walking horse, 1551, im Y	£675	£1850
Galloping horse,		
1551-52, im tun	£725	£1900

Edward VI, fine silver issue Sixpence

	F	VF
Walking horse,		
1553, im tun	£1300	£3750
Shillings, im Y, tun	£125	£450
Sixpences, London (Tower), im y, tun	£125	£525
York, im mullet	£200	£775
Threepences, London (Tower), im tun	£200	£800
York, im mullet	£400	£1450
Pennies, sovereign type	£1250	£4000
Farthings, portcullis type	£1500	*

Mary Groat

MARY 1553-54	F	VF
Groats, im pomegranate	£125	£425
Halfgroats, similar	£750	£2250
Pennies, reverse VERITAS TEMP FILIA	£700	£2000
Reverse CIVITAS LONDON	£700	£2000

PHILIP AND MARY 1554-58		
Shillings, full titles, without date	£425	£1750
Full titles, without date also without XII	£450	£1850
Full titles, dated 1554	£425	£1750
Dated 1554, English titles	£450	£1850
Dated 1555, English titles only	£425	£1800
Dated 1554, English titles		
only, also without XII	£475	£2000
Dated 1555, English titles		
only, also without XII	£750	*
Dated 1554 but date below bust	£2500	*
1555 but date below bust	£2750	*
1555 similar to previous		
but without ANG	£3000	*
Sixpences, full titles, 1554	£400	£1450
Full titles, undated		ext. rare
English titles, 1555	£450	£1650
Similar but date below bust, 1554	£800	*
English titles, 1557	£425	£1750
Similar, but date below bust, 1557	£1000	*
Groats, im lis	£150	£450
Halfgroats, im lis	£500	£1600

Philip and Mary Halfgroat

Pennies, im lis	£475	£1475
Base pennies, without portrait	£75	£225

ELIZABETH I 1558-1603		
Hammered coinage, first issue 1558-61		
Shillings ELIZABETH		
Wire-line circles	£575	£2400
Beaded inner circles	£250	£875
ET for Z	£150	£450

	F	VF
Groats		
Wire-line inner circles	£150	£650
Beaded inner circles	£75	£325
ET for Z	£70	£285
Halfgroats		
Wire-line inner circles	£165	£700
Beaded inner circles	£50	£150
Pennies		
Wire-line inner circles	£200	£850
Beaded inner circles	£35	£95
Countermarked shillings of Edward VI, 1560-61		
with portcullis mark		
(current for 4½d) F	£2650	*
with greyhound mark		
(current for 2½d) F	£3250	*

Hammered coinage, second issue 1561-82		
Sixpences, dated 1561-82	£65	£200
Threepences, 1561-82	£45	£145
Halfgroats, undated	£50	£170
Threehalfpences, 1561-62,		
1564-70, 1572-79, 1581-82	£45	£165
Pennies, undated	£35	£100
Threefarthings, 1561-62, 1568,		
1572-78, 1581-82	£75	£225

Elizabeth I 1601 Crown

Hammered coinage, third issue 1583-1603		
Crowns, im 1	£1650	£3500

	F	VF
im 2	£2850	£7500
Halfcrowns, im 1	£975	£2500
im 2 F	£3000	£8500
Shillings ELIZAB	£120	£450
Sixpences, 1582-1602	£60	£185
Halfgroats, E D G ROSA etc	£25	£80
Pennies	£25	£80
Halfpennies	£25	£75

There are many different initial marks, such as lis, bell or lion, featured on the hammered coins of Elizabeth I, and these marks enable collectors to date those coins which are not themselves dated. For more details see J J North's *English Hammered Coinage, Volume 2.*

Elizabeth I milled coinage 1561 Sixpence

Milled Coinage

Shillings		
Large size	£400	£1250
Intermediate	£325	£875
Small	£275	£750
Sixpences		
1561	£135	£425
1562	£120	£385
1563-64, 1566	£125	£395
1567-68	£125	£350
1570-71	£375	£1250
Groats, undated	£150	£575
Threepences, 1561, 1562-64	£150	£500
Halfgroats	£185	£625
Threefarthings	ext. rare	*

■ THE STUART KINGS

JAMES I 1603-25
First coinage 1603-04

	F	VF
Crowns, reverse begins EXURGAT	£950	£3000
Halfcrowns	£1250	£3500
Shillings, varieties	£90	£400
Sixpences, dated 1603-04, varieties	£70	£225
Halfgroats, undated	£35	£100
Pennies	£25	£70

Second coinage 1604-19

	F	VF
Crowns reverse begins QVAE DEVS	£875	£2850
Halfcrowns	£1350	£3650

James I second coinage Shilling

	F	VF
Shillings, varieties	£80	£325
Sixpences, dated 1604-15, varieties	£50	£175
Halfgroats, varieties	£20	£50
Pennies	£20	£50
Halfpennies	£15	£45

James I third coinage Shilling

Third coinage 1619-25

	F	VF
Crowns	£625	£1750
Plume over reverse shield	£825	£2250
Halfcrowns	£225	£750
Plume over reverse shield	£500	£1475
Shillings	£100	£325
Plume over reverse shield	£225	£750
Sixpences dated 1621-24	£75	£225
Halfgroats	£20	£50
Pennies	£20	£50
Halfpennies	£15	£35

CHARLES I 1625-1649
Tower Mint 1625-1643

Crowns, obverse King on horseback, reverse shield

		F	VF
1st horseman/square shield im lis, cross-calvary		£750	£2000
Horseman/square shield, plume above shield im lis, cross-calvary, castle		£1000	£3250
2nd horseman/oval shield im plume, rose harp, some varieties	from	£650	£1700
3rd horseman/round shield im bell, crown, tun, anchor, triangle, star, portcullis, triangle-in-circle, some varieties,	from	£650	£1700

Halfcrowns, obverse King on horseback, reverse shield

	F	VF
4th bust/oval or round shield im harp, portcullis, bell, crown, tun, many varieties, from	£50	£175
5th bust/square shield im tun, anchor, triangle, many varieties	£60	£200
6th bust/square shield im anchor, triangle, star, triangle-in-circle, many varieties	£45	£165
Sixpences		
1st bust/square shield, date above, 1625 im lis, cross-calvary,		
1626 im cross-calvary,	£100	£350
2nd bust/square shield, date above, 1625, 1626 im cross-calvary, 1626, 1627 im negro's head, 1628, 1629 im castle, 1629 im heart,		
1630 im heart, plume	£110	£425
3rd bust/oval shield, im plume, rose,	£70	£225
4th bust/oval or round shield, im harp, portcullis, bell, crown, tun	£50	£150

Charles I Tower mint Crown, plume on rev

		F	VF
1st horseman/square shield im lis, cross-calvary, negro's head, castle, anchor, many varieties	from	£225	£725
2nd horseman/oval shield im plume, rose, harp, portcullis, many varieties	from	£125	£385
3rd horseman/round shield im bell, crown, tun, portcullis, anchor, triangle, star, many varieties,	from	£75	£200
4th horseman/round shield im star, triangle in circle		£70	£200

Charles I Tower mint Sixpence im crown

		F	VF
5th bust/square shield im tun, anchor, triangle, many varieties	from	£60	£200
6th bust/square shield im triangle, star		£50	£200
Halfgroats, crowned rose both sides im lis, cross-calvary, negro's head		£25	£80
2nd bust/oval shield im plume, rose		£25	£80
3rd bust/oval shield im rose, plume		£30	£90
4th bust/oval or round shield, im harp, crown, portcullis, bell, tun, anchor, triangle, star, many varieties	from	£20	£50
5th bust/round shield, im anchor		£30	£90
Pennies, uncrowned rose both sides im one or two pellets, lis, negro's head		£20	£60
2nd bust/oval shield im plume		£25	£75
3rd bust/oval shield im plume, rose		£20	£60
4th bust/oval shield im harp, one or two pellets, portcullis, bell, triangle		£15	£50
5th bust/oval shield im one or two pellets, none		£15	£50
Halfpennies, uncrowned rose both sides im none		£15	£40

Charles I Tower mint Halfcrown, im triangle

Shillings

		F	VF
1st bust/square shield im lis, cross-calvary, some varieties		£125	£500
2nd bust/square shield im cross-calvary, negro's head, castle, anchor, heart, plume many varieties,	from	£90	£395
3rd bust/oval shield im plume, rose		£70	£250

Tower Mint, under Parliament 1643-48
Crowns, obverse King on horseback, reverse shield

	F	VF
4th horseman/round shield im P, R, eye sun	£700	£1850
5th horseman/round shield im sun, sceptre	£850	£2250

Charles I Parliament Shilling,

Halfcrowns, obverse King on horseback, reverse shield		
3rd horseman/round shield im P, R, eye sun	£50	£200
im P, foreshortened horse	£150	£450
5th tall horseman/round shield im sun, sceptre	£75	£250
Shillings, reverse all square shield		
6th bust, crude, im P, R, eye, sun	£45	£165
7th bust, tall, slim, im sun, sceptre	£60	£245
8th bust, shorter, older, im sceptre	£70	£285
Sixpences, reverse all square shields		
6th bust im P, R, eye sun	£70	£200
7th bust im R, eye, sun, sceptre	£60	£185
8th bust (crude style) im eye, sun	£125	£400
Halfgroats, 4th bust/round shield im P, R, eye sceptre	£20	£70
7th bust, old/round shield im eye, sun, sceptre	£20	£70
Pennies, 7th bust/oval shield im one or two pellets	£20	£70

Charles I Briot's issue Crown

Briot's first milled issue 1631-32, im flower and B	F	VF
Crowns	£950	£2500
Halfcrowns	£525	£1500
Shillings	£350	£850
Sixpences	£165	£450
Halfgroats	£65	£140
Pennies	£70	£180

Briot's second milled issue 1638-39, im anchor and B, anchor and mullet		
Halfcrowns	£350	£850
Shillings	£150	£450
Sixpences	£90	£240

Briot's first milled issue Sixpence

Briot's hammered issue 1638-39, im anchor, triangle over anchor		
Halfcrowns	£825	£2000
Shillings	£350	£875

Charles I 1645 Exeter Crown

Provincial Mints

		F	VF
York 1642-44, im lion			
Halfcrowns, varieties	from	£300	£750
Shillings		£225	£650
Sixpences		£275	£850
Threepences		£70	£175

Aberystwyth 1638-42 im open book			
Halfcrowns, varieties	from	£950	£3500
Shillings		£475	£1500
Sixpences		£400	£1100
Groats		£75	£180

Charles I Aberystwyth Groat

	F	VF
Threepences	£50	£145
Halfgroats	£55	£150
Pennies	£70	£225
Halfpennies	£200	£525

Aberystwyth-Furnace 1647-48, im crown			
Halfcrowns	from	£2500	£7000
Shillings		£3500	*
Sixpences		£1500	£3750
Groats		£275	£650
Threepences		£250	£575
Halfgroats		£350	£850
Pennies		£750	£2000

Shrewsbury 1642 im plume without band			
Pounds, varieties	from	£2850	£7000
Halfpounds		£1450	£3500
Crowns		£950	£2850
Halfcrowns		£725	£2000
Shillings		£1650	£5500

Oxford 1642-46 im plume with band			
Pounds, varieties	from	£2500	£6500
Halfpounds		£1100	£2750
Crowns		£1000	£2650
Halfcrowns		£325	£750
Shillings		£375	£1100
Sixpences		£300	£850
Groats		£175	£500
Threepences		£125	£350
Halfgroats		£125	£350
Pennies		£225	£600

Bristol 1643-45 im Bristol monogram, acorn, plumelet			
Halfcrowns, varieties	from	£400	£1000

Charles I York Shilling

	F	VF
Shillings	£485	£1200
Sixpences	£325	£925
Groats	£195	£485
Threepences	£200	£500
Halfgroats	£225	£675
Pennies	£425	£950

Charles I 1644 Bristol Halfcrown

Late 'Declaration' issues 1645-6
Ashby de la Zouch
These bear the marks A, B and plume.

Halfcrowns, varieties	from	£2250	*
Shillings, varieties		£1000	*
Sixpences, varieties		£1000	*
Groats, varieties		£700	£1850
Threepences, varieties		£225	£525
Halfgroats, varieties		£500	£1250

Truro 1642-43 im rose, bugle			
Crowns, varieties	from	£475	£1000
Halfcrowns		£1250	£3250
Shillings		£3750	*

Charles I 1646 Bridgnorth-on-Severn Halfcrown

Exeter 1643-46 im Ex, rose, castle		**F**	**VF**
Halfpounds			ext. rare
Crowns, varieties	from	£450	£1050
Halfcrowns		£450	£1000
Shillings		£400	£1000
Sixpences		£375	£900
Groats		£150	£375
Threepences		£150	£375
Halfgroats		£300	£750
Pennies		£400	£1000

Worcester 1643-4 im castle, helmet, leopard's head, lion, two lions, lis, rose, star

Halfcrowns, many varieties	from	£950	£2750

Salopia (Shrewsbury) 1644 im helmet, lis, rose in legend

Halfcrowns, many varieties	from	£1100	£3000

Worcester or Salopia (Shrewsbury) im bird, boar's head, lis, castle, cross and annulets, helmet, lion, lis, pear, rose, scroll

Shillings, varieties	£2250	£5250
Sixpences	£1850	£5000
Groats	£675	£2000
Threepences	£425	£975
Halfgroats	£475	£1200

'HC' mint (probably Hartlebury Castle, Worcester, 1646) im pear, three pears

Halfcrowns	£1650	£4000

Chester 1644 im cinquefoil, plume, prostrate gerb, three gerbs

Halfcrowns, varieties	£1250	£3500
Shillings	£2250	7500
Threepences	£950	£2750

Welsh Marches mint? 1644

Halfcrowns	£1000	£2950

Carlisle besieged 1644-45	**F**	**VF**
Three shillings	£8500	£20000
Shillings F	£6500	£13500

Newark besieged 1645-6, surrendered May 1646

Halfcrowns, F	£825	£1750

Charles I 1645 Newark Halfcrown

Shillings, 1645-46, varieties F	£675	£1500
Ninepences, 1645-46	£650	£1400
Sixpences	£750	£1750

Pontefract besieged 1648-49

Two shillings, 1648	£6250	£16500
Shillings, 1648, varieties	£2250	£5750

Charles I 1648 Pontefract Shilling

Scarborough besieged 1644-45

Many odd values issued were issued in Scarborough, all of which are extremely rare. The coin's value was decided by the intrinsic value of the piece of metal from which it was made.

Examples: 5s 8d, 2s 4d, 1s 9d, 1s 3d, 7d F

Collectors can expect to pay at least £12000 or more in F and £19500 in VF for any of these.

COMMONWEALTH 1649-60

Crowns, im sun 1649, 51-54, 56	£800	£1900
Halfcrowns, im sun 1649, 1651-6	£250	£650
im anchor 1658-60	£1250	£2750

Commonwealth 1656 Halfcrown

	F	VF
Shillings, im sun 1649, 1661-87	£175	£425
im anchor 1658-60	£850	£1750
Sixpences, im sun 1649, 1651-7	£150	£375
im anchor 1658-6	£675	£1600
Halfgroats undated	£35	£100
Pennies undated	£30	£80
Halfpennies	£30	£80

CHARLES II 1660-85
Hammered coinage 1660-62

		F	VF
Halfcrowns, three issues	from	£250	£850
Shillings, three issues	from	£165	£500

Charles II hammered issue Shilling

		F	VF
Sixpences, three issues		£135	£450
Fourpences, third issue only		£35	£90
Threepences, third issue	from	£30	£70
Twopences, three issues	from	£25	£65
Pennies, three issues	from	£25	£65

'ROYAL' AND 'ROSE' BASE METAL FARTHINGS

Until 1613 English coins were struck only in gold or silver, because the monarchy thought base metal issues would dimish the royal prerogative of coining.

However silver coins became far too small and farthings so tiny that they had to be discontinued.

So to meet demands for small change, James I authorised Lord Harington to issue copper farthing tokens.

Subsequently this authority passed in turn to the Duke of Lennox, the Duchess of Richmond and Lord Maltravers.

It ceased by order of Parliament in 1644.

■ ROYAL FARTHING TOKENS

JAMES I	Fair	F	VF	EF
Type 1 Harington, c1613. Larger flan with tin-washed surface, mint-mark between sceptres below crown	£10	£20	£75	£200
Type 2 Harington, c1613. Larger flan, no tin wash	£15	£15	£40	£120
Type 3 Lennox, 1614-25. IACO starts at 1 o'clock position	£3	£10	£25	£95
Type 4 Lennox, 1622-25. Oval flan, IACO starts at 7 o'clock	£8	£26	£65	£200

CHARLES I	Fair	F	VF	EF
Type 1 Richmond, 1625-34 single arched crown	£2	£8	£25	£85
Type 2 Transitional, c1634 double arched crown	£6	£20	£50	£160
Type 3 Maltravers, 1634-36 inner circles	£3	£10	£30	£85
Type 4 Richmond, 1625-34 as Type 1 but oval	£8	£25	£60	£180
Type 5 Maltravers, 1634-36 double arched crown	£10	£30	£70	£160

■ ROSE FARTHING TOKENS

These have a rose on the reverse.

	Fair	F	VF	EF
Type 1 Small thick flan	£3	£10	£30	£100
Type 2 Small thick flan, but single arched crown	£2	£7	£25	£85
Type 3 Small thick flan, but sceptres below crown	£10	£25	£50	£110

ABOVE: (from left to right) James I Harington farthings, types 1, 2 and 3

ABOVE: (from left to right) Charles I Richmond, Maltravers and rose farthings

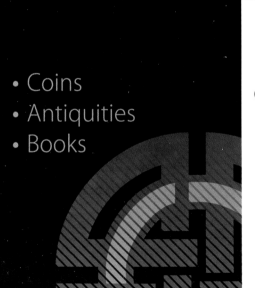

MILLED COINAGE FROM 1656

This listing gives a general indication of value throughout the entire milled series.

As such, only some of the varieties, dates and errors are mentioned.

Again, the prices shown in this guide are the approximate amounts collectors can expect to pay for coins, not dealers' buying prices. Standards of grading also vary.

Information for this guide is drawn from auction results and dealers' lists, with the aim of determining firm valuations, but prices still vary enormously from sale to sale and from one dealer's list to another.

The prices given here aim at a reasonable assessment of the market at the time of compilation.

With some denominations in the silver series, the column headings which indicate condition change at the beginning of the lists of George III coins. The condition, or grade, of a coin is of great importance in determining its market value. Refer to the pages on grading (pp52-53) and terms used in this book (pp54-55).

■ CROMWELL GOLD PATTERNS

These were struck by order of Cromwell, with the consent of the Council of State.

Thomas Simon made the dies, and the coins were struck on Peter Blondeau's machine.

The fifty shillings and the broad were struck from the same dies, but the fifty shillings has the edge inscription PROTECTOR LITERIS LITERAE NUMMIS CORONA ER SALUS, while the broad is not as thick and has a grained edge.

No original strikings of the half broad are known, but some were struck from dies made by John Tanner in 1738.

All three denominations are dated 1656.

	F	VF	EF	Unc
Fifty shillings	*	£45000	£80000	*
Broad	*	£6750	£30000	£23000
Half-broad	*	*	£15000	*

Oliver Cromwell gold Broad 1656

■ FIVE GUINEAS

CHARLES II	F	VF	EF	Unc
1668-78 pointed end of trnctn of bust	£2750	£4750	£16500	*
1668, 69, 75 as above, eleph below bust	£2750	£4750	£16500	*
1675-8 as above, eleph & castle below bust	£2500	£4750	£16500	*
1678-84 rounded end to trnctn	£2500	£4750	£16000	*
1680-4 as above, eleph & castle	£2850	£5250	£16000	*

Charles II 1670 proof Five Guineas

JAMES II	F	VF	EF	Unc
1686 sceptres in wrong order on rev	£2750	£4750	£16000	*
1687-8 sceptres correct	£2500	£4750	£16000	*
1687-8 eleph & castle	£2750	£5250	£16500	*

WILLIAM AND MARY	F	VF	EF	Unc
1691-4 no prov mark	£3000	£5250	£15000	*
1691-4 eleph & castle	£3000	£5250	£15000	*

William and Mary 1692 elephant & castle Five Guineas

WILLIAM III	F	VF	EF	Unc
1699-1700 no				
prov mark	£2500	£3950	£13500	*
1699 eleph & castle	£2500	£4750	£14500	*
1701 new bust				
'fine work'	£2750	£3750	£11000	£25000

ANNE
Pre-Union with Scotland

1703 VIGO below bust	*	*	£175000	*
1705-6 plain below	£3000	£4500	£18750	*

Post-Union with Scotland

1706	£2750	£4500	£13000	£20000
1709 larger lettering				
wider shield and				
crowns	£2850	£4750	£13500	*
1711, 1713-4				
broader bust	£2850	£4750	£13500	*

The pre-Union reverse has separate shields, top and right, for England and Scotland, while post-Union reverses have the English and Scottish arms side by side on the top and bottom shields.

GEORGE I

1716, 17, 20, 26	£4250	£6250	£25000	*

George I 1716 Five Guineas

GEORGE II

1729, 31, 35,				
38, 41 YH	£2750	£3750	£11000	*
1729 YH,				
E.I.C. below head	£2750	£4250	£11000	*
1746 OH, LIMA				
below	£2750	£4000	£10000	£20000
1748, 53 OH				
plain below	£3000	£4250	£10000	£17500

GEORGE III	F	VF	EF	Unc
1770, 73, 77 patterns only	*	*	£95000	£175000

■ TWO GUINEAS

CHARLES II

1664, 65, 69, 71 pointed				
end to trnctn	£1650	£3500	£9500	*
1664 elephant below	£1650	£3500	£9500	*
1675-84 rounded end				
to trnctn	£1500	£3000	£9000	*
1676, 78, 82-84				
eleph & castle				
below bust	£1650	£3500	£9750	*
1678 eleph below				ext. rare

JAMES II

1687	£2000	£4250	£11500	*
1688/7	£2000	£4500	£11500	*

WILLIAM AND MARY

1691, 93, 94 eleph				
& castle	£1975	£3750	£8000	£11000
1693, 94 no				
prov mark	£1975	£2750	£7500	£11000

WILLIAM III

1701	£1900	£4000	£10000	*

ANNE
(none struck before union)

1709, 11, 13, 14	£1450	£2250	£5750	£9250

GEORGE I

1717, 20, 26	£1500	£2500	£6000	£8500

GEORGE II

1734, 35, 38, 39, YH F	£700	£1250	£2500	£4000
1739-40 intermediate				
hd F	£750	£1250	£2500	£4000
1748, 53, OH	£800	£1450	£3500	£4750

GEORGE III

1768, 73, 77 patterns only	*	*	£25000	£40000

■ GUINEAS

CHARLES II

1663 pointed trnctn	£1750	£4500	£15000	*
1663 eleph	£1100	£3500	£10000	*
1664 trnctn indented	£1100	£3500	£10000	*
1664 eleph	*	*	£16500	*
1664-73 sloping pointed				
trnctn	£900	£2850	£8500	*
1664, 65, 68 eleph	£1200	£3000	£9750	*
1672-84 rounded trnctn	£800	£2450	£7250	*
1674-84 eleph & castle	£1100	£2750	£9500	*
1677-8 eleph				ext. rare

Charles II 1663 Guinea, elephant below bust

JAMES II	F	VF	EF	Unc
1685-6 1st bust	£725	£1750	£5250	£9000
1685 1st bust eleph & castle	£800	£2250	£6250	*
1686-8 2nd bust	£750	£1750	£5250	£9000
1686-8 2nd bust eleph & castle	£850	£2250	£6750	*

WILLIAM AND MARY				
1689-94 no prov mark	£750	£2000	£5750	£8250
1689-94 eleph & castle	£800	£2500	£5750	*
1692 eleph	£1250	£2950	£8000	*

WILLIAM III				
1695-6 1st bust	£600	£1500	£4250	£6250
1695, 7 eleph & castle	*	*	*	*
1697-1701 2nd bust	£625	£1500	£4250	£6000
1698-1701 eleph & castle	*	*	* ext. rare	
1701 3rd bust 'fine work'	£800	£2250	£6000	*

ANNE				
Pre-Union				
1702, 1705-07 plain below bust	£875	£2000	£5000	£7500
1703 VIGO below	£4500	£9000	£25000	*

Post-Union				
1707-8 1st bust	£750	£1650	£4500	£6500
1707 eleph & castle	£950	£2500	£6500	*
1707-9 2nd bust	£650	£1350	£3500	£5000
1708-9 eleph & castle	£950	£2500	£6500	*
1710-1714 3rd bust	£575	£1000	£2850	£4000

Pre-Union reverse has separate shields, top and right, for England and Scotland. Post-Union reverses have the English and Scottish arms side by side on both the top and bottom shields.

GEORGE I				
1714 1st hd PR. EL. (Prince Elector) in rev legend	£1100	£2750	£5000	£7000
1715 2nd hd, tie with two ends	£550	£1000	£2950	£4250

	F	VF	EF	Unc
1715-16 3rd hd, hair not curling round trnctn	£550	£1100	£3000	£4750
1716-23 4th hd, tie with loop	£550	£1100	£3000	£4750
1721-2 eleph & castle	*			ext. rare
1723-7 5th hd, smaller, older bust	£475	£975	£2850	£4500
1726 eleph & castle	£1650	£4000	*	*

GEORGE II				
1727 1st YH, small lettering	£750	£2000	£5500	£8000
1727-28 1st YH larger lettering	£750	£2150	£5750	£8500
1729-32 2nd YH	£650	£1375	£3500	*
1729, 31-32 E.I.C. below	£750	£2150	£5750	*
1732-38 larger lettering	£600	£1150	£3000	£5000
1732 E.I.C. below	£750	£1750	£4500	*
1739-40, 43 intermediate hd	£500	£950	£2850	£4000
1739 E.I.C. below	£750	£1750	£5000	*
1745-6 larger lettering	£500	£1150	£2750	£4250
1745 LIMA below	£2000	£3950	£8000	*
1746-53, 55-56, 58-59, 60, OH	£500	£1150	£2750	£4250

GEORGE III				
1761 1st hd	£900	£2850	£4750	*
1763-64 2nd hd	£650	£2000	£4500	*
1765-73 3rd hd	£300	£650	£1500	£3000
1774-79, 81-86 4th hd	£275	£400	£925	£1750
1789-99 5th hd, 'spade' rev	£265	£385	£750	£1200
1813 6th hd, rev shield in Garter ('Military guinea')	£725	£1500	£2950	£4500

George II 1760 Guinea

George III 1813 Guinea

■ HALF-GUINEAS

CHARLES II	F	VF	EF	Unc
1669-72 bust with pointed trnctn	£650	£1500	£4750	*
1672-84 rounded truncation	£650	£1500	£4750	*
1676-78, 80, 82, 84 eleph & castle	£750	£1800	£5250	*

JAMES II				
1686-88 no prov mark	£675	£1500	£4500	*
1686 eleph & castle	£2000	*	*	*

WILLIAM AND MARY				
1689 1st busts	£650	£1650	£4500	*
1690-4 2nd busts	£600	£1650	£4500	*
1691-2 eleph & castle	£650	£1650	£5000	*
1692 eleph	£1500	*	*	

William and Mary 1689 Half-guinea

WILLIAM III				
1695 no prov mark	£475	£950	£2850	*
1695-6 eleph & castle	£650	£1500	£3750	*
1697-1701 larger harp on rev	£475	£900	£2850	*
1698 eleph & castle	£600	£1650	£4750	*

ANNE
Pre-Union

1702, 05 plain below bust	£750	£1950	£5250	*
1703 VIGO below	£3250	£9000	£18500	*

Post-Union

1707-1714 plain	£375	£700	£2250	£3250

Pre-Union reverse has separate shields, top and right, for England and Scotland. Post-Union reverses have the English and Scottish arms side by side on the top and bottom shields.

GEORGE I				
1715, 17-24 1st hd	£300	£575	£2000	£3000
1721 eleph & castle	*	*	* ext. rare	
1725-27 smaller older hd	£275	£425	£1450	£2350

GEORGE II	F	VF	EF	Unc
1728-39 YH			£375	£875
	£2850		*	
1729-32, 39 E.I.C. below	£550	£1350	£3850	*
1740, 43, 45-46 intermediate hd	£375	£700	£2250	*
1745 LIMA below	£1350	£2850	£6250	*
1747-53, 55-56, 58-60 OH	£275	£500	£1600	£3000

George II 1756 Half-guinea

GEORGE III				
1762-63 1st hd	£575	£1375	£3250	£5000
1764-66, 68-69, 72-75 2nd hd	£225	£525	£1350	£2250
1774-75 3rd hd	£850	£1750	£3950	*
1775-79, 81, 83-86 4th hd	£195	£325	£800	£1500
1787-91, 93-98, 1800 5th hd	£175	£250	£575	£850
1801-03 6th hd	£130	£185	£400	£675
1804, 06, 08-11, 13 7th hd	£130	£195	£425	£775

■ THIRD-GUINEAS

GEORGE III				
1797-1800 1st hd	£90	£150	£300	£475
1801-03 date close to crown on rev	£90	£150	£300	£475
1804-05, 08-11 2nd hd	£90	£150	£300	£475

■ QUARTER-GUINEAS

GEORGE I				
1718	£110	£185	£385	£525

GEORGE III				
1762	£120	£200	£400	£600

George III 1762 Quarter-guinea

MILLED COINAGE

■ FIVE POUNDS

	F	VF	EF	Unc
GEORGE III				
1820 pattern F	*	*	*	£125000
GEORGE IV				
1826 proof	*	*	£8250	£13000
VICTORIA				
1839 proof, 'Una and the Lion' rev F	*	*	£18500	£35000

Victoria 1839 proof Five Pound with 'Una and the Lion'

	F	VF	EF	Unc
1887 JH F	£875	£950	£1100	£1650
1887 proof	*	*	£1500	£3000
1887 proof no B.P.	*	*	£1750	£3500
1893 OH F	£900	£1050	£1500	£2250
1893 proof	*	*	£1850	£3750
EDWARD VII				
1902 F	£875	£975	£1100	£1500
1902 proof	*	*	£1000	£1400
GEORGE V				
1911 proof F	*	*	*	£2650
GEORGE VI				
1937 proof	*	*	*	£1350

In 1984 the Royal Mint issued the first of an annual issue of Brilliant Uncirculated £5 coins.

These bear the symbol 'U' in a circle to the left of the date on the reverse to indicate the standard of striking.

BV indicates bullion value, at the time of going to press gold is approximately £780 per troy oz.

ELIZABETH II Sovereign Issues	Unc
1953 proof	ext. rare
1980 proof, originally issued in Royal Mint set	BV

	Unc
1981 proof	BV
1982 proof, originally issued in Royal Mint set	BV
1984 proof	BV
1984 BU	BV
1985 proof	BV
1985 BU	BV
1986 BU	BV
1987 new effigy, BU	BV
1988 BU	£950
1989 proof, 500th anniversary of the sovereign, originally issued in Royal Mint set	£1200
1989 BU, 500th anniversary of the sovereign	BV
1990 proof, originally issued in Royal Mint set	BV
1990 BU	BV
1991 proof, originally issued in Royal Mint set	BV
1991 BU	BV
1992 proof, originally issued in Royal Mint set	BV
1992 BU	BV
1993 proof, originally issued in Royal Mint set	BV
1993 BU	BV
1994 proof, originally issued in Royal Mint set	BV
1994 BU	BV
1995 proof, originally issued in Royal Mint set	BV
1995 BU	BV
1996 proof, originally issued in Royal Mint set	BV
1996 BU	BV
1997 proof, originally issued in Royal Mint set	BV
1997 BU	BV
1998 proof, originally issued in Royal Mint set	BV
1998 BU	BV
1999 proof, originally issued in Royal Mint set	BV
1999 BU	BV
2000 proof, originally issued in Royal Mint set	BV
2000 BU	BV
2001 proof, originally issued in Royal Mint set	BV
2001 BU	BV
2002 shield reverse, proof, originally issued in Royal Mint set	BV
2002 BU	BV
2003 proof, originally issued in Royal Mint set	BV
2003 BU	BV
2004 proof, originally issued in Royal Mint set	BV
2004 BU	BV
2005 proof, originally issued in Royal Mint set	BV
2005 BU	BV
2006 proof, originally issued in Royal Mint set	BV
2006 BU	BV
2007 proof, originally issued in Royal Mint set	BV
2008 proof, originally issued in Royal Mint four coin set	BV
2009 proof, Countdown to London 2012	£1150
2009 proof, Henry VIII	£1150

■ TWO POUNDS

	F	VF	EF	Unc
GEORGE III				
1820 pattern F	*	*	£13000	£25000

GEORGE IV	F	VF	EF	Unc
1823 St George on rev F	*	£800	£1500	£2950
1826 proof, shield rev	*	*	£3500	£5750

George IV 1823 Two Pounds

WILLIAM IV

1831 proof	*	*	£3950	£7500

VICTORIA

	F	VF	EF	Unc
1887 JH F	£385	£425	£495	£600
1887 proof	*	*	£725	£1350
1893 OH F	£425	£525	£675	£875
1893 proof	*	*	£800	£1350

EDWARD VII

	F	VF	EF	Unc
1902 F	£385	£425	£525	£700
1902 proof	*	*	£500	£650

GEORGE V

1911 proof F	*	*	*	£925

GEORGE VI

1937 proof	*	*	*	£700

ELIZABETH II

	Unc
1953 proof	ext. rare
1980 proof, originally issued in Royal Mint set	BV
1982 proof, originally issued in Royal Mint set	BV
1983 proof	BV
1985 proof, originally issued in Royal Mint set	BV
1987 proof	BV
1988 proof	BV
1989 500th anniversary of the sovereign, proof	£500
1990 proof	BV
1991 proof	BV
1992 proof	BV
1993 proof	BV
1996 proof	BV
1998 proof, originally issued in Royal Mint set	BV
2000 proof, originally issued in Royal Mint set	BV
2002 shield rev, proof, originially issued in Royal Mint set	BV
2003 proof, originally issued in Royal Mint set	BV
2004 proof, originally issued in Royal Mint set	BV
2005 proof, originally issued in Royal Mint set	BV
2006 proof, originally issued in Royal Mint set	BV
2007 proof, originally issued in Royal Mint set	BV
2008 proof, originally issued in Royal Mint set	BV

2009 proof, issued in Royal Mint set	£350
2009 250th Anniversary Birth Robert Burns	£550

■ SOVEREIGNS

George III 1817 Sovereign

Early sovereigns can attain higher prices in exceptional grade.

GEORGE III	F	VF	EF	Unc
1817 F	£300	£475	£1350	£1900
1818	£700	£1350	£3000	*
1819	£28000	£45000	*	*
1820	£285	£450	£1250	£2000

GEORGE IV
Type Laureate head/St George

	F	VF	EF	Unc
1821	£300	£475	£1000	£1825
1821 proof	*	*	£1950	£4000
1822 F	£300	£475	£1000	£1950
1823	£1000	£1750	£4500	*
1824	£375	£475	£1250	£2150
1825	£575	£1100	£3750	£6000

Type bare head/shield

	F	VF	EF	Unc
1825 F	£300	£475	£975	£1750
1826	£300	£475	£95	£1650
1826 proof	*	*	£1350	£2750
1827 F	£300	£475	£975	£1750
1828 F	£3000	£5250	£16000	*
1829	£300	£525	£1200	£2150
1830	£300	£525	£1200	£2150

WILLIAM IV

	F	VF	EF	Unc
1831	£475	£850	£2250	£3850
1831 proof	*	*	£2250	£4250
1832 F	£350	£595	£1300	£2000
1833	£400	£650	£1650	£2750

William IV 1833 Sovereign

	F	VF	EF	Unc
1835	£400	£650	£1650	£2750
1836	£400	£625	£1475	£2500
1837	£425	£600	£1475	£2500

VICTORIA	F	VF	EF	Unc
Type I, YH/shield				
1838	£500	£850	£1875	£3000
1838 wreath leaves different	£1850	*	*	*
1839	£1000	£1750	£3250	*
1839 proof	*	*	£2250	£4750
1841	£3250	£5000	*	*
1842	*	*	£475	£1100
1843	*	*	£375	£850
1843 narrow shield	£3250	£5500	*	*
1844	*	*	£475	£1100
1845	*	*	£475	£1100
1846	*	*	£475	£1100
1847	*	*	£425	£850
1848	*	*	£475	£1100
1849	*	*	£500	*
1850	*	*	£475	£1100
1851	*	*	£425	£850
1852	*	*	£425	£850
1853	*	*	£295	£750
1853 proof	*	*	£4750	£9250
1854	*	*	£425	£850
1855	*	*	£285	£625
1856	*	*	£295	£750
1857	*	*	£285	£625
1858	*	*	£285	£625
1859	*	*	£255	£625
1859 'Ansell'	£525	£1600	£5000	*

Victoria 1859 'Ansell' Sovereign

	F	VF	EF	Unc
1860	*	*	£350	£750
1861	*	*	£285	£600
1862	*	*	£285	£600
1863	*	*	£285	£485
1863 die number below wreath on rev	*	*	£285	£525
1863 '827' on trnctn	£4000	£6000	*	*
1864 die no	*	*	£285	£525
1865 die no	*	*	£285	£525
1866 die no	*	*	£285	£525
1868 die no	*	*	£285	£525
1869 die no	*	*	£285	£525
1870 die no	*	*	£285	£525
1871 die no	*	*	£275	£400
1871 S (Sydney mint) below wreath	*	*	£300	*
1872	*	*	£200	£300
1872 die no	*	*	£275	£400

	F	VF	EF	Unc
1872 M (Melbourne mint) below wreath	*	*	£275	£1000
1872 S	*	*	£375	£1000
1873 die no	*	*	£200	£400
1873 S	*	*	£250	£500
1874 die no	£925	£2750	£5750	£8000
1874 M	*	*	£400	*
1875 S	*	*	£375	*
1877 S	*	*	£375	£900
1878 S	*	*	£375	£900
1879 S	*	*	£375	*
1880 M	£300	£825	£2250	*
1880 S	*	*	£375	*
1881 M	*	*	£400	*
1881 S	*	*	£400	*
1882 M	*	*	£400	*
1882 S	*	*	£400	*
1883 M	*	£400	£1000	*
1883 S	*	*	£285	£800
1884 M	*	*	£375	£900
1884 S	*	*	£285	£800
1885 M	*	*	£285	£800
1885 S	*	*	£285	£800
1886 M	£700	£1750	£6000	*
1886 S	*	*	£285	£800
1887 M	£600	£1500	£4000	*
1887 S	*	*	£400	£1450

Type II, YH/St George and dragon

	F	VF	EF	Unc
1871	*	*	£225	£475

Victoria 1871 St George Sovereign

	F	VF	EF	Unc
1871 S below hd	*	*	£800	*
1872	*	*	£200	£475
1872 M below hd	*	£265	£750	£2000
1872 S	*	*	£265	£800
1873	*	*	£200	£475
1873 M	*	*	£265	£800
1873 S	*	*	£265	£625
1874	*	*	£225	£475
1874 M	*	*	£265	£700
1874 S	*	*	£265	*
1875 M	*	*	£265	£700
1875 S	*	*	£265	*
1876	*	*	£225	£575
1876 M	*	*	£265	£800
1876 S	*	*	£265	£800
1877 M	*	*	£265	£800
1878	*	*	£225	£475
1878 M	*	*	£265	£750

	F	VF	EF	Unc
1879	£400	£600	£2750	*
1879 M	*	*	£265	£750
1879 S	*	*	£700	£1650
1880	*	*	£225	£475
1880 M	*	*	£225	£750
1880 S	*	*	£400	*
1881 M	*	*	£265	£800
1881 S	*	*	£265	£825
1882 M	*	*	£265	£800
1882 S	*	*	£265	£650
1883 M	*	*	£265	£750
1883 S	*	*	£300	*
1884	*	*	£200	£450
1884 M	*	*	£265	£750
1884 S	*	*	£265	£750
1885	*	*	£225	£475
1885 M	*	*	£265	£750
1885 S	*	*	£265	£750
1886 M	*	*	£265	£750
1886 S	*	*	£265	£750
1887 M	*	*	£265	£800
1887 S	*	*	£265	£750

Victoria 1887 Jubilee Head Sovereign

Jubilee head coinage

	F	VF	EF	Unc
1887 F	*	*	£195	£250
1887 proof	*	*	£475	£925
1887 M (Melbourne mint) on ground below dragon	*	*	£195	£395
1887 S (Sydney mint) on ground below dragon	*	*	£275	£650
1888	*	*	£195	£250
1888 M	*	*	£195	£395
1888 S	*	*	£195	£395
1889	*	*	£195	£250
1889 M	*	*	£195	£395
1889 S	*	*	£195	£395
1890	*	*	£195	£250
1890 M	*	*	£195	£395
1890 S	*	*	£195	£250
1891	*	*	£195	£250
1891 M	*	*	£195	£395
1891 S	*	*	£195	£395
1892	*	*	£195	£250
1892 M	*	*	£195	£395
1892 S	*	*	£195	£395
1893 M	*	*	£195	£395
1893 S	*	*	£195	£395

Old head coinage

	F	VF	EF	Unc
1893	*	*	*	£255
1893 proof	*	*	£550	£850
1893 M	*	*	£225	£400
1893 S	*	*	£225	£375
1894	*	*	*	£225
1894 M	*	*	£200	£295
1894 S	*	*	£200	£295
1895	*	*	*	£225
1895 M	*	*	£200	£295
1895 S	*	*	£225	£375
1896	*	*	*	£225
1896 M	*	*	£200	£295
1896 S	*	*	£225	£375
1897 M	*	*	£200	£295
1897 S	*	*	£200	£295
1898	*	*	*	£225
1898 M	*	*	£200	£295
1898 S	*	*	£225	£375
1899	*	*	*	£225
1899 M	*	*	£200	£295
1899 P (Perth mint) on ground below dragon	*	*	£400	£600
1899 S	*	*	£200	£295
1900	*	*	*	£225
1900 M	*	*	£200	£295
1900 P	*	*	£200	£295
1900 S	*	*	£200	£295
1901	*	*	*	£225
1901 M	*	*	£195	£275
1901 P	*	*	£225	£350
1901 S	*	*	£200	£295

EDWARD VII

	F	VF	EF	Unc
1902	*	*	*	£225
1902 proof	*	*	*	£325
1902 M	*	*	*	£225
1902 P	*	*	*	£225
1902 S	*	*	*	£225
1903	*	*	*	£225
1903 M	*	*	*	£225
1903 P	*	*	*	£225
1903 S	*	*	*	£225
1904	*	*	*	£225
1904 M	*	*	*	£225
1904 P	*	*	*	£225
1904 S	*	*	*	£225
1905	*	*	*	£225
1905 M	*	*	*	£225
1905 P	*	*	*	£225
1905 S	*	*	*	£225
1906	*	*	*	£225
1906 M	*	*	*	£225
1906 P	*	*	*	£225
1906 S	*	*	*	£225
1907	*	*	*	£225
1907 M	*	*	*	£225
1907 P	*	*	*	£225
1907 S	*	*	*	£225

	F	VF	EF	Unc
1908	*	*	*	£225
1908 C on ground below dragon F	*	*	£3000	£4500
1908 M	*	*	*	£225
1908 P	*	*	*	£225
1908 S	*	*	*	£225
1909	*	*	*	£225
1909 C	*	*	£300	£825
1909 M	*	*	*	£225
1909 P	*	*	*	£225
1909 S	*	*	*	£225
1910	*	*	*	£225
1910 C	*	*	£300	£825
1910 M	*	*	*	£225
1910 P	*	*	*	£225
1910 S	*	*	*	£225

GEORGE V

	F	VF	EF	Unc
1911	*	*	*	£200
1911 proof	*	*	*	£500
1911 C	*	*	*	£225
1911 M	*	*	*	£225
1911 P	*	*	*	£225
1911 S	*	*	*	£225
1912	*	*	*	£200
1912 M	*	*	*	£225
1912 P	*	*	*	£225
1912 S	*	*	*	£225
1913	*	*	*	£200
1913 C F	*	£300	£750	£1450
1913 M	*	*	*	£225
1913 P	*	*	*	£225
1913 S	*	*	*	£225
1914	*	*	*	£200
1914 C	*	£250	£385	£650
1914 M	*	*	*	£225
1914 P	*	*	*	£225
1914 S	*	*	*	£225
1915	*	*	*	£200
1915 M	*	*	*	£225
1915 P	*	*	*	£225
1915 S	*	*	*	£225
1916	*	*	*	£225
1916 C F	*	£6000	£12000	£16500
1916 M	*	*	*	£200
1916 P	*	*	*	£225
1916 S	*	*	*	£225
1917 F	*	£2950	£5000	£8000
1917 C	*	*	£200	£275
1917 M	*	*	*	£225
1917 P	*	*	*	£225
1917 S	*	*	*	£225
1918 C	*	*	£200	£275
1918 I on ground below dragon*	*	*	£200	£275
1918 M	*	*	*	£225
1918 P	*	*	*	£200
1918 S	*	*	*	£225
1919 C	*	*	£200	£275
1919 M	*	*	*	£200
1919 P	*	*	*	£225
1919 S	*	*	*	£225
1920 M	£900	£2000	£3750	*
1920 P	*	*	*	£225
1920 S			highest	rarity
1921 M	£2250	£4250	£8500	£14750
1921 P	*	*	*	£265
1921 S	*	£600	£950	£1500
1922 M	£2250	£3850	£6750	£10000
1922 P	*	*	*	£225
1922 S	£3500	£5000	£7000	*
1923 M	*	*	*	£225
1923 S	£2250	£3750	£6750	£12000
1923 SA (Pretoria Mint) on ground below dragon	*	£2250	£3750	£4750
1923 SA proof	*	*	*	£1650
1924 M	*	*	*	£225
1924 P	*	*	*	£225
1924 S	*	£475	£875	£1650
1924 SA	*	*	£4250	£6750
1925	*	*	*	£200
1925 M	*	*	*	£275
1925 P	*	*	*	£275
1925 S	*	*	*	£275
1925 SA	*	*	*	£200
1926 M	*	*	*	£275
1926 P	*	£425	£975	£1850
1926 S	£3750	£7000	£13750	£20000
1926 SA	*	*	*	£200
1927 P	*	*	£250	£425
1927 SA	*	*	*	£200
1928 M	£425	£700	£1500	£2500
1928 P	*	*	*	£265
1928 SA	*	*	*	£200
1929 M	*	£700	£1650	£2750
1929 P	*	*	*	£265
1929 SA	*	*	*	£200
1930 M	*	*	£225	£325
1930 P	*	*	£225	£325
1930 SA	*	*	*	£200
1931 M	*	*	£425	£650
1931 P	*	*	*	£250
1931 SA	*	*	*	£200
1932	*	*	*	£200

GEORGE VI

	F	VF	EF	Unc
1937 proof only	*	*	*	£1850

George VI 1937 proof Sovereign

ELIZABETH II	F	VF	EF	Unc
1953 proof				ext. rare

	F	VF	EF	Unc
1957	*	*	*	£200
1958	*	*	*	£195
1959	*	*	*	£195
1962	*	*	*	£195
1963	*	*	*	£195
1964	*	*	*	£195
1965	*	*	*	£195
1966	*	*	*	£195
1967	*	*	*	£195
1968	*	*	*	£195
1974	*	*	*	£195
1976	*	*	*	£195
1977	*	*	*	£195
1978	*	*	*	£195
1979	*	*	*	£195
1979 proof				£225
1980	*	*	*	£195
1980 proof				£225
1981	*	*	*	£195
1981 proof				£225
1982	*	*	*	£195
1982 proof				£225
1983 proof				£225
1984 proof				£225
1985 proof				£225
1986 proof				£225
1987 proof				£225
1988 proof				£225
1989 500th anniversary of sovereign, proof				£1100
1990 proof				£225
1991 proof				£225
1992 proof				£225
1993 proof				£225
1994 proof				£225
1995 proof				£225
1996 proof				£225
1997 proof				£225
1998 proof				£225
1999 proof				£225
2000 proof				£225
2000 BU				£225
2001 proof				£225
2001 BU				£225
2002 shield, proof				£275
2002 BU				£225
2003 proof				£225
2003 BU				£225
2004 Proof				£225
2004 BU				BV
2005 proof				£225
2005 BU				BV
2006 proof				£225
2006 BU				BV
2007 proof				£225
2007 BU				BV
2008 BU				BV
2008 proof				£225
2009 BU				BV
2009 proof				£275
2010 proof				£350
2010 BU				£245

■ HALF-SOVEREIGNS

GEORGE III	F	VF	EF	Unc
1817	£100	£150	£350	£575
1818	£100	£165	£400	£700
1820	£100	£165	£400	£650

GEORGE IV	F	VF	EF	Unc
Laureate hd/ornate shield date				
1821	£350	£850	£1950	£2950
1821 proof	*	*	£2250	£3750
1823 plain shield	£95	£195	£450	£800
1824	£125	£185	£425	£725
1825	£125	£185	£425	£725
Bare hd, date/shield and full legend				
1826	£125	£185	£425	£725
1826 proof	*	*	£925	£1500
1827	£125	£185	£475	£800
1828	£135	£185	£450	£725

WILLIAM IV	F	VF	EF	Unc
1831 proof	*	*	£1450	£2350
1834 reduced size	£165	£300	£825	£1500
1835 normal size	£150	£250	£650	£1250
1836 sixpence obv die	£850	£1650	£3750	£4750
1836	£165	£300	£825	£1500
1837	£165	£300	£825	£1500

VICTORIA	F	VF	EF	Unc
1838	*	£125	£575	£925
1839 proof only	*	*	£1200	£1850
1841	*	£125	£500	£900
1842	*	£125	£350	£675
1843	*	£125	£400	£750
1844	*	£125	£350	£675
1845	£175	£350	£1500	*
1846	*	£125	£350	£675
1847	*	£125	£350	£675
1848	*	£150	£350	£700
1849	*	£125	£325	£575
1850	£150	£300	£1250	*
1851	*	£125	£300	£575
1852	*	£125	£300	£575
1853	*	£125	£300	£575
1853 proof	*	*	£3000	£5250
1855	*	£125	£300	£575
1856	*	£125	£250	£575
1857	*	£125	£300	£575
1858	*	£125	£300	£575
1859	*	£125	£275	£575
1860	*	£125	£275	£575
1861	*	£125	£275	£575
1862	£500	£1250	£4000	*
1863	*	£125	£240	£575
1863 die no	*	£150	£350	£750
1864 die no	*	£125	£250	£500

	F	VF	EF	Unc
1865 die no	*	£125	£250	£500
1866 die no	*	£125	£250	£500
1867 die no	*	£125	£250	£500
1869 die no	*	£125	£250	£500
1870 die no	*	£125	£225	£425
1871 die no	*	£125	£225	£425
1871 S below shield	£135	£165	£750	*
1872 die no	*	£125	£225	£425
1872 S	£135	£165	£750	*
1873 die no	*	£125	£225	£425
1873 M below shield	£135	£165	£750	*
1874 die no	*	£125	£225	£425
1875 die no	*	£125	£225	£425
1875 S	£135	£165	£750	*
1876 die no	*	£125	£225	£425
1877 die no	*	£125	£225	£425
1877 M	£135	£165	£750	*
1878 die no	*	£125	£225	£425
1879 die no	*	£125	£225	£425
1879 S	£135	£165	£750	*
1880	*	£125	£225	£425
1880 die no	*	£125	£275	£525
1880 S	£135	£165	£750	*
1881 S	£150	£200	£900	*
1881 M	£165	£300	*	*
1882 S	£200	£500	£3000	*
1882 M	£135	£165	£750	*
1883	*	£125	£225	£425
1883 S	£135	£165	£750	*
1884	*	£125	£225	£425
1884 M	£165	£300	*	*
1885	*	£125	£225	£425
1885 M	£165	£350	*	*
1886 S	£165	£300	*	*
1886 M	£165	£200	£850	£3000
1887 S	£135	£165	£750	*
1887 M	£165	£350	*	*

JH/shield

	F	VF	EF	Unc
1887	*	*	£125	£165
1887 proof	*	*	£350	£550
1887 M	*	£150	£375	£675
1887 S	*	£150	£375	£675
1889 S	*	£175	£550	*
1890	*	*	£125	£165
1891	*	*	£125	£165
1891 S	*	*	£750	*
1892	*	*	£125	£165
1893	*	*	£125	£165
1893 M	*	£175	£550	*

OH/St George and dragon

	F	VF	EF	Unc
1893	*	*	£110	£160
1893 proof	*	*	£395	£700
1893 M				ext. rare
1893 S	*	£150	£350	*
1894	*	*	£110	£160
1895	*	*	£110	£160
1896	*	*	£110	£160

	F	VF	EF	Unc
1896 M	*	£150	£450	*
1897	*	*	£100	£160
1897 S	*	£150	£350	*
1898	*	*	£110	£160
1899	*	*	£110	£160
1899 M	£100	£135	£350	*
1899 P proof only	*	*	*	ext. rare
1900	*	*	£110	£160
1900 M	£100	£150	£450	*
1900 P	£100	£250	£800	*
1900 S	*	£135	£350	£1100
1901	*	*	£110	£160
1901 P proof only	*	*	*	ext. rare

EDWARD VII

	F	VF	EF	Unc
1902	*	*	£95	£130
1902 proof	*	*	£125	£200
1902 S	*	*	£200	£750
1903	*	*	£95	£130
1903 S	*	*	£225	*
1904	*	*	£95	£130
1904 P	*	*	*	ext.rate
1905	*	*	£95	£130
1906	*	*	£95	£130
1906 M	*	£250	£900	*
1906 S	*	*	£150	£600
1907	*	*	£95	£130
1907 M	*	*	£185	*
1908	*	*	£95	£130
1908 M	*	*	£200	£750
1908 P	*	£250	*	*
1908 S	*	*	£125	£450
1909	*	*	£95	£130
1909 M	*	*	£200	£750
1909 P	*	£250	£725	*
1910	*	*	£95	£130
1910 S	*	*	£110	£450

GEORGE V

	F	VF	EF	Unc
1911	*	*	*	£120
1911 proof	*	*	£225	£350
1911 P	*	*	£110	£250
1911 S	*	*	£110	£250
1912	*	*	*	£120
1912 S	*	*	£100	£200
1913	*	*	*	£120
1914	*	*	*	£120
1914 S	*	*	*	£120
1915	*	*	*	£120
1915 M	*	*	£100	£150
1915 P	*	*	£110	£265
1915 S	*	*	*	£130
1916 S	*	*	*	£130
1918 P	*	£450	£1500	£3250
1923 SA proof	*	*	*	£500
1925 SA	*	*	*	£120
1926 SA	*	*	*	£120

GEORGE VI

	F	VF	EF	Unc
1937 proof	*	*	*	£450

ELIZABETH II

	Unc
1953 proof	ext. rare
1980 proof	£110
1982 proof	£110
1982 BU	BV
1983 proof	£110
1984 proof	£110
1985 proof	£110
1986 proof	£110
1986 proof	£110
1987 proof	£110
1988 proof	£110
1989 500th anniversary of the sovereign, proof	£425
1990 proof	£110
1991 proof	£110
1992 proof	£110
1993 proof	£110
1994 proof	£110
1995 proof	£110
1996 proof	£110
1997 proof	£110
1998 proof	£110
1999 proof	£110
2000 proof	£110
2000 BU	BV
2001 proof	£110
2001 BU	£BV
2002 shield, proof	£175
2002 BU	BV
2003 proof	£110
2003 BU	BV
2004 proof	£110
2004 BU	£BV
2005 proof	BV
2005 BU	BV
2006 proof	£110
2006 BU	BV
2007 proof	£110
2007 BU	BV
2008 BU	BV
2008 proof	£120
2009 BU	BV
2009 proof	£140
2010 BU	£140
2010 proof	£175

■ CROWNS

CROMWELL

	F	VF	EF
1658	£1850	£2850	£5250
1658 Dutch copy	£1900	£2950	£6850
1658 Tanner's copy	*	£3750	£8000

CHARLES II

	F	VF	EF
1662 1st bust	£200	£725	£4500
1663	£200	£725	£4500
1664 2nd bust	£225	£850	£5000
1665	£825	£2250	*
1666	£250	£750	£4000
1666 eleph	£525	£2000	£11000

	F	VF	EF
1667	£185	£575	£3250
1668	£185	£575	£3250
1668/7	£185	£575	£3250
1668/5			ext. rare
1669	£325	£1200	*
1669/8	£375	£1350	*
1670	£175	£600	£3250
1670/69	£400	£700	*
1671	£185	£575	£3250
1671 3rd bust	£185	£575	£3250
1672	£185	£575	£3250
1673	£185	£575	£3250
1673/2	£250	£675	£3250
1674	*	*	ext. rare
1675	£700	£2250	*
1675/3	£600	£1875	*
1676	£185	£575	£3250
1677	£185	£575	£3250
1677/6	£185	£575	£3250
1678/7	£275	£700	*
1679	£185	£575	£3250
1679 4th bust	£185	£575	£3250
1680 3rd bust	£250	£675	£3650
1680/79 3rd bust	£250	£675	£3650
1680 4th bust	£250	£675	£3650
1680/79	£250	£675	*
1681 eleph & castle	£3500	£5750	*
1681	£250	£675	£3650
1682	£250	£675	£3650
1682/1	£250	£675	£3650
1683	£275	£800	*
1684	£250	£750	*

JAMES II

	F	VF	EF
1686 1st bust	£350	£1000	*
1687 2nd bust	£200	£600	£2000
1688	£200	£600	£2000
1688/7	£200	£600	£2000

WILLIAM & MARY

	F	VF	EF
1691	£450	£1250	£3750
1692	£475	£1250	£3750
1692/2 inv QVINTO	£450	£1250	£3750
1692/2 inv QVARTO	£600	£1500	*

WILLIAM III

	F	VF	EF
1695 1st bust	£110	£325	£1475
1696	£100	£325	£1500
1696 GEI error	£400	£900	*
1696/5	£200	£500	*
1696 2nd bust			unique
1696 3rd bust	£110	£325	£1475
1697	£700	£2250	£15000
1700 3rd bust var	£110	£325	£1500

ANNE

	F	VF	EF
1703 1st bust VIGO	£375	£1000	£3250
1705	£600	£1850	£4500
1706	£275	£625	£2500

MILLED COINAGE

1707	£275	£625	£2500
1707 2nd bust	£175	£475	£1950
1707 E	£175	£475	£1950
1708	£175	£475	£1950
1708 E	£175	£495	*
1708/7	£175	£500	*
1708 plumes	£275	£625	£2500
1713 3rd bust	£275	£625	£2500

GEORGE I

1716 rev r & p	£325	£800	£3000

George I 1716 Crown

1718	£385	£900	£3500
1718/6	£400	£975	£3750
1720	£400	£975	£3750
1720/18	£385	£900	£3500
1723 SS C	£385	£900	£3500
1726 small r & p	£750	£1500	£4750

GEORGE II

1732 YH	£400	£750	£2650
1732 proof	*	*	£6500
1734	£400	£750	£2650
1735	£400	£750	£2650
1736	£375	£750	£2650
1739	£295	£650	£2150
1741	£375	£675	£2500
1743 OH	£295	£650	£2500

William & Mary 1691 Crown

	F	VF	EF
1746 OH LIMA	£400	£700	£2250
1746 OH proof	*	£3500	£7000
1750	£400	£800	£2250
1751	£425	£775	£2400

GEORGE III	F	VF	EF	Unc
Oval counterstamp	£200	£325	£750	£1100
Octagonal counterstamp	£550	£900	£1750	*
1804 Bank of England Dollar	£125	£250	£550	£750

Collectors should beware of contemporary forgeries on these three coins. The counterstamps are usually on Spanish-American dollars.

1818 LVIII	£25	£60	£295	£650
1818 LVIII error edge	£250	*	*	*
1818 LIX	£25	£60	£295	£650
1819 LIX	£25	£60	£295	£650
1819 LIX no edge stops	£50	£140	£400	*
1819/8 LIX	*	£150	£475	*
1819 LIX no stop after TUTAMEN	£45	£150	£475	*
1820 LX	*	*	£325	£650
1820/19 LX	£50	£200	£500	*

GEORGE IV

1821 1st hd SECUNDO	£35	£150	£825	£1750

George IV 1821 Crown

1821 SECUNDO proof	*	*	*	£3750
1821 TERTIO error edge	*	*	*	£4250
1822 SECUNDO	£60	£175	£825	£1875
1822 SECUNDO proof	*	*	*	*
1822 TERTIO	£50	£175	£825	£1875
1822 TERTIO proof	*	*	*	£4250
1823 proof only	*	*	*	ext. rare
1826 2nd head proof	*	*	£2650	£4500

	F	VF	EF	Unc
WILLIAM IV proof only				
1831 W.W.	*	*	£8500	£12500
1831 W.WYON	*	*	£9000	£13500
1834 W.W.	*	*	£9750	£16500
VICTORIA				
1839 proof	*	*	£3950	£7500
1844 star stops	£35	£100	£750	£2650
1844 star stops proof	*	* ext. rare		*
1844 cinquefoil stops	£35	£100	£750	£2650
1845	£35	£100	£750	£2650
1845 proof	*	*	*	£10500
1847	£35	£100	£850	£2850

Victoria 1847 Gothic Crown

	F	VF	EF	Unc
1847 Gothic	£425	£600	£1250	£3000
1847 Gothic plain edge	*	£750	£1500	£3250
1853 SEPTIMO	*	*	£5000	£7500
1853 plain	*	*	£5750	£8500
1887 JH	£15	£25	£65	£135
1887 JH proof	*	*	£400	£750
1888 close date	£20	£30	£90	£200
1888 wide date	£32	£100	£250	£475
1889	£20	£35	£85	£200
1890	£20	£35	£85	£225
1891	£20	£35	£90	£250
1892	£20	£35	£100	£275
1893 LVI	£20	£35	£165	£300
1893 LVI proof	*	*	£475	£825
1893 LVII	£20	£65	£235	£500
1894 LVII	£20	£40	£200	£425
1894 LVIII	£20	£40	£200	£425
1895 LVIII	£20	£40	£175	£375
1895 LIX	£20	£40	£165	£350
1896 LIX	£30	£60	£275	£550
1896 LX	£20	£40	£200	£400
1897 LX	£20	£40	£165	£385
1897 LXI	£20	£40	£165	£350
1898 LXI	£20	£40	£200	£475
1898 LXII	£20	£40	£165	£375
1899 LXII	£20	£40	£185	£385
1899 LXIII	£20	£40	£195	£450
1900 LXIII	£20	£40	£165	£395

	F	VF	EF	Unc
1900 LXIV	£20	£40	£140	£375
EDWARD VII				
1902	£30	£65	£125	£185
1902 matt proof	*	*	£125	£175
GEORGE V				
1927 proof	*	*	£165	£285
1928	£85	£150	£275	£385
1929	£85	£165	£285	£450
1930	£85	£150	£275	£400
1931	£85	£150	£275	£400
1932	£140	£250	£475	£700
1933	£85	£140	£275	£385
1934	£975	£1975	£3250	£4250
1935	£5	£7	£10	£20
1935 raised edge proof	*	*	*	£425
1935 gold proof	*	*	*	£19500
1935 proof in good silver (.925)	*	*	*	£1750
1935 specimen	*	*	*	£60
1936	£125	£250	£400	£650
GEORGE VI				
1937	*	*	£18	£30
1937 proof	*	*	*	£65
1937 'VIP' proof	*	*	*	£1250
1951	*	*	*	£10
1951 'VIP' proof	*	*	*	£600
ELIZABETH II				
1953	*	*	*	£8
1953 proof	*	*	*	£35
1953 'VIP' proof	*	*	*	£475
1960	*	*	*	£10
1960 'VIP' proof	*	*	*	£500
1960 polished dies	*	*	*	£25
1965 Churchill	*	*	*	£1.00
1965 Churchill 'satin' finish	*	*	*	£1250

For issues from 1972 onwards see under 25 pence in Decimal Coinage section.

George V 1935 raised edge proof Crown

■ DOUBLE-FLORINS

VICTORIA	F	VF	EF	Unc
1887 Roman 'I'	£8	£15	£50	£110
1887 Roman 'I' proof	*	*	£200	£395
1887 Arabic 'I'	£8	£15	£45	£100
1887 Arabic 'I' proof	*	*	£200	£395
1888	£8	£17	£60	£150
1888 inv 'I'	£15	£30	£165	£400
1889	£8	£17	£60	£150
1889 inv 'I'	£15	£35	£165	£400
1890	£8	£17	£65	£150

■ THREE SHILLING BANK TOKENS

Contemporary forgeries of these pieces, as well as of other George III coins, were produced in quite large numbers. Several varieties exist for the pieces dated 1811 and 1812. Prices given here are for the commonest types of these years.

GEORGE III				
1811	*	£45	£135	£225
1812 draped bust	*	£45	£110	£225
1812 laureate hd	*	£45	£110	£225
1813	*	£45	£135	£225
1814	*	£45	£135	£225
1815	*	£45	£135	£225
1816	*	£250	£975	£1650

■ HALFCROWNS

CROMWELL	F	VF	EF
1656	£2250	£4250	£9250
1658	£975	£1850	£3250

Cromwell 1658 Halfcrown

CHARLES II			
1663 1st bust	£225	£625	£3750
1664 2nd bust	£250	£1000	£4650
1666/3 3rd bust	£850	*	*
1666/3 eleph	£850	£2500	*
1667/4			ext. rare
1668/4	£225	£950	*

	F	VF	EF
1669	£325	£1100	*
1669/4	£200	£750	*
1670	£125	£475	£3000
1671 3rd bust var	£110	£425	£3000
1671/0	£125	£500	£3000
1672	£125	£425	£3000
1672 4th bust	£125	£425	£3000
1673	£125	£425	£3000
1673 plume below	£5250	*	*
1673 plume both sides	£7000	*	*
1674	£125	£425	£3000
1674/3	£250	£700	*
1675	£120	£375	£2750
1676	£120	£375	£2750
1677	£120	£375	£2750
1678	£175	£650	*
1679	£110	£350	£2250
1680	£150	£525	*
1681	£120	£350	£2750
1681/0	£225	£650	£2850
1681 eleph & castle	£2500	£5250	£20000
1682	£125	£500	*
1682/79	£300	£875	*
1683	£125	£425	£3000
1683 plume below	ext. rare	*	*
1684/3	£300	£875	

JAMES II			
1685 1st bust	£150	£650	£2750
1686	£175	£600	£2500
1686/5	£250	£850	*
1687	£175	£600	£2500
1687/6	£525	£600	£2500
1687 2nd bust	£150	£600	£2500
1688	£175	£675	£3250

WILLIAM AND MARY			
1689 1st busts 1st shield	£95	£395	£1750
1689 1st busts 2nd shield	£95	£395	£1750
1690	£140	£475	£2250

William and Mary 1690 Halfcrown

1691 2nd busts 3rd shield	£110	£400	£1850
1692	£110	£400	£1850
1693	£110	£400	£1850

	F	VF	EF
1693 2nd busts 3rd shield 3 inv	£125	£475	£1950
1693 3 over 3 inv	£110	£400	£1850

WILLIAM III

	F	VF	EF
1696 1st bust large shield early hp	£60	£250	£975
1696 B	£85	£300	£1350
1696 C	£125	£450	£1750
1696 E	£125	£425	£1650
1696 N	£200	£700	*
1696 Y	£95	£375	£1500
1696 y/E			ext. rare
1696 large shield ord hp	£125	£475	£1350
1696 C	£125	£425	£1475
1696 E	£120	£425	£1450
1696 N	£250	£675	*
1696 small shield	£65	£275	£1000
1696 B	£85	£300	£1375
1696 C	£150	£500	£1850
1696 E	£150	£500	£1850
1696 N	£125	£425	£1650
1696 y	£125	£400	£1625
1696 2nd bust			unique
1697 1st bust large shield	£65	£225	£900
1697 B	£90	£300	£1375
1697 C	£90	£295	£1450
1697 E	£80	£275	£1250
1697 E/C	£150	£525	*
1697 N	£90	£300	£1375
1697 y	£85	£275	£1250
1698	£65	£200	£775
1699	£110	£350	£1500
1700	£60	£165	£725
1701	£70	£250	£1150
1701 eleph & castle	£2750	*	*
1701 plumes	£250	£775	£3500

ANNE

	F	VF	EF
1703 plain	£700	£1850	£9000
1703 VIGO	£175	£425	£1500
1704 plumes	£250	£675	*
1705	£185	£575	£2000
1706 r & p	£100	£285	£1350
1707	£100	£275	£1275
1707 plain	£65	£200	£975
1707 E	£65	£225	£1200
1708 plain	£65	£200	£750
1708 E	£65	£275	£1350
1708 plumes	£110	£375	£1500
1709 plain	£70	£250	£875
1709 E	£400	*	*
1710 r & p	£100	£300	£1200
1712	£65	£200	£975
1713 plain	£75	£300	£1300
1713 r & p	£75	£275	£1100
1714	£75	£275	£1100
1714/3	£125	£400	£1475

GEORGE I

	F	VF	EF
1715 proof	*	*	£5000

	F	VF	EF
1715 r & p	£200	£525	£2500
1717	£175	£525	£2250
1720	£275	£650	£2950
1720/17	£200	£525	£2500
1723 SS C	£200	£450	£1900
1726 small r & p	£2500	£4500	£12500

George III oval countermarked Spanish 4 Reales (Half-Dollar)

GEORGE II

	F	VF	EF
1731 YH proof	*	£2000	£4000
1731	£125	£365	£1350
1732	£125	£365	£1350
1734	£140	£425	£1500
1735	£125	£365	£1350
1736	£150	£425	£1500
1739	£95	£225	£975
1741	£95	£275	£975
1741/39	£100	£300	£1000
1743 OH	£80	£195	£875
1745	£80	£195	£875
1745 LIMA	£65	£175	£675
1746 LIMA	£65	£175	£700
1746 plain, proof	*	*	£4000
1750	£150	£400	£1650
1751	£150	£475	£1750

GEORGE III	F	VF	EF	Unc
Oval counterstamp, usually on Spanish Half-Dollar	£250	£395	£750	*
1816 large hd	£10	£50	£275	£425
1817	£10	£50	£275	£425
1817 small hd	£10	£50	£245	£425
1818	£10	£50	£300	£475
1819	£10	£50	£275	£425
1819/8				ext. rare
1820	£10	£60	£300	£475

Victoria 1839 proof Halfcrown

George IV 1820 Halfcrown

GEORGE IV	F	VF	EF	Unc
1st hd				
1820 1st rev	£15	£60	£300	£625
1821	£15	£60	£295	£575
1821 proof	*	*	£850	£2000
1823	£750	£1750	£5000	*
1823 2nd rev	£15	£60	£350	£750
1824	£25	£70	£350	£750
2nd hd				
1824 3rd rev				ext. rare
1825	£15	£70	£265	£550
1826	£15	£50	£265	£550
1826 proof	*	*	£550	£950
1828	£25	£85	£350	£800
1829	£20	£60	£295	£675

WILLIAM IV				
1831				ext. rare
1831 proof	*	*	£850	£1500

William IV 1831 proof Halfcrown

1834 ww	£30	£110	£495	£975
1834 ww in script	£15	£50	£265	£600
1835	£25	£80	£300	£750
1836	£15	£50	£275	£600
1836/5	£45	£150	£525	*
1837	£35	£110	£495	£975

VICTORIA

From time to time Halfcrowns bearing dates ranging from
1861 to 1871 are found (usually worn), but except for
rare proofs in 1853, 1862 and 1864, no Halfcrowns were
struck between 1850 and 1874, so pieces dated from
this period are now considered to be contemporary or
later forgeries.

Young Head	F	VF	EF	Unc
1839 plain and				
ornate fillets, ww	*	£1250	£4000	*
1839 plain and ornate				
fillets, plain edge proof	*	*	£875	£1800
1839 plain fillets,				
ww inc	*	£1450	£4000	*
1840	£35	£75	£400	£850
1841	£400	£825	£2450	£3950
1842	£35	£75	£400	£900
1843	£60	£150	£675	£1700
1844	£35	£60	£395	£825
1845	£35	£60	£395	£825
1846	£30	£60	£395	£825
1848	£125	£225	£975	£2250
1848/6	£110	£350	£850	*
1849 large date	£35	£140	£600	£1250
1849 small date	£70	£175	£750	£1450
1850	£35	£110	£575	£1275
1853 proof	*	*	*	£2500
1862 proof	*	*	*	£5500
1864 proof	*	*	*	£5500
1874	£15	£35	£150	£400
1875	£15	£35	£160	£425
1876	£15	£35	£185	£500
1876/5	£15	£50	£375	£750
1877	£15	£30	£175	£475
1878	£15	£30	£175	£475
1879	£15	£35	£195	£495
1880	£15	£30	£150	£395
1881	£15	£30	£150	£400
1882	£15	£30	£150	£395
1883	£15	£30	£150	£395
1884	£15	£30	£150	£395
1885	£15	£30	£150	£395
1886	£15	£30	£150	£395

	F	VF	EF	Unc
1887	£15	£30	£165	£400

Jubilee Head

	F	VF	EF	Unc
1887	£5	£15	£35	£65
1887 proof	*	*	£95	£255
1888	£6	£20	£65	£130
1889	£6	£20	£65	£145
1890	£6	£25	£75	£165
1891	£6	£25	£75	£180
1892	£6	£25	£75	£200

Old Head

	F	VF	EF	Unc
1893	£7	£20	£45	£135
1893 proof	*	*	£150	£300
1894	£7	£20	£85	£245
1895	£7	£20	£70	£195
1896	£7	£20	£70	£195
1897	£7	£15	£50	£150
1898	£7	£20	£70	£175
1899	£7	£20	£60	£160
1900	£7	£20	£50	£135
1901	£7	£20	£50	£120

Edward VII 1909 Halfcrown

EDWARD VII

	F	VF	EF	Unc
1902	£8	£25	£65	£135
1902 matt proof	*	*	*	£135
1903	£80	£300	£2000	£4000
1904	£35	£165	£800	£1850
1905 F	£300	£1250	£5000	£8250
1906	£12	£30	£225	£625
1907	£12	£40	£225	£625
1908	£15	£60	£425	£1100
1909	£12	£45	£350	£875
1910	£12	£30	£175	£425

GEORGE V

	F	VF	EF	Unc
1911	*	£10	£60	£200
1911 proof	*	*	*	£185
1912	*	£15	£60	£200
1913	*	£15	£70	£245
1914	*	*	£25	£80
1915	*	*	£20	£65
1916	*	*	£20	£65
1917	*	*	£30	£75
1918	*	*	£20	£60

	F	VF	EF	Unc
1919	*	*	£20	£60
1920	*	*	£30	£125
1921	*	*	£40	£100
1922	*	*	£30	£100
1923	*	*	£12	£45
1924	*	*	£30	£100
1925	*	£45	£295	£800
1926	*	*	£45	£125
1926 mod eff	*	*	£60	£150
1927	*	*	£25	£60
1927 new rev, proof only	*	*	*	£70
1928	*	*	£10	£27
1929	*	*	£10	£28
1930	£7	£35	£285	£850
1931	*	*	£12	£45
1932	*	*	£15	£50
1933	*	*	£10	£35
1934	*	*	£35	£125
1935	*	*	£8	£20
1936	*	*	£8	£17

GEORGE VI

	F	VF	EF	Unc
1937	*	*	*	£14
1937 proof	*	*	*	£25
1938	*	*	£4	£35
1939	*	*	*	£17
1940	*	*	*	£14
1941	*	*	*	£14
1942	*	*	*	£12
1943	*	*	*	£14
1944	*	*	*	£12
1945	*	*	*	£12
1946	*	*	*	£10
1947	*	*	*	£10
1948	*	*	*	£10
1949	*	*	*	£17
1950	*	*	*	£24
1950 proof	*	*	*	£25
1951	*	*	*	£24
1951 proof	*	*	*	£25
1952			2 known	

ELIZABETH II

	F	VF	EF	Unc
1953	*	*	*	£12
1953 proof	*	*	*	£15
1954	*	*	£4	£45
1955	*	*	*	£10
1956	*	*	*	£10
1957	*	*	*	£8
1958	*	*	*	£28
1959	*	*	*	£45
1960	*	*	*	£4
1961	*	*	*	£4
1962	*	*	*	£4
1963	*	*	*	£2
1964	*	*	*	£2
1965	*	*	*	£2
1966	*	*	*	£1
1967	*	*	*	£1

■ FLORINS

The first Florins produced in the reign of Victoria bore the legend VICTORIA REGINA and the date, omitting DEI GRATIA or 'By the Grace of God'. They are therefore known as 'godless' Florins.

The date of a Victorian Gothic Florin is shown in Roman numerals in Gothic lettering on the obverse, for example mdcclvii (1857). Gothic Florins were issued between 1851–1887.

VICTORIA	F	VF	EF	Unc
1848 'Godless' proof with milled edge	*	*	*	£2250
1848 'Godless' proof with plain edge	*	*	*	£1200
1849 'Godless' ww obliterated by circle	£25	£50	£190	£425
1849 'Godless' ww inside circle	£15	£40	£140	£300
1851 proof only	*	*	*	£8500
1852	£15	£40	£135	£325
1853	£15	£40	£135	£325
1853 no stop after date	£20	£50	£150	£395
1853 proof	*	*	*	£2250
1854	£350	£825	£3500	*
1855	£20	£55	£195	£450
1856	£20	£55	£195	£450
1857	£20	£45	£175	£400
1858	£20	£45	£175	£400
1859	£20	£40	£175	£400
1859 no stops after date	£20	£50	£175	£375
1860	£20	£50	£200	£450
1862	£150	£350	£1500	*
1863	£500	£875	£2750	*
1864	£20	£50	£200	£450
1865	£30	£80	£275	£575
1865 colon after date	*	*		ext. rare
1866	£20	£50	£200	£425
1866 colon after date				ext. rare
1867	£20	£50	£200	£450
1868	£25	£70	£275	£575
1869	£25	£70	£275	£575
1870	£20	£50	£200	£425
1871	£20	£50	£200	£425
1872	£15	£35	£140	£325
1873	£15	£35	£175	£350

	F	VF	EF	Unc
1874	£15	£35	£200	£425
1874 xxiv/iii die	£75	£175	£400	*
1875	£15	£45	£175	£395
1876	£15	£45	£175	£395
1877	£15	£45	£195	£425
1877 no ww	*	*	*	*
1877 42 arcs	*	*	*	*
1878	£15	£40	£175	£375
1879 die no	*	*	*	ext.rare
1879 ww 42 arcs	£80	£175	£450	*
1879 ww 48 arcs	£15	£40	£175	£350
1879 no ww, 38 arcs	£15	£45	£150	£350
1880	£15	£40	£150	£350
1881	£15	£40	£150	£350
1881 xxri error	£15	£40	£150	£350
1883	£15	£40	£140	£300
1884	£15	£40	£140	£300
1885	£15	£40	£140	£300
1886	£15	£40	£140	£300
1887 33 arcs	*	*	*	ext.rare
1887 46 arcs	£20	£50	£200	£425
1887 JH	*	£10	£25	£55
1887 JH	*	*	*	£120
1888	*	£10	£40	£95
1889	*	£10	£50	£150
1890	£8	£15	£100	£300
1891	£20	£50	£200	£475
1892	£20	£60	£250	£525
1893 OH	*	£12	£50	£100
1893 proof	*	*	*	£200
1894	*	£12	£85	£200
1895	*	£12	£70	£150
1896	*	£12	£70	£150
1897	*	£12	£60	£125
1898	*	£12	£70	£150
1899	*	£12	£70	£150
1900	*	£12	£50	£120
1901	*	£12	£50	£120

EDWARD VII	F	VF	EF	Unc
1902	*	£12	£55	£110
1902 matt proof	*	*	*	£85
1903	*	£25	£135	£400
1904	*	£35	£175	£475
1905	£45	£140	£700	£1500
1906	*	£20	£110	£375
1907	*	£25	£120	£400
1908	*	£40	£265	£625
1909	*	£35	£225	£575
1910	*	£15	£85	£265

GEORGE V	F	VF	EF	Unc
1911	*	*	£40	£110
1911 proof	*	*	*	£110
1912	*	*	£50	£135
1913	*	*	£70	£175
1914	*	*	£25	£60
1915	*	*	£40	£100
1916	*	*	£20	£65

Victoria 1871 Gothic Florin

	F	VF	EF	Unc
1917	*	*	£25	£70
1918	*	*	£20	£50
1919	*	*	£25	£70
1920	*	*	£25	£95
1921	*	*	£20	£75
1922	*	*	£18	£50
1923	*	*	£18	£50
1924	*	*	£27	£55
1925	£15	£35	£135	£400
1926	*	*	£40	£85
1927 proof	*	*	*	£120
1928	*	*	£7	£25
1929	*	*	£7	£30
1930	*	*	£25	£60
1931	*	*	£12	£40
1932	£15	£60	£250	£650

1954	*	*	*	£45
1955	*	*	*	£7
	F	VF	EF	Unc
1956	*	*	*	£7
1957	*	*	*	£45
1958	*	*	*	£30
1959	*	*	*	£35
1960	*	*	*	£4
1961	*	*	*	£4
1962	*	*	*	£2
1963	*	*	*	£2
1964	*	*	*	£2
1965	*	*	*	£2
1966	*	*	*	£1
1967	*	*	*	£1

George V 1932 Florin

1933	*	*	£12	£40
1935	*	*	£8	£20
1936	*	*	£5	£20

GEORGE VI
1937	*	*	*	£9
1937 proof	*	*	*	£15
1938	*	*	£4	£30
1939	*	*	*	£12
1940	*	*	*	£10
1941	*	*	*	£10
1942	*	*	*	£8
1943	*	*	*	£8
1944	*	*	*	£8
1945	*	*	*	£8
1946	*	*	*	£8
1947	*	*	*	£8
1948	*	*	*	£8
1949	*	*	*	£18
1950	*	*	*	£18
1950 proof	*	*	*	£12
1951	*	*	*	£20
1951 proof	*	*	*	£20

ELIZABETH II
1953	*	*	*	£6
1953 proof	*	*	*	£10

■ **EIGHTEENPENCE BANK TOKENS**

GEORGE III
1811	£9	£25	£80	£165
1812 laureate bust	£9	£25	£80	£165
1812 laureate hd	£9	£25	£80	£165
1813	£9	£25	£90	£175
1814	£9	£25	£90	£175
1815	£9	£25	£90	£175
1816	£9	£25	£90	£175

■ **SHILLINGS**

Cromwell 1658 Shilling

CROMWELL	F	VF	EF
1658	£750	£1500	£2750
1658 Dutch copy	*	*	*

Charles II 1671 Shilling, plumes both sides

CHARLES II	F	VF	EF
1663 1st bust	£135	£375	£1850
1663 1st bust var	£135	£375	£1850
1666 1st bust	*	*	*
1666 eleph	£450	£1750	£6000
1666 guinea head, eleph	£2500	*	*
1666 2nd bust	£1700	*	*
1668 1st bust var	£400	£1650	*
1668 2nd bust	£135	£375	£1850
1668/7	£150	£450	£1900
1669/6 1st bust var	ext. rare	*	*
1669 2nd bust	ext. rare	*	*
1670	£150	£525	£2000
1671	£150	£525	£2000
1671 plumes both sides	£625	£1650	£4000
1672	£150	£525	£2000
1673	£150	£525	£2000
1673/2	£150	£525	£2000
1673 plumes both sides	£625	£1650	£4000
1674	£150	£525	£2000
1674/3	£150	£525	£2000
1674 plumes both sides	£625	£1650	£4000
1674 plumes rev only	£700	£1750	£4500
1674 3rd bust	£525	£1500	*
1675	£525	£1500	*
1675/3	£525	£1500	*
1675 2nd bust	£275	£675	£2250
1675/4	£275	£675	£2250
1675 plumes both sides	£625	£1650	£4000
1676	£150	£525	£2000
1676/5	£150	£525	£2000
1676 plumes both sides	£625	£1650	£4000
1677	£150	£525	£2000
1677 plumes obv only	£750	£1750	£4850
1678	£150	£525	£2000
1678/7	£150	£525	£2000
1679	£150	£525	£2000
1679/7	£150	£525	£2000
1679 plumes	£625	£1650	£4000
1679 plumes obv only	£750	£1750	£4850
1680 plumes	£750	£1750	£4850
1680/79 plumes	£750	£1750	£4850
1681	£300	£850	*
1681/0	£300	£850	*
1681/0 eleph & castle	£2750	*	*
1682/1	£800	*	*
1683	£800	*	*
1683 4th bust	£800	*	*
1684	£275	£675	£2250

James II 1687 Shilling

JAMES II	F	VF	EF
1685	£200	£525	£1950
1685 no stops on rev	£200	£525	£2000
1685 plume on rev			ext. rare
1686	£200	£525	£1950
1686/5	£200	£525	£1950
1686 V/S	£200	£525	£2000
1687	£200	£525	£1950
1687/6	£200	£525	£1950
1688	£200	£525	£1950
1688/7	£200	£525	£2000

WILLIAM AND MARY			
1692	£225	£525	£1950
1693	£225	£525	£1950

WILLIAM III			
1695 1st bust	£30	£100	£500
1696	£30	£90	£425
1696 no stops on rev	£100	£325	*
1669 in error	£850	*	*
1696 B	£45	£150	£595
1696 C	£55	£175	£625
1696 E	£55	£175	£625
1696 N	£55	£175	£625
1696 y	£55	£175	£625
1696 Y	£65	£200	£700
1696 2nd bust		unique	
1696 3rd bust C	£145	£375	£1250
1696 E		ext. rare	
1697 1st bust	£30	£90	£395
1697 no stops on rev	£85	£295	*
1697 B	£45	£150	£595
1697 C	£45	£150	£595

William III 1699 roses Shilling

	F	VF	EF
1697 E	£45	£150	£595
1697 N	£45	£150	£595
1697 y	£45	£145	£575
1697 Y	£60	£200	£875
1697 3rd bust	£30	£90	£395
1697 B	£60	£200	£825
1697 C	£50	£150	£500
1697 E	£60	£200	£875
1697 N	£60	£200	£875
1697 y	£60	£200	£875
1697 3rd bust var	£30	£90	£395
1697 B	£60	£200	£875
1697 C	£120	£325	£1100

	F	VF	EF
1698 plain	£60	£200	£800
1698 plumes	£200	£575	£1750
1698 4th bust	£165	£450	£1600
1699 4th bust	£165	£475	£1650
1699 5th bust	£100	£350	£1100
1699 plumes	£200	£500	£2250
1699 roses	£200	£475	£1850
1700	£30	£90	£385
1700 no stops on rev	£55	£150	£475
1700 plume below bust			ext. rare
1701	£75	£275	£800
1701 plumes	£200	£585	£1750

	F	VF	EF
1711 3rd bust	£175	£475	£1200
1711 4th bust	£30	£90	£375
1712 r&p	£50	£165	£575
1713/2	£65	£195	£675
1714	£55	£165	£575
1714/3	£60	£250	£675

George I 1721/0 roses & plumes Shilling

GEORGE I

	F	VF	EF
1715 1st bust r&p	£50	£195	£750
1716 r&p	£150	£375	£1200
1717 r&p	£55	£195	£775
1718 r&p	£55	£185	£750
1719 r&p	£150	£375	£1200
1720 r&p	£55	£165	£750
1720/18	£150	£325	£1100
1720 plain	£50	£165	£550
1720 large 0	£50	£165	£575
1721 plain	£175	£500	£1300
1721 r&p	£80	£250	£800
1721/0 r&p	£55	£195	£750
1721/19 r&p	£85	£250	£875
1721/18 r&p	ext. rare	*	*
1722 r&p	£50	£175	£750
1723 r&p	£65	£175	£775
1723 SSC	£30	£80	£300
1723 SSC C/SS	£35	£110	£365
1723 SSC French arms at date	£175	£500	£1500
1723 2nd bust SS C	£50	£120	£350
1723 r&p	£55	£195	£800
1723 WCC	£575	£1500	£4250
1724 r&p	£55	£195	£800
1724 WCC	£575	£1500	£4250
1725 r&p	£55	£195	£800
1725 no obv stops	£75	£250	£875
1725 WCC	£575	£1500	£4250
1726 r&p	£500	£1500	*
1726 WCC	£575	£1500	£4250
1727 r&p	£500	£1250	*
1727 r&p no stops on obv	£500	£1200	*

GEORGE II

	F	VF	EF
1727 YH plumes	£100	£350	£1200
1727 r&p	£75	£200	£850
1728	£150	£395	£1200
1728 r&p	£85	£250	£850
1729 r&p	£85	£250	£850
1731 r&p	£65	£200	£750

Anne 1702 Shilling

ANNE

	F	VF	EF
1702 1st bust	£80	£275	£900
1702 plumes	£85	£300	£800
1702 VIGO	£80	£275	£750
1703 2nd bust VIGO	£80	£275	£725
1704	£400	£1250	*
1704 plumes	£120	£350	£1250
1705	£135	£450	£1500
1705 plumes	£85	£300	£950
1705 r&p	£80	£325	£950
1707 r&p	£90	£365	£900
1707 E	£75	£225	£875
1707 E*	£90	£250	£900
1707 E* local dies	£175	£500	*
1707 3rd bust	£25	£145	£400
1707 plumes	£70	£275	£875
1707 E	£65	£225	£775
1707 Edin bust E*	£350	*	*
1708 2nd bust E	£100	£450	£1300
1708 E*	£90	£250	£925
1708/7 E*			ext. rare
1708 r&p	£125	£350	£1100
1708 3rd bust	£30	£90	£375
1708 plumes	£85	£300	£875
1708 r&p	£120	£350	£1200
1708 E	£75	£225	£875
1708/7 E	£100	£300	£925
1708 Edin bust E*	£120	£350	£1200
1709	£60	£100	£400
1709 Edin bust E	£250	£850	*
1709 Edin bust E*	£100	£300	£1100
1710 3rd bust r&p	£85	£300	£900
1710 4th bust proof			ext. rare
1710 r&p	£65	£200	£775

	F	VF	EF
1731 plumes	£120	£400	£1100
1732 r&p	£85	£250	£850
1734 r&p	£70	£185	£750
1735 r&p	£70	£185	£750
1736 r&p	£70	£185	£750
1736/5 r&p	£85	£250	£850
1737 r&p	£50	£185	£750
1739 r&p roses	£40	£165	£625
1741 roses	£40	£165	£625
1741/39 roses	£100	£250	£950

George II 1729 young head Shilling

	F	VF	EF
1743 OH roses	£40	£145	£575
1743/1 roses	£65	£175	£675
1745	£30	£110	£485
1745/3 roses	£65	£175	£600
1745 LIMA	£25	£90	£485
1746 LIMA	£80	£200	£675
1746/5 LIMA	£80	£200	£675
1746 proof	*	£700	£1375
1747 roses	£40	£110	£485
1750	£55	£165	£600
1750/6	£70	£185	£675
1751	£80	£225	£750
1758	£15	£45	£125

George III 1763 'Northumberland' Shilling

GEORGE III

	F	VF	EF	Unc
1763 'Northumberland'	*	£450	£900	£1500
1786 proof or pattern	*	*	*	£5000
1787 no hearts	£15	£30	£70	£165
1787 no hearts no stop over head	£20	£45	£100	£225
1787 no hearts no stops at date	£20	£65	£150	£285
1787 no stops on obv	£250	£600	*	*

	F	VF	EF	Unc
1787 hearts	£15	£25	£70	£165
1798 'Dorrien and Magens'	*	£5500	£12000	£16500
1816	*	£5	£70	£140
1817	*	£5	£70	£140
1817 GEOE error	£75	£150	£525	*
1818	£4	£25	£125	£250
1819	*	£4	£85	£165
1819/8	*	*	£120	£275
1820	*	£4	£85	£165

GEORGE IV

	F	VF	EF	Unc
1820 1st head 1st rev pattern or proof	*	*	*	£4250
1821 1st rev	£10	£30	£185	£450
1821 proof	*	*	£450	£875
1823 1st head 2nd rev	£20	£50	£285	£650
1824 2nd rev	£8	£35	£185	£450
1825 2nd rev	£15	£40	£185	£450
1825 2nd head	£10	£25	£150	£300
1826	*	£25	£120	£265

George IV 1824 Shilling

	F	VF	EF	Unc
1826 proof	*	*	£200	£450
1827	£10	£50	£300	£675
1829	*	£40	£200	£525

WILLIAM IV

	F	VF	EF	Unc
1831 proof	*	*	*	£725
1834	£10	£30	£165	£395
1835	£10	£35	£175	£425
1836	£15	£25	£165	£395
1837	£25	£75	£225	£550

William IV 1836 Shilling

VICTORIA

	F	VF	EF	Unc
1838 YH	£10	£25	£175	£425
1839	£20	£50	£250	£575

	F	VF	EF	Unc
1839 2nd YH	£10	£30	£165	£340
1839 proof	*	*	*	£650
1840	£15	£45	£200	£425
1841	£15	£45	£210	£425
1842	£12	£30	£150	£325
1843	£15	£45	£210	£425
1844	£12	£30	£150	£325
1845	£12	£30	£135	£375
1846	£10	£30	£150	£325
1848/6	£60	£125	£600	£1100
1849	£12	£30	£135	£375
1850	£300	£900	£2500	*
1850/49	£300	£975	£2600	*
1851	£40	£150	£475	£975
1852	£10	£20	£110	£265
1853	£10	£20	£110	£265
1853 proof	*	*	*	£800
1854	£75	£350	£1200	£2250
1855	£10	£20	£110	£265
1856	£10	£20	£110	£265
1857	£10	£20	£110	£265
1857 F:G:	£250	*	*	*
1858	£10	£20	£110	£265
1859	£10	£20	£110	£265
1860	£10	£25	£150	£325
1861	£10	£25	£150	£325
1862	£15	£45	£200	£425

Victoria 1860 Shilling

	F	VF	EF	Unc
1863	£40	£85	£400	£875
1863/1	£60	£200	£675	*
1864	£12	£25	£120	£265
1865	£12	£25	£120	£265
1866	£12	£25	£120	£265
1866 BBRITANNIAR error	£60	£225	£750	*
1867	£12	£25	£120	£265
1867 3rd YH, die no	£150	£385	£1200	*
1868	£10	£25	£120	£265
1869	£15	£40	£150	£325
1870	£10	£25	£120	£265
1871	£10	£20	£120	£265
1872	£10	£20	£120	£265
1873	£10	£20	£120	£265
1874	£10	£20	£120	£265
1875	£10	£20	£120	£265
1876	£10	£25	£120	£265
1877	£10	£20	£120	£265

	F	VF	EF	Unc
1878	£12	£28	£150	£325
1879 no die		ext. rare		
1879 4th YH	£8	£20	£120	£265
1880	£10	£15	£80	£195
1880 longer line below SHILLING	*	*	*	*
1881	£10	£20	£80	£195
1881 longer line below SHILLING	£10	£20	£80	£165
1881 longer line below SHILLING, large rev lettering	£10	£20	£80	£165
1882	£15	£20	£120	£235
1883	£10	£20	£70	£195
1884	£10	£20	£70	£195
1885	£10	£20	£70	£195
1886	£10	£20	£70	£195
1887	£10	£25	£110	£265
1887 JH	*	£5	£12	£35
1887 proof	*	*	*	£150
1888/7	*	£8	£45	£90
1889	£40	£100	£425	*
1889 large JH	*	£8	£50	£120
1890	*	£8	£50	£120
1891	*	£8	£50	£135
1892	*	£8	£50	£145
1893 OH	*	*	£35	£80
1893 proof	*	*	*	£165
1893 small obv letters	*	*	£40	£80
1894	*	*	£45	£100
1895	*	*	£40	£120
1896	*	*	£40	£100

Victoria 1896 Shilling

	F	VF	EF	Unc
1897	*	*	£40	£90
1898	*	*	£40	£90
1899	*	*	£40	£90
1900	*	*	£40	£90
1901	*	*	£40	£90

EDWARD VII

	F	VF	EF	Unc
1902	*	*	£40	£70
1902 matt proof	*	*	£40	£80
1903	*	£20	£150	£425
1904	*	£15	£110	£325
1905	£70	£200	£1250	£2850
1906	*	*	£65	£185
1907	*	*	£70	£200

	F	VF	EF	Unc
1908	£8	£20	£175	£525
1909	£8	£20	£175	£525
1910	*	*	£45	£125

GEORGE V

	F	VF	EF	Unc
1911	*	*	£20	£60
1911 proof	*	*	*	£70
1912	*	*	£30	£80
1913	*	*	£65	£160
1914	*	*	£20	£55
1915	*	*	£20	£50
1916	*	*	£20	£50
1917	*	*	£20	£75
1918	*	*	£20	£50
1919	*	*	£25	£70
1920	*	*	£20	£70
1921	*	*	£25	£100
1922	*	*	£20	£70
1923	*	*	£15	£55
1923 nickel	*	*	*	£1200
1924	*	*	£25	£60
1924 nickel	*	*	*	£1200
1925	*	*	£45	£120
1926	*	*	£25	£70
1926 mod eff	*	*	£18	£48
1927	*	*	£20	£50
1927 new type	*	*	£12	£40
1927 new type proof	*	*	*	£60
1928	*	*	*	£25
1929	*	*	£8	£25
1930	*	*	£25	£85
1931	*	*	£8	£30
1932	*	*	£8	£30
1933	*	*	£8	£30
1934	*	*	£13	£45
1935	*	*	£4	£20
1936	*	*	£4	£20

GEORGE VI

	F	VF	EF	Unc
1937 Eng	*	*	*	£9
1937 Eng proof	*	*	*	£12
1937 Scot	*	*	*	£9
1937 Scot proof	*	*	*	£12
1938 Eng	*	*	£5	£30
1938 Scot	*	*	£5	£25
1939 Eng	*	*	*	£10
1939 Scot	*	*	*	£10
1940 Eng	*	*	*	£10
1940 Scot	*	*	*	£10
1941 Eng	*	*	£2	£12
1941 Scot	*	*	£2	£12
1942 Eng	*	*	*	£10
1942 Scot	*	*	*	£10
1943 Eng	*	*	*	£10
1943 Scot	*	*	*	£10
1944 Eng	*	*	*	£8
1944 Scot	*	*	*	£9
1945 Eng	*	*	*	£6
1945 Scot	*	*	*	£6

	F	VF	EF	Unc
1946 Eng	*	*	*	£6
1946 Scot	*	*	*	£6
1947 Eng	*	*	*	£6
1947 Scot	*	*	*	£6
1948 Eng	*	*	*	£7
1948 Scot	*	*	*	£7
1949 Eng	*	*	*	£20
1949 Scot	*	*	*	£20
1950 Eng	*	*	*	£17
1950 Eng proof	*	*	*	£20
1950 Scot	*	*	*	£17
1950 Scot proof	*	*	*	£20
1951 Eng	*	*	*	£17
1951 Eng proof	*	*	*	£20
1951 Scot	*	*	*	£17
1951 Scot proof	*	*	*	£20

ELIZABETH II

	F	VF	EF	Unc
1953 Eng	*	*	*	£5
1953 Eng proof	*	*	*	£10
1953 Scot	*	*	*	£5
1953 Scot proof	*	*	*	£10
1954 Eng	*	*	*	£5
1954 Scot	*	*	*	£5
1955 Eng	*	*	*	£5
1955 Scot	*	*	*	£5
1956 Eng	*	*	*	£10
1956 Scot	*	*	*	£9
1957 Eng	*	*	*	£4
1957 Scot	*	*	*	£20
1958 Eng	*	*	*	£50
1958 Scot	*	*	*	£4
1959 Eng	*	*	*	£4
1959 Scot	*	*	*	£70
1960 Eng	*	*	*	£2
1960 Scot	*	*	*	£3
1961 Eng	*	*	*	£2
1961 Scot	*	*	*	£10
1962 Eng	*	*	*	£1
1962 Scot	*	*	*	£1
1963 Eng	*	*	*	£1
1963 Scot	*	*	*	£1
1964 Eng	*	*	*	£1
1964 Scot	*	*	*	£1
1965 Eng	*	*	*	£1
1965 Scot	*	*	*	£1
1966 Eng	*	*	*	£1
1966 Scot	*	*	*	£1

■ SIXPENCES

CROMWELL	F	VF	EF
1658		highest rarity	
1658 Dutch copy	*	£4000	£6500

CHARLES II	F	VF	EF
1674	£50	£225	£750
1675	£50	£245	£785

	F	VF	EF
1675/4	£50	£245	£785
1676	£50	£250	£825
1676/5	£50	£250	£825
1677	£50	£225	£750
1678/7	£50	£245	£785
1679	£50	£250	£825
1680	£70	£250	£825
1681	£50	£245	£785
1682	£65	£285	£875
1682/1	£50	£245	£785
1683	£50	£225	£750
1684	£65	£245	£750

James II 1686 Sixpence

JAMES II

	F	VF	EF
1686 early shields	£100	£350	£900
1687 early shields	£100	£350	£900
1687/6	£100	£350	£900
1687 later shields	£100	£350	£900
1687/6	£100	£375	£1000
1688	£100	£375	£1000

WILLIAM AND MARY

	F	VF	EF
1693	£110	£375	£950

William and Mary 1693 Sixpence

	F	VF	EF
1693 3 upside down	£125	£425	£1000
1694	£140	£400	£1000

WILLIAM III

	F	VF	EF
1695 1st bust early hp	£30	£95	£375
1696	£25	£70	£200
1696 no obv stops	£40	£125	£450
1696/5	£30	£100	£450
1696 B	£30	£80	£350
1696 C	£35	£100	£450
1696 E	£35	£100	£450
1696 N	£35	£100	£450
1696 y	£30	£95	£425

	F	VF	EF
1696 Y	£40	£100	£425
1696 1st bust later hp	£50	£135	£400
1696 B	£75	£200	*
1696 C	£60	£225	£500
1696 N	£70	£225	£525
1696 2nd bust	£185	£500	£1750
1696 3rd bust, early hp, E		ext. rare	
1696 3rd bust, early hp, y		ext. rare	
1697 1st bust early hp	£25	£60	£275
1697 B	£40	£100	£425
1697 C	£60	£150	£500
1697 E	£40	£110	£425
1697 N	£40	£110	£425
1697 y	£40	£110	£425
1697 2nd bust	£145	£395	£1200
1697 3rd bust later hp	£25	£75	£250
1697 B	£40	£100	£425
1697 C	£60	£185	£650
1697 E	£65	£120	£450
1697 Y	£60	£150	£500
1698	£45	£95	£300
1698 plumes	£80	£175	£575
1699	£85	£200	£625
1699 plumes	£70	£165	£500
1699 roses	£75	£185	£585

William III 1699 plumes Sixpence

	F	VF	EF
1700	£25	£60	£225
1700 plume below bust	£2750	*	*
1701	£40	£85	£325

ANNE

	F	VF	EF
1703 VIGO	£40	£110	£325
1705	£60	£185	£525
1705 plumes	£50	£165	£475
1705 r&p	£45	£150	£450
1707	£40	£140	£425
1707 plain	£25	£75	£275
1707 E	£25	£100	£385
1707 plumes	£35	£100	£375

Anne 1707 plumes Sixpence

	F	VF	EF
1708 plain	£30	£95	£285
1708 E	£35	£110	£450
1708/7 E	£60	£165	£525
1708 E*	£40	£150	£500
1708/7 E*	£60	£185	£550
1708 Edin bust E*	£60	£185	£550
1708 plumes	£45	£125	£450
1710 r&p	£45	£135	£450
1711	£20	£75	£200

George I 1726 roses and plumes Sixpence

GEORGE I

	F	VF	EF
1717 r&p	£50	£175	£575
1720/17 r&p	£50	£175	£575
1723 SS C, small letters on obv	£25	£85	£250
1723 SS C, large letters on both sides	£25	£85	£250
1726 small r&p	£35	£200	£625

George II 1728 roses and plumes Sixpence

GEORGE II

	F	VF	EF
1728 YH	£65	£225	£550
1728 plumes	£45	£150	£450
1728 YH r&p	£25	£110	£400
1731	£25	£110	£400
1732	£25	£110	£400
1734	£35	£125	£465
1735	£35	£125	£425
1735/4	£35	£125	£485
1736	£30	£125	£400
1739 roses	£25	£100	£325
1739 O/R	£60	£185	£475
1741	£25	£110	£325
1743 OH roses	£25	£110	£325
1745	£25	£110	£325
1745/3	£30	£125	£350
1745 LIMA	£20	£85	£225
1746	£20	£85	£225
1746 plain proof	*	*	£900

	F	VF	EF
1750	£35	£135	£325
1751	£35	£175	£400
1757	£10	£20	£60
1757	£10	£20	£60
1758/7	£15	£35	£70

GEORGE III

	F	VF	EF	Unc
1787 hearts	£10	£20	£50	£100
1787 no hearts	£10	£20	£50	£100
1816	£8	£12	£60	£110
1817	£8	£12	£60	£110
1818	£8	£18	£65	£140
1819	£8	£15	£60	£130
1819/8	£8	£15	£60	£130
1819 small 8	£10	£20	£100	£150
1820	£8	£15	£60	£120
1820 I inv	£30	£100	£375	£600

GEORGE IV

	F	VF	EF	Unc
1820 1st head 1st rev pattern or proof	*	*	*	£2500
1821	£8	£20	£125	£300
1821 BBITANNIAR error	£100	£250	£675	*
1824 1st head 2nd rev	£8	£20	£120	£325
1825	£8	£20	£120	£325
1826	£20	£60	£285	£550
1826 2nd head 3rd rev	£5	£14	£100	£285
1826 proof	*	*	*	£365
1827	£15	£45	£325	£550
1828	£8	£20	£185	£425
1829	£6	£20	£110	£300

William IV 1831 proof Sixpence

WILLIAM IV

	F	VF	EF	Unc
1831	£10	£20	£110	£250
1831 proof	*	*	*	£325
1834	£10	£30	£120	£250
1835	£10	£20	£120	£250
1836	£15	£35	£175	£325
1837	£12	£30	£175	£325

VICTORIA

	F	VF	EF	Unc
1838 1st YH	£5	£17	£100	£220
1839	£8	£17	£100	£220
1839 proof	*	*	*	£485
1840	£8	£15	£110	£240
1841	£8	£15	£120	£265
1842	£8	£15	£110	£240
1843	£8	£15	£110	£240

	F	VF	EF	Unc
1844	£8	£15	£110	£240
1845	£8	£15	£110	£265
1846	£8	£15	£110	£240
1848	£25	£110	£465	£825
1848/6	£20	£100	£425	£800
1850	£8	£18	£110	£240
1850 5/3	£17	£45	£200	£400
1851	£8	£12	£110	£240
1852	£8	£12	£110	£240
1853	£6	£17	£95	£180
1853 proof	*	*	*	£525
1854	£90	£250	£800	*
1855	£8	£15	£110	£240
1855/3	£10	£17	£120	£285
1856	£8	£15	£110	£240
1857	£8	£15	£110	£240
1858	£8	£15	£110	£240
1859	£8	£15	£110	£240
1859/8	£8	£20	£110	£250
1860	£8	£17	£110	£240
1862	£45	£110	£475	£875
1863	£40	£85	£365	£725
1864	£8	£15	£110	£240
1865	£8	£15	£110	£240
1866	£7	£15	£110	£240
1866 no die no				ext. rare
1867	£10	£20	£125	£265
1868	£10	£15	£110	£240
1869	£12	£25	£135	£300
1870	£12	£20	£135	£300

Victoria 1871 proof Sixpence

	F	VF	EF	Unc
1871	£7	£12	£80	£215
1871 no die no	£5	£12	£80	£200
1872	£7	£12	£80	£215
1873	£7	£12	£80	£215
1874	£7	£12	£80	£215
1875	£7	£12	£80	£215
1876	£9	£20	£120	£295
1877	£7	£12	£80	£215
1877 no die no	£5	£12	£70	£200
1878	£7	£10	£80	£215
1878/7	£40	£115	£600	*
1878 DRITANNIAR error	£65	£185	£750	*
1879 die no	£10	£20	£95	£250
1879 no die no	£7	£10	£80	£215
1880 2nd YH	£7	£15	£80	£215
1880 3rd YH	£5	£8	£70	£125
1881	£5	£10	£60	£110
1882	£8	£25	£100	£285

	F	VF	EF	Unc
1883	£5	£10	£70	£125
1884	£5	£10	£45	£110
1885	£5	£10	£45	£110
1886	£5	£10	£45	£110
1887	£5	£10	£45	£110
1887 JH shield rev	£2	£5	£10	£28
1887 proof	*	*	*	£110
1887 new rev	£2	£5	£10	£30
1888	£3	£5	£28	£75
1889	£3	£7	£28	£75
1890	*	£8	£28	£75
1891	*	£8	£35	£85
1892	*	£10	£40	£100
1893	£250	£650	£2150	*
1893 OH	*	£5	£20	£60
1893 proof	*	*	*	£150
1894	*	£5	£35	£100
1895	*	£5	£32	£75
1896	*	£5	£30	£65
1897	*	£5	£30	£65
1898	*	£5	£30	£65
1899	*	£5	£30	£65
1900	*	£5	£25	£55
1901	*	£5	£25	£55

EDWARD VII

	F	VF	EF	Unc
1902	*	£5	£35	£65
1902 matt proof	*	*	*	£65
1903	*	£7	£45	£110
1904	*	£15	£80	£195
1905	*	£15	£90	£200
1906	*	£9	£45	£100
1907	*	£9	£45	£110
1908	*	£10	£55	£125
1909	*	£9	£45	£110
1910	*	£6	£35	£75

GEORGE V

	F	VF	EF	Unc
1911	*	*	£15	£45
1911 proof	*	*	*	£65
1912	*	*	£28	£70
1913	*	*	£35	£75
1914	*	*	£12	£40
1915	*	*	£12	£45
1916	*	*	£12	£35
1917	*	*	£35	£100
1918	*	*	£12	£30
1919	*	*	£15	£50
1920	*	*	£12	£55
1920 debased	*	*	£12	£55
1921	*	*	£12	£50
1922	*	*	£12	£50
1923	*	*	£15	£50
1924	*	*	£12	£50
1925	*	*	£12	£35
1925 new rim	*	*	£12	£30
1926	*	*	£12	£35
1926 mod eff	*	*	£9	£30
1927	*	*	£10	£28

	F	VF	EF	Unc
1927 new rev proof	*	*	*	£40
1928	*	*	£7	£20
1929	*	*	£7	£20
1930	*	*	£7	£25
1931	*	*	£7	£20
1932	*	*	£12	£35
1933	*	*	£5	£20
1934	*	*	£8	£25
1935	*	*	£5	£15
1936	*	*	£5	£15

GEORGE VI

	F	VF	EF	Unc
1937	*	*	£1	£7
1937 proof	*	*	*	£10
1938	*	*	£4	£15
1939	*	*	£2	£10
1940	*	*	£2	£10
1941	*	*	£2	£10
1942	*	*	£1	£7
1943	*	*	£1	£7
1944	*	*	£1	£7
1945	*	*	£1	£7
1946	*	*	£1	£7
1947	*	*	*	£7
1948	*	*	£1	£5
1949	*	*	£1	£8
1950	*	*	£1	£8
1950 proof	*	*	*	£10
1951	*	*	£1	£12
1952	*	£5	£20	£80

ELIZABETH II

	F	VF	EF	Unc
1953	*	*	*	£5
1953 proof	*	*	*	£7
1954	*	*	*	£5
1955	*	*	*	£3
1956	*	*	*	£4
1957	*	*	*	£3
1958	*	*	*	£6
1959	*	*	*	£2
1960	*	*	*	£4
1961	*	*	*	£4
1962	*	*	*	£1
1963	*	*	*	£1
1964	*	*	*	£1
1965	*	*	*	£1
1966	*	*	*	£1
1967	*	*	*	£1

■ GROATS (FOURPENCES) 'BRITANNIA' TYPE

Earlier dates are included in Maundy sets (see p136).

WILLIAM IV

	F	VF	EF	Unc
1836	*	*	£45	£100
1836 proof	*	*	*	£625
1837	*	*	£60	£120
1837 proof	*	*	*	£825

VICTORIA	F	VF	EF	Unc
1838	*	£5	£40	£110
1838 8/8 on side	*	£15	£60	£165
1839	*	£8	£40	£110
1839 proof	*	*	*	£275
1840	*	£10	£40	£110
1840 narrow 0	*	£12	£40	*
1841	*	£10	£50	£125
1841 1 for last 1	*	*	*	*
1842	*	£8	£50	£125
1842/1	*	£15	£70	£180
1843	*	£5	£50	£125
1843 4/5	*	£15	£65	£185
1844	*	£8	£50	£125
1845	*	£8	£50	£125
1846	*	£8	£50	£125
1847/6	£25	£70	£325	*
1848	*	£8	£45	£120
1848/6	£10	£25	£75	*
1848/7	*	£20	£90	£265
1849	*	£10	£45	£120
1849/8	*	£10	£50	£125
1851	£15	£65	£275	*
1852	£40	£100	£350	*

Victoria 1852 Groat

	F	VF	EF	Unc
1853	£35	£90	£400	*
1853 proof	*	*	*	£575
1854	*	£8	£45	£120
1854 5/3	*	£20	£85	*
1855	*	£8	£45	£120
1857 proof	*	*	*	£1150
1862 proof	*	*	*	£1750
1888 JH	*	£20	£40	£90

■ SILVER THREEPENCES

Earlier dates are included in Maundy sets.

WILLIAM IV

	F	VF	EF	Unc
1834	*	£10	£70	£160
1835	*	£10	£65	£145
1836	*	£10	£65	£165
1837	*	£20	£85	£19

Victoria 1866 Threepence

VICTORIA	F	VF	EF	Unc		F	VF	EF	Unc
1838	*	£15	£50	£140	1892	*	£3	£12	£30
1839	*	£20	£85	£175	1893	£12	£40	£100	£275
1840	*	£15	£60	£150	1893 OH	*	*	£6	£20
1841	*	£15	£85	£175	1893 proof	*	*	*	£65
1842	*	£15	£85	£175	1894	*	£2	£10	£30
1843	*	£15	£55	£120	1895	*	£2	£10	£30
1844	*	£15	£85	£175	1896	*	£2	£10	£30
1845	*	£10	£40	£90	1897	*	*	£5	£25
1846	*	£15	£95	£195	1898	*	*	£5	£30
1847	£45	£125	£400	£800	1899	*	*	£5	£30
1848	£35	£100	£400	£750	1900	*	*	£5	£18
1849	*	£15	£85	£175	1901	*	*	£5	£20
1850	*	£10	£50	£95					
1851	*	£10	£45	£135	EDWARD VII				
1852	£45	£175	£450	*	1902	*	*	£7	£15
1853	*	£20	£95	£185	1902 matt proof	*	*	*	£20
1854	*	£10	£60	£110	1903	*	£2	£15	£40
1855	*	£15	£85	£165	1904	*	£6	£25	£80
1856	*	£10	£60	£110	1905	*	£6	£25	£70
1857	*	£15	£70	£165	1906	*	£3	£20	£70
1858	*	£12	£50	£110	1907	*	£2	£15	£40
1858 BRITANNIAB error		ext. rare			1908	*	£2	£12	£35
1858/6	£10	£25	£150	*	1909	*	£2	£25	£50
1859	*	£8	£50	£110	1910	*	£2	£10	£30
1860	*	£15	£60	£165					
1861	*	£8	£50	£110	GEORGE V				
1862	*	£8	£50	£110	1911	*	*	£6	£17
1863	*	£10	£80	£150	1911 proof	*	*	*	£30
1864	*	£10	£50	£100	1912	*	*	£6	£17
1865	*	£10	£70	£150	1913	*	*	£6	£17
1866	*	£8	£50	£100	1914	*	*	£4	£15
1867	*	£8	£50	£100	1915	*	*	£4	£20
1868	*	£8	£50	£100	1916	*	*	£3	£12
1868 RRITANNIAR error		ext. rare			1917	*	*	£3	£12
1869	£10	£30	£100	£185	1918	*	*	£3	£12
1870	*	£6	£50	£95	1919	*	*	£3	£12
1871	*	£7	£60	£110	1920	*	*	£3	£17
1872	*	£5	£55	£110	1920 debased	*	*	£3	£17
1873	*	£5	£35	£75	1921	*	*	£3	£20
1874	*	£5	£35	£75	1922	*	*	£10	£45
1875	*	£5	£35	£75	1925	*	£1	£10	£45
1876	*	£5	£35	£75	1926	*	£3	£15	£60
1877	*	£5	£35	£75	1926 mod eff	*	£1	£8	£30
1878	*	£5	£35	£75	1927 new rev proof	*	*	*	£95
1879	*	£5	£35	£75	1928	*	£2	£15	£45
1880	*	£6	£40	£70	1930	*	£1	£8	£30
1881	*	£6	£40	£70	1931	*	*	£1	£9
1882	*	£8	£45	£100	1932	*	*	£1	£9
1883	*	£5	£30	£60	1933	*	*	£1	£9
1884	*	£5	£30	£55	1934	*	*	£1	£9
1885	*	£5	£25	£55	1935	*	*	£1	£9
1886	*	£5	£25	£50	1936	*	*	£1	£9
1887 YH	*	£6	£35	£65					
1887 JH	*	£2	£5	£15	GEORGE VI				
1887 proof	*	*	*	£40	1937	*	*	£2	£5
1888	*	£2	£12	£35	1937 proof	*	*	*	£10
1889	*	£2	£10	£30	1938	*	*	£2	£6
1890	*	£2	£10	£30	1939	*	£1	£5	£20
1891	*	£2	£10	£30	1940	*	*	£2	£8

F	VF	EF	Unc	
1941	*	*	£2	£12
1942	*	£2	£6	£35
1943	*	£3	£17	£55
1944	*	£6	£28	£80
1945	*	*	*	*

Some of the Threepences were issued for use in the Colonies. Note: all specimens of 1945 were probably melted down but it appears that one or two still exist.

■ SMALL SILVER FOR COLONIES

These tiny coins were struck for issue in some of the Colonies but they were never issued for circulation in Britain. However, they are often included in collections of British coins, so we have given the prices.

Twopences

Other dates are included in Maundy sets.

VICTORIA	F	VF	EF	Unc
1838	*	£5	£20	£45
1838 2nd 8 like S	*	£8	£30	£75
1848	*	£5	£20	£50

Threehalfpences

WILLIAM IV		VF	EF	Unc
1834	*	£5	£40	£75
1835	*	£5	£65	£165
1835/4	*	£10	£40	£95
1836	*	£5	£35	£60
1837	£10	£25	£100	£265

VICTORIA		VF	EF	Unc
1838	*	£8	£25	£65
1839	*	£8	£25	£65
1840	*	£15	£65	£135
1841	*	£8	£30	£80
1842	*	£8	£30	£80
1843	*	£8	£20	£60
1843/34	£5	£20	£65	£150
1860	£4	£15	£45	£110
1862	£4	£15	£45	£110
1870 proof				£750

■ NICKEL-BRASS THREEPENCES

Edward VIII 1937 Threepence, extremely rare

The 1937 Edward VIII threepences, struck in 1936 ready for issue, were melted after Edward's abdication.

A few, however, escaped into circulation to become highly prized collectors' pieces.

George VI 1937 threepences were struck in large numbers, and are consequently worth much less.

EDWARD VIII	F	VF	EF	BU
1937	*	*	£35000	*

GEORGE VI	F	VF	EF	BU
1937	*	*	£1	£6
1938	*	*	£3	£28
1939	*	*	£6	£50
1940	*	*	£2	£20
1941	*	*	£1	£8
1942	*	*	£1	£8
1943	*	*	£1	£8
1944	*	*	£1	£8
1945	*	*	£1	£12
1946	*	£10	£100	£500
1948	*	*	£5	£45
1949	*	£10	£100	£450
1950	*	*	£15	£85
1951	*	*	£25	£110
1952	*	*	*	£12

ELIZABETH II	F	VF	EF	BU
1953	*	*	*	£5
1953 proof	*	*	*	£8
1954	*	*	*	£5
1955	*	*	*	£7
1956	*	*	*	£7
1957	*	*	*	£4
1958	*	*	*	£10
1959	*	*	*	£3
1960	*	*	*	£3
1961	*	*	*	£1
1962	*	*	*	£1
1963	*	*	*	£1
1964	*	*	*	£1
1965	*	*	*	£1
1966	*	*	*	£1
1967	*	*	*	*

■ COPPER TWOPENCE

GEORGE III	F	VF	EF	BU
1797	£20	£75	£275	*

■ COPPER PENNIES

GEORGE III	F	VF	EF	BU
1797 10 leaves	£5	£35	£225	*
1797 11 leaves	£5	£45	£225	*
1806	£3	£8	£90	£300
1806 no incuse curl	£3	£8	£90	£325
1807	£3	£8	£90	£350

George III 1806 Penny

GEORGE IV

	F	VF	EF	BU
1825	£5	£25	£175	£485
1826	£3	£12	£150	£300
1826 thin line down St Andrew's cross	£5	£25	£175	£485
1826 thick line	£5	£40	£225	*
1827	£200	£550	£3000	*

William IV 1831

WILLIAM IV

	F	VF	EF	BU
1831	£10	£50	£285	£1000
1831 .ww inc		ext. rare		
1831 w.w inc	£15	£75	£375	*
1834	£15	£75	£365	£1375
1837	£20	£90	£450	£2000

Victoria 1841 Penny

VICTORIA	F	VF	EF	BU
1839 proof	*	*	*	£950
1841	£20	£60	£300	£800
1841 no colon after REG	£3	£15	£65	£275
1843	£90	£300	£1350	£3500
1843 no colon after REG	£65	£200	£1250	£2650
1844	£3	£15	£100	£325
1845	£8	£20	£145	£485
1846 DEF far colon	£3	£15	£110	£395
1846 DEF close colon	£3	£15	£135	£425
1847 DEF close colon	£3	£15	£95	£275
1847 DEF far colon	£3	£15	£85	£250
1848	£3	£15	£95	£300
1848/6	£15	£75	£420	*
1848/7	£3	£15	£95	£300
1849	£100	£350	£1650	£2850
1851 DEF far colon	£3	£18	£125	£475
1851 DEF close colon	£4	£15	£110	£385
1853 OT	£2	£10	£80	£215
1853 PT	£2	£10	£85	£285
1854 PT	£2	£10	£80	£215
1854/3	£15	£40	£165	£395
1854 OT	£2	£10	£80	£215
1855 OT	£2	£10	£80	£215
1855 PT	£2	£10	£80	£215
1856 PT	£50	£175	£600	£2000
1856 OT	£60	£225	£750	£2250
1857 OT	£2	£10	£80	£215
1857 PT	£2	£10	£80	£215
1857 small date	£2	£10	£85	£285
1858	£2	£10	£65	£195
1858 small date	£3	£10	£85	£285
1858/3	£20	£65	£350	*
1858/7	£2	£5	£85	£285
1858 no ww	£2	£5	£65	£250
1858 no ww (large 1 and 5, small 8s)	£3	£8	£65	£250
1859	£3	£10	£85	£285
1859 small date	£4	£15	£100	£295
1860/59	£300	£700	£2650	*

◼ BRONZE PENNIES

For fuller details of varieties in bronze pennies see *English Copper, Tin and Bronze Coins in the British Museum 1558-1958* by C W Peck, *The Bronze Coinage of Great Britain* by M J Freeman and *The British Bronze Penny 1860-1970* by Michael Gouby.

The die pairings used below are from the latter publication, a must for the penny collector. There are a large number of varieties and die combinations for this series, and only the more significant of these are listed below.

VICTORIA	F	VF	EF	BU
1860 BB, dies C/a	£100	£300	£700	*
1860 BB dies C/b	£40	£100	£245	£500
1860 BB rev rock to left of lighthouse, dies C/c	£80	£200	£750	*
1860 obv BB/rev TB, dies C/d	£400	£750	£1500	£3000

Victoria 1860 bronze Penny

	F	VF	EF	BU
1860 obv TB/rev BB, dies D/b	£300	£600	£1350	*
1860 TB, signature on cape, dies D/d	*	£15	£60	£235
1860 TB, rev L.C.W. inc below foot, dies E/e	£300	£575	£1000	£2500
1860 TB, rev L.C.W inc below shield, dies F/d	*	£15	£90	£225
1860 TB obv, no signature on cape, dies H/d	*	£150	£400	£900

1861 bronze Penny

	F	VF	EF	BU
1861 signature on cape, rev LCW below shield, dies D/d	£80	£225	£450	£1500
1861 signature on cape, rev no signature, dies D/g	£80	£225	£450	£1500
1861 signature below cape, L.C.W. below shield, dies F/d	*	£10	£90	£300
1861 signature below cape, rev no signature, dies F/g	£80	£350	£850	*
1861 obv no signature, L.C.W. below shield, dies H/d	*	£20	£100	£300
1861 date: 6 over 8	£400	£1250	£2500	*
1861 no signature either side, dies J/g	*	£12	£75	£275
1862 obv signature, rev no LCW, dies D/g	£450	£875	£1875	*
1862 obv no signature dies J/g	*	£10	£75	£275
1862 date: small figures (½d size)	£475	£1500	£2750	*

	F	VF	EF	BU
1863 dies J/g	*	£10	£60	£200
1863 die no 2 below date	£2000	*	*	*
1863 die no 3 below date	£1450	£3000	*	*
1863 die no 4 below date	£1350	*	*	*
1863 die no 5 below date **unique**				
1864 upper serif to 4 in date	£20	£135	£1000	*
1864 crosslet serif to 4 in date	£25	£150	£1450	£4000
1865	*	£25	£150	£525
1865/3	£40	£125	£525	£1450
1866	*	£15	£90	£425
1867	£10	£35	£200	£750
1868	£10	£40	£225	£875
1869	£150	£450	£1750	£4000
1870	£10	£40	£200	£575
1871	£30	£85	£525	£1500
1872	*	£12	£85	£300
1873	*	£12	£85	£350
1874	*	£20	£125	£400
1874 H dies J/g	*	£12	£80	£325
1874 rev lighthouse tall and thin, dies J/j	£20	£95	£300	£600
1874 H dies J/j	£25	£95	£250	£675
1874 obv, aged portrait, dies K/g	*	£20	£85	£325
1874 H	*	£20	£85	£325
1875 dies L/k	*	£15	£80	£285
1875 H	£30	£200	£875	£2250
1876 H	*	£15	£85	£275
1877	*	£8	£75	£225
1878	*	£35	£175	£500
1879	*	*	£75	£200
1880 no rock to left of lighthouse, dies M/k	£12	£35	£125	£375
1880 rocks to left of lighthouse, dies M/n	£12	£45	£150	£495
1881	*	*	£200	£575
1881 new obv, dies P/k	£45	£145	£350	*
1881 H	*	*	£65	£285
1882 H	*	*	£65	£235
1882 no H	£575	£1000	*	*
1883	*	*	£60	£225
1884	*	*	£50	£165
1885	*	*	£50	£165
1886	*	*	£50	£165
1887	*	*	£45	£140
1888	*	*	£50	£165
1889 14 leaves	*	*	£45	£140
1889 15 leaves	*	*	£50	£165
1890	*	*	£40	£125
1891	*	*	£40	£125
1892	*	*	£40	£145
1893	*	*	£40	£125
1894	*	*	£60	£225
1895 2mm	*	£50	£325	£750

	F	VF	EF	BU
1895	*	*	£15	£65
1896	*	*	£12	£60
1897	*	*	£12	£60
1897 higher horizon	£40	£120	£450	*
1898	*	*	£15	£65
1899	*	*	£15	£60
1900	*	*	£12	£55
1901	*	*	£10	£35

EDWARD VII

	F	VF	EF	BU
1902 low horizon	*	£15	£100	£275
1902	*	*	£10	£45
1903	*	*	£20	£70
1904	*	*	£35	£140
1905	*	*	£30	£95
1906	*	*	£20	£75
1907	*	*	£20	£80
1908	*	*	£17	£75
1909	*	*	£20	£80
1910	*	*	£17	£65

George V 1933 Penny

GEORGE V

	F	VF	EF	BU
1911	*	*	£12	£45
1912	*	*	£12	£50
1912 H	*	*	£55	£185
1913	*	*	£15	£55
1914	*	*	£12	£50
1915	*	*	£12	£50
1916	*	*	£12	£50
1917	*	*	£12	£50
1918	*	*	£12	£50
1918 H	*	£35	£250	£525
1918 KN	*	£45	£375	£725
1919	*	*	£12	£45
1919 H	*	£35	£325	£725
1919 KN	*	£75	£600	*
1920	*	*	£12	£45
1921	*	*	£12	£45
1922	*	*	£12	£45
1922 rev as 1927		ext. rare		
1926	*	*	£20	£80
1926 mod eff	*	£50	£800	£2000
1927	*	*	£7	£30
1928	*	*	£7	£28

	F	VF	EF	BU
1929	*	*	£7	£30
1930	*	*	£10	£35
1931	*	*	£10	£30
1932	*	*	£20	£75
1933		highest rarity		
1934	*	*	£15	£40
1935	*	*	£4	£15
1936	*	*	£4	£15

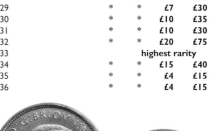

Edward VIII proof Penny

EDWARD VIII

proof penny   **highest rarity**

GEORGE VI

	F	VF	EF	BU
1937	*	*	*	£5
1938	*	*	*	£5
1939	*	*	£1	£6
1940	*	*	£7	£35
1944	*	*	£5	£20
1945	*	*	£4	£15
1946	*	*	*	£9
1947	*	*	*	£4
1948	*	*	*	£5
1949	*	*	*	£5
1950	*	£7	£20	£60
1951	*	£7	£28	£45
1952 proof				unique

George VI 1952 Penny, unique

ELIZABETH II	F	VF	EF	BU
1953	*	£1	£2	£15
1953 proof	*	*	*	£20
1954		unique		
1961	*	*	*	£2
1962	*	*	*	£1
1963	*	*	*	£1
1964	*	*	*	£0.50
1965	*	*	*	£0.50
1966	*	*	*	£0.50
1967	*	*	*	£0.25

■ COPPER OR TIN HALFPENNIES

Charles II 1675 Halfpenny

CHARLES II	Fair	F	VF	EF
1672	£8	£45	£225	£1350
1672 CRAOLVS error		ext. rare		*
1673	£8	£45	£200	£1350
1673 CRAOLVS error		ext. rare		*
1673 no stops on rev	£10	£65	£325	*
1673 no stops on obv	£12	£60	£300	*
1675	£10	£50	£200	£1475
1675 no stops on obv	£10	£60	£300	*
1675 5/3	£35	£120	£400	*

JAMES II				
1685 tin	£65	£250	£550	£3250
1686 tin	£70	£250	£600	*
1687 tin	£65	£250	£550	*
1687 D/D	*	*	*	*

WILLIAM AND MARY				
1689 tin, ET on right	£650	£1250	£2500	*
1689 tin, ET on left	*	*	*	*

	Fair	F	VF	EF
1690 tin, date on edge	£65	£200	£525	£2750
1691 tin, date in exergue and on edge	£65	£200	£525	£2750
1691/2 tin, 1691 in exergue 1692 on edge		ext. rare		*
1692 tin, date in exergue and on edge	£65	£75	£450	*
1694 copper	£12	£50	£250	£1350
1694 GVLIEMVS error	£150	*	*	*
1694 no stop after MARIA	£25	£65	£300	£1400
1694 BRITANNIA with last I/A	£30	£125	£350	*
1694 no stop on rev	£20	£60	£300	£1350

William III 1696 Halfpenny

WILLIAM III
Type 1, date in exergue

	Fair	F	VF	EF
1695	£10	£35	£175	£1250
1695 BRITANNIA, A's unbarred	£50	£175	*	*
1695 no stop on rev	£10	£50	£225	*
1696	£10	£35	£175	£1250
1696 GVLIEMVS, no stop on rev		ext. rare		*
1696 TERTVS error	£85	£200	*	*
1697	£10	£45	£175	£1250
1697 no stops	£35	£150	*	*
1697 I/E on TERTIVS	£35	£150	*	*
1697 GVLILMVS no stop on rev		ext. rare		*
1697 no stop after TERTIVS	£15	£40	£150	£1250
1698	£15	£45	£200	*

Type 2, date in legend

	Fair	F	VF	EF
1698	£10	£45	£225	£1250
1699	£10	£30	£225	£1100
1699 BRITANNIA, A's unbarred	£35	£150	*	*
1699 GVLIEMVS error	£35	£150	*	*

Type 3, Britannia's hand on knee, date in exergue

	Fair	F	VF	EF
1699	£10	£30	£200	£1150
1699 stop after date	£35	£150	*	*

	Fair	F	VF	EF
1699 BRITANNIA, A's unbarred	£20	£70	£250	*
1699 GVILELMVS	£50	£225	*	*
1699 TERTVS	£50	£225	*	*
1699 no stop on rev	£35	£150	*	*
1699 no stops on obv	£15	£60	£250	*
1699 no stops after GVLIELMVS	£15	£60	£250	*
1700	£8	£20	£200	£1100
1700 no stops on obv	£20	£70	£250	*
1700 no stops after GVLIELMVS	£20	£70	£250	*
1700 BRITANNIA, A's unbarred	£8	£20	£200	£1100
1700 no stop on reverse	£8	£25	£200	£1100
1700 GVLIELMS error	£20	£70	£250	*
1700 GVLIEEMVS error	£12	£45	£185	*
1700 TER TIVS error	£8	£20	£200	£1100
1700 I/V on TERTIVS	£50	£225	*	*
1701 BRITANNIA, A's unbarred	£8	£20	£200	£1100
1701 no stops on obv	£50	£225	*	*
1701 GVLIELMVS TERTIVS, V's inverted A's	£12	£45	£225	*

GEORGE I
Type 1

	Fair	F	VF	EF
1717	£10	£35	£250	£875
1717 no stops on obv	£15	£65	£475	*

George I 1717 Halfpenny

	Fair	F	VF	EF
1718	£10	£30	£225	£800
1718 no stop on obv	£15	£65	£475	*
1719 on large flan of type 2	£250	*	*	*
1719 on large flan of type 2, edge grained			ext. rare	*

Type 2

	Fair	F	VF	EF
1719 both shoulder straps ornate	£5	£25	£150	£825
1719 both shoulder straps ornate, edge grained			ext. rare	*
1719 bust with left strap plain	£5	£25	£150	£800
1720	£5	£25	£150	£750
1721	£5	£25	£150	£725
1721/0	£5	£25	£150	£725

	Fair	F	VF	EF
1721 stop after date	£5	£25	£150	£725
1722	£5	£25	£150	£725
1722 GEORGIVS, V inverted A	£15	£90	£300	*
1723	£5	£25	£150	£725
1723 no stop on reverse	£15	£90	£300	*
1724	£5	£25	£150	£650

George II 1733 Halfpenny

GEORGE II
Young Head

	Fair	F	VF	EF
1729	*	£20	£85	£400
1729 no stop on rev	*	£25	£90	£425
1730	*	£20	£85	£375
1730 GEOGIVS, no stop on reverse	*	£25	£110	£450
1730 stop after date	£5	£20	£85	£375
1730 no stop after REX or on rev	*	£25	£110	£450
1731	*	£20	£85	£365
1731 rev no stop	*	£25	£100	£400
1732	*	£20	£75	£350
1732 rev no stop	*	£25	£100	£400
1733	*	£18	£70	£350
1734	*	£18	£70	£350
1734/3	*	£25	£150	*
1734 no stops on obv	*	£25	£150	*
1735	*	£18	£70	£350
1736	*	£18	£75	£350
1737	*	£18	£75	£350
1738	*	£18	£70	£325
1739	*	£18	£70	£325

Old Head

	Fair	F	VF	EF
1740	*	£7	£55	£285
1742	*	£7	£55	£285
1742/0	*	£10	£80	£325
1743	*	£7	£55	£285
1744	*	£7	£55	£285
1745	*	£7	£55	£285
1746	*	£7	£55	£285
1747	*	£7	£55	£285
1748	*	£7	£55	£285
1749	*	£7	£55	£285
1750	*	£7	£55	£295
1751	*	£7	£55	£275

	Fair	F	VF	EF
1752	*	£7	£55	£275
1753	*	£7	£55	£275
1754	*	£7	£55	£275

George II 1777 Halfpenny

GEORGE III

	F	VF	EF	BU
1770	£5	£45	£200	£700
1771	£5	£45	£200	£700
1771 no stop on rev	£7	£45	£200	£700
1771 ball below spear head	£5	£45	£200	£700
1772	£5	£45	£200	£700
1772 GEORIVS error	£10	£80	£275	*
1772 ball below spear head	£5	£45	£200	£700
1772 no stop on rev	£5	£45	£200	£700
1773	£5	£45	£200	£700
1773 no stop after REX	£5	£45	£200	£700
1773 no stop on reverse	£5	£45	£200	*
1774	£5	£45	£200	£700
1775	£5	£45	£200	£850
1799 five inc gunports	*	£8	£60	£175
1799 six relief gunports	*	£8	£60	£175
1799 nine relief gunports	*	£8	£60	£200
1799 no gunports	*	£8	£60	£185
1799 no gunports and raised line along hull	*	£8	£60	£185
1806 no berries on olive branch	*	£8	£55	£175
1806 line under SOHO three berries	*	£8	£55	£175
1807	*	£8	£45	£175

GEORGE IV

	F	VF	EF	BU
1825	*	£30	£135	£350
1826 two inc lines down cross	*	£15	£85	£250
1826 raised line down centre of cross	*	£20	£100	£275
1827	*	£15	£85	£250

WILLIAM IV

	F	VF	EF	BU
1831	*	£20	£110	£275
1834	*	£20	£110	£275
1837	*	£15	£100	£265

VICTORIA

	F	VF	EF	BU
1838	£3	£8	£50	£175
1839 proof	£1	*	*	£325
1839 proof, rev inv	£1	*	*	£375
1841	£3	£8	£50	£175
1843	£15	£45	£150	£425
1844	£3	£8	£55	£175
1845	£75	£150	£750	*
1846	£3	£8	£50	£175
1847	£3	£8	£50	£175
1848	£5	£30	£125	£325
1848/7	£5	£20	£95	£200
1851	£3	£8	£50	£175
1851 seven inc dots on and above shield	£2	£5	£35	£175
1852	£3	£8	£50	£175
1852 seven inc dots on and above shield	£2	£8	£50	£175
1853 proof	*	*	*	£425
1853/2	£4	£25	£110	£295
1854	£3	£5	£45	£130

Victoria 1853 proof Halfpenny

	F	VF	EF	BU
1855	£2	£5	£45	£135
1856	£3	£8	£50	£175
1857	£2	£5	£45	£135
1857 seven inc dots on and above shield	£1	£5	£35	£135
1858	£2	£5	£45	£135
1858/6	£3	£10	£45	£150
1858/7	£2	£5	£45	£150
1858 small date	£1	£5	£35	£150
1859	£2	£5	£45	£150
1859/8	£6	£12	£85	£200
1860 proof only	*	*	*	£6500

■ BRONZE HALFPENNIES

For fuller details of varieties in bronze Halfpennies and Farthings see *English Copper, Tin and Bronze Coins in the British Museum 1558-1958* by C W Peck and *The Bronze Coinage of Great Britain* by M J Freeman. There are a large number of varieties and die combinations for this series, only the more significant are listed below.

Victoria 1860 bronze Halfpenny

VICTORIA	F	VF	EF	BU
1860 BB	*	£5	£40	£125
1860 rev TB/obv BB		ext. rare		*
1860 TB, 4 berries	*	£5	£50	£175
1860 TB, double inc leaf veins	*	£15	£80	£265
1861 obv 5 berries	*	£30	£100	£325
1861 obv 4 berries, rev L.C.W. on rock	*	£20	£95	£265
1861 rev no signature	£12	£50	£150	*
1861 rev no signature, breastplate has inc lines	*	£30	£100	£325
1861 obv 4 double incuse leaf veins, rev no signature, breastplate has inc lines	*	£20	£95	£265
1861 same obv, rev L.C.W. on rock	*	£5	£50	£175
1861 obv 7 double incuse leaf veins, rev L.C.W. on rock	*	£5	£60	£185
1861 rev no signature	*	£5	£40	£125
1861 obv 16 leaves, rev rounded to top lighthouse	*	£20	£95	£265
1861 rev pointed top to lighthouse	*	£5	£50	£175
1861 no signature	*	£8	£50	£150
1861 HALP error	£185	£475	*	*
1861 6/8	£200	£525	*	*
1862	*	£5	£35	£150
1862 letter A left of lighthouse base	£395	*	*	*
1862 letter B left of lighthouse base	£550	*	*	*
1862 letter C left of lighthouse base	£650	*	*	*
1863	*	£5	£55	£185
1864	*	£6	£100	£275
1865	*	£10	£85	£395
1865/3	£30	£90	£285	£775
1866	*	£8	£65	£245
1867	*	£8	£80	£300
1868	*	£8	£75	£265
1869	£20	£65	£295	£825
1870	*	£5	£55	£195
1871	£20	£65	£295	£825
1872	*	£5	£55	£175
1873	*	£8	£65	£225
1874	*	£15	£100	£395
1874 H	*	£5	£50	£160

	F	VF	EF	BU
1875	*	£5	£50	£165
1875 H	*	£5	£60	£190
1876 H	*	£5	£50	£165
1877	*	£5	£50	£165
1878	*	£15	£90	£385
1879	*	£5	£45	£150
1880	*	£4	£45	£165
1881	*	£4	£45	£165
1881 H	*	£4	£40	£165
1882 H	*	£4	£40	£165
1883	*	£4	£40	£165
1884	*	£2	£35	£145
1885	*	£2	£35	£145
1886	*	*	£35	£145
1887	*	*	£35	£145
1888	*	*	£35	£145
1889	*	*	£35	£145
1889/8	*	£20	£110	£325
1890	*	*	£35	£120
1891	*	*	£35	£120
1892	*	*	£35	£120
1893	*	*	£35	£120
1894	*	£5	£50	£185
1895 OH	*	*	£5	£60
1896	*	*	£5	£45
1897 normal horizon	*	*	£5	£45
1897 higher horizon	*	*	£5	£45
1898	*	*	£6	£45
1899	*	*	£5	£45
1900	*	*	£2	£25
1901	*	*	£2	£20
EDWARD VII				
1902 low horizon	*	£25	£100	£275
1902	*	*	£8	£25
1903	*	*	£10	£50
1904	*	*	£15	£75
1905	*	*	£12	£60
1906	*	*	£12	£50
1907	*	*	£9	£50
1908	*	*	£9	£50
1909	*	*	£12	£60
1910	*	*	£9	£50
GEORGE V				
1911	*	*	£7	£30
1912	*	*	£8	£40
1913	*	*	£8	£40
1914	*	*	£8	£45
1915	*	*	£8	£45
1916	*	*	£5	£45
1917	*	*	£5	£30
1918	*	*	£5	£30
1919	*	*	£5	£30
1920	*	*	£5	£35
1921	*	*	£5	£30
1922	*	*	£5	£40
1923	*	*	£5	£35
1924	*	*	£5	£35

	Fair	F	VF	EF
1925	*	*	£5	£35
1925 mod eff	*	*	£5	£45
1926	*	*	£5	£35
1927	*	*	£3	£30
1928	*	*	£3	£20
1929	*	*	£3	£20
1930	*	*	£3	£20
1931	*	*	£3	£20
1932	*	*	£3	£20
1933	*	*	£3	£20
1934	*	*	£3	£25
1935	*	*	£3	£20
1936	*	*	£3	£15

GEORGE VI

1937	*	*	*	£5
1938	*	*	*	£9
1939	*	*	*	£16
1940	*	*	*	£16
1941	*	*	*	£6
1942	*	*	*	£4
1943	*	*	*	£4
1944	*	*	*	£5
1945	*	*	*	£4
1946	*	*	*	£12
1947	*	*	*	£6
1948	*	*	*	£6
1949	*	*	*	£8
1950	*	*	*	£8
1951	*	*	*	£17
1952	*	*	*	£5

ELIZABETH II

1953	*	*	*	£2
1954	*	*	*	£5
1955	*	*	*	£4
1956	*	*	*	£5
1957	*	*	*	£2
1958	*	*	*	£2
1959	*	*	*	£1
1960	*	*	*	£1
1962	*	*	*	*
1963	*	*	*	*
1964	*	*	*	*
1965	*	*	*	*
1966	*	*	*	*
1967	*	*	*	*

■ COPPER FARTHINGS

OLIVER CROMWELL

	Fair	F	VF	EF
Patterns only	*	£2500	£5000	£7500

CHARLES II

	Fair	F	VF	EF
1671 patterns only	*	*	£350	£750
1672	£2	£35	£175	£625
1672 no stop on obv	£5	£45	£250	£750
1672 loose drapery				

at Britannia's elbow	£4	£35	£200	£775
1673	£1	£35	£175	£650
1673 CAROLA error	£30	£125	£400	*
1673 BRITINNIA error			ext. rare	
1673 no stops on obv	£30	£125	*	*
1673 rev no stop	£25	£125	*	*
1674	*	£35	£175	£675
1675	*	£35	£175	£650
1675 no stop after CAROLVS	£45	£165	*	*
1679	*	£25	£175	£700
1679 no stop on rev	£7	£75	£300	*
1694 tin, various edge readings	£35	£175	£550	£3000
1685 tin			ext. rare	*	*

James II 1685 tin Farthing

JAMES II

1684 tin		ext. rare		*
1685 tin, various edge readings	£60	£165	£600	£2650
1686 tin, various edge readings	£70	£185	£600	£3000
1687 tin, draped bust, various readings		ext. rare	*	*

WILLIAM AND MARY

1689 tin, date in exergue and on edge, many varieties	£250	£500	*	*
1689/90 tin, 1689 in exergue, 1690 on edge	*	*	*	*
1689/90 tin, 1690 in exergue, 1689 on edge	*	*	*	*
1690 tin, various types	£40	£150	£475	£2650
1691 tin, small and large figures	£40	£150	£475	£2650
1692 tin	£40	£150	£475	£2650
1694 copper, many varieties	£10	£50	£165	£800

William and Mary 1694 Farthing

WILLIAM III	Fair	F	VF	EF
Type 1, date in exergue				
1695	£2	£40	£160	£725
1695 GVLIELMV error	£60	£185	*	*
1696	*	£40	£145	£700
1697	*	£40	£145	£700
1698	£50	£175	£450	*
1699	£2	£40	£150	£700
1700	£2	£40	£145	£700
Type 2, date in legend				
1698	£5	£45	£175	£750
1699	£5	£45	£185	£775

ANNE				
1714 patterns F	*	*	£475	£875

George I 1717 'dump' Farthing

GEORGE I				
Smaller flan, 'dump type'				
1717	*	£150	£375	£875
1718		unique		
1718 silver proof	*	*	*	£1750
Larger flan				
1719 large lettering on obv	£3	£35	£200	£600
1719 small lettering on obv	£3	£35	£200	£625
1719 last A over I in BRITANNIA	£10	£60	£295	*

George I 1721 Farthing

	Fair	F	VF	EF
1719 legend continuous over bust	£20	£60	*	*
1720 large lettering on obv	£20	£60	£275	*
1720 small lettering on obv	£2	£20	£110	£525
1721	£2	£20	£110	£500
1721/0	£5	£40	£125	£525
1722 large lettering on obv	*	£25	£125	£550

	Fair	F	VF	EF
1722 small lettering on obv	*	£20	£110	£500
1723	*	£20	£125	£525
1723 R/R REX	£12	£75	£150	£650
1724	£5	£25	£125	£550

GEORGE II	Fair	F	VF	EF
1730	*	£10	£55	£285
1731	*	£10	£55	£285
1732	*	£12	£60	£325
1733	*	£10	£50	£285
1734	*	£10	£55	£325
1734 no stops on obv	*	£12	£70	£375
1735	*	£10	£40	£265
1735 3/3	*	£12	£70	£375
1736	*	£10	£50	£285
1736 triple tie-riband	*	£15	£70	£375
1737 small date	*	£10	£45	£265
1737 large date	*	£10	£45	£265
1739	*	£10	£45	£285
1739/5	*	£10	£55	£325
1741 OH	*	£10	£45	£200
1744	*	£10	£55	£250
1746	*	£10	£45	£200
1746 V/U		ext. rare	*	*
1749	*	£10	£45	£175
1750	*	£10	£55	£200
1754/0	*	£20	£80	£265
1754	*	£8	£40	£125

GEORGE III	F	VF	EF	BU
1771	£5	£45	£200	£550
1773	£5	£30	£175	£400
1774	£5	£30	£175	£400
1775	£5	£30	£175	£400
1799	*	*	£50	£110
1806	*	£3	£50	£115
1807	*	£4	£50	£120

GEORGE IV				
1821	*	£8	£45	£130
1822	*	£8	£45	£130
1823	*	£8	£45	£130
1825	*	£8	£45	£130
1825 D/U in DEI	*	£50	£175	*
1826 date on rev	*	£10	£60	£150
1826 date on obv	*	£9	£50	£135
1826 I for 1 in date	£15	£65	£300	£575
1827	*	£9	£50	£140
1828	*	£9	£55	£135
1829	*	£10	£60	£180
1830	*	£9	£50	£135

WILLIAM IV				
1831	*	£7	£55	£150
1834	*	£7	£55	£150
1835	*	£7	£50	£165
1836	*	£7	£50	£165
1837	*	£7	£55	£165

VICTORIA	F	VF	EF	BU
1838	*	£5	£35	£150
1839	*	£5	£35	£145
1840	*	£5	£35	£145
1841	*	£5	£35	£145
1842	*	£35	£100	£350
1843	*	£5	£40	£145
1843 I for I	£40	£200	£575	*
1844	£35	£100	£600	£2000
1845	*	£6	£30	£130
1846	*	£6	£60	£150
1847	*	£5	£40	£130
1848	*	£6	£40	£130
1849	*	£50	£325	*
1850	*	£5	£35	£130
1851	*	£15	£50	£165
1851 D/D sideways	£10	£75	£300	£850
1852	*	£12	£55	£165
1853 w.w. raised	*	£5	£35	£120
1853 w.w. inc	*	£20	£85	£275
1854	*	£5	£35	£95
1855	*	£6	£45	£130
1855 w.w. raised	*	£6	£40	£130
1856 w.w. inc	*	£7	£55	£165
1856 R/E in VICTORIA	£10	£50	£275	*
1857	*	£5	£40	£120
1858	*	£5	£40	£120
1859	*	£15	£50	£195
1860 proof	*	*	*	£7000

Victoria 1859 copper Farthing

■ BRONZE FARTHINGS

VICTORIA	F	VF	EF	BU
1860 BB	*	£2	£20	£85
1860 TB/BB (mule)	£100	£200	£450	*
1860 TB	*	£1	£15	£75
1861	*	£1	£12	£75
1862 small 8	*	£1	£12	£65
1862 large 8	£40	£100	£225	*
1863	£20	£40	£150	£375
1864	*	£3	£30	£110
1865	*	£3	£25	£85
1865-5/2	*	£5	£35	£135
1866	*	£2	£20	£80
1867	*	£3	£30	£100
1868	*	£3	£30	£100

	F	VF	EF	BU
1869	*	£8	£40	£125
1872	*	£2	£20	£80
1873	*	£3	£20	£80
1874 H	*	£5	£30	£90
1874 H G sideways/Gs	£65	£175	£475	*
1875 large date	*	£10	£35	£125
1875 small date	£8	£20	£90	£300
1875 older features	*	£20	£80	£250
1875 H	*	£2	£15	£70
1875 H older features	£60	£175	£300	*
1876 H	*	£10	£35	£120
1877 proof only				£5000
1878	*	£2	£10	£75
1879	*	£2	£20	£80
1879 large 9	*	£1	£12	£90
1880	*	£2	£25	£95
1881	*	£5	£20	£75
1881 H	*	£2	£20	£75
1882 H	*	£2	£20	£75
1883	*	£5	£35	£110
1884	*	*	£12	£50
1886	*	*	£12	£50
1887	*	*	£20	£75
1890	*	*	£12	£55
1891	*	*	£12	£55
1892	*	£9	£35	£120
1893	*	*	£10	£60
1894	*	*	£12	£70
1895	*	£15	£60	£200
1895 OH	*	*	£3	£25
1896		*	£5	£30
1897 bright finish	*	*	£3	£30
1897 black finish higher horizon	*	*	£2	£30
1898	*	*	£3	£30
1899	*	*	£2	£30
1900	*	*	£2	£30
1901	*	*	£2	£15

EDWARD VII	F	VF	EF	BU
1902	*	*	£3	£20
1903 low horizon	*	*	£4	£20
1904	*	*	£4	£20
1905	*	*	£4	£20
1906	*	*	£4	£20
1907	*	*	£4	£20
1908	*	*	£4	£20
1909	*	*	£4	£20
1910	*	*	£8	£25

GEORGE V	F	VF	EF	BU
1911	*	*	£4	£15
1912	*	*	£4	£15
1913	*	*	£4	£15
1914	*	*	£4	£15
1915	*	*	£4	£15
1916	*	*	£4	£15
1917	*	*	£4	£10
1918 black finish	*	*	£6	£20

	F	VF	EF	BU
1919 bright finish	*	*	£3	£9
1919	*	*	£3	£10
1920	*	*	£3	£10
1921	*	*	£3	£10
1922	*	*	£3	£10
1923	*	*	£3	£10
1924	*	*	£3	£10
1925	*	*	£3	£10
1926 mod eff	*	*	£2	£6
1927	*	*	£2	£6
1928	*	*	*	£3
1929	*	*	*	£3
1930	*	*	*	£3
1931	*	*	*	£3
1932	*	*	*	£3
1933	*	*	*	£3
1934	*	*	*	£5
1935	*	*	£1	£7
1936	*	*	*	£2

GEORGE VI

	F	VF	EF	BU
1937	*	*	*	£2
1938	*	*	*	£7
1939	*	*	*	£3
1940	*	*	*	£3
1941	*	*	*	£3
1942	*	*	*	£3
1943	*	*	*	£3
1944	*	*	*	£3
1945	*	*	*	£3
1946	*	*	*	£3
1947	*	*	*	£3
1948	*	*	*	£3
1949	*	*	*	£3
1950	*	*	*	£3
1951	*	*	*	£3
1952	*	*	*	£3

ELIZABETH II

	F	VF	EF	BU
1953	*	*	*	£2
1954	*	*	*	£2
1955	*	*	*	£2
1956	*	*	*	£4

■ **FRACTIONS OF FARTHINGS**

Copper Half-Farthings

GEORGE IV

	F	VF	EF	BU
1828 Britannia breaks legend	£5	£20	£100	£275
1828 Britannia below legend	£8	£35	£110	£300
1830 trident breaks legend	£5	£25	£100	£275
1830 trident to base of legend	£20	£60	£225	*

WILLIAM IV	F	VF	EF	BU
1837	£40	£125	£300	*

VICTORIA

	F	VF	EF	BU
1839	*	£6	£40	£100
1842	*	£6	£40	£100
1843	*	*	£15	£70
1844	*	*	£15	£70
1844 E/N	£3	£12	£75	£250
1847	*	£5	£20	£85
1851	*	£5	£40	£100
1852	*	£5	£40	£100
1853	*	£8	£45	£125
1853 proof				£325
1854	*	£20	£80	£200
1856	*	£20	£80	£200
1856 large date	£40	£95	£300	*
1868 bronze proof	*			£475
1868 copper-nickel proof	*			£600

Copper Third-Farthings

GEORGE IV

	F	VF	EF	BU
1827	*	£10	£55	£150

WILLIAM IV

	F	VF	EF	BU
1835	*	£12	£85	£200

VICTORIA

	F	VF	EF	BU
1844	*	£25	£85	£300
1844 RE for REG	£25	£60	£325	*

Bronze Third-Farthings

VICTORIA

	F	VF	EF	BU
1866	*	*	£15	£60
1868	*	*	£15	£60
1876	*	*	£15	£65
1878	*	*	£15	£60
1881	*	*	£15	£65
1884	*	*	£10	£60
1885	*	*	£10	£60

EDWARD VII

			EF	BU
1902	*	*	£8	£28

GEORGE V

			EF	BU
1913	*	*	£8	£28

Copper Quarter-Farthings

VICTORIA

	F	VF	EF	BU
1839	£8	£15	£40	£125
1851	£8	£15	£40	£145
1852	£8	£15	£40	£110
1853	£8	£18	£50	£125
1853 proof	*	*	*	£550
1868 bronze-proof	*	*	*	£400
1868 copper-nickel proof	*	*	*	£475

MAUNDY SETS

These sets are given out by the monarch each year on Maundy Thursday, the day before Good Friday.

The number of recipients and the amount they receive matches the sovereign's age that year.

Maundy coins are newly minted every year, and are legal tender.

The ceremony has been known in England since about 600. The first recorded occasion when the sovereign distributed alms at a Maundy service was in 1210, when King John did so at Knaresborough, North Yorkshire.

Extremely Fine prices are for evenly matched sets.

CHARLES II	F	VF	EF
1670-74	£125	£225	£525
1675-76	£125	£225	£525
1677	£125	£225	£525
1678	£125	£250	£575
1679	£125	£225	£525
1680	£125	£225	£525
1681	£125	£250	£575
1682	£125	£225	£525
1683	£125	£225	£525
1684	£125	£225	£525

JAMES II			
1686-88	£125	£295	£650

WILLIAM AND MARY			
1689	£475	£850	£1650
1691	£145	£295	£700
1692	£150	£295	£750
1693	£150	£295	£750
1694	£145	£285	£650

WILLIAM III			
1698	£135	£250	£650
1699-1700	£135	£275	£675
1701	£135	£250	£650

ANNE			
1703	£125	£165	£550
1705	£125	£165	£550
1706	£125	£150	£500
1708	£125	£175	£550
1709	£125	£165	£500
1710	£150	£195	£600
1713	£125	£150	£550

GEORGE I			
1723	£120	£185	£550
1727	£120	£150	£525

GEORGE II			
1729	£95	£165	£400
1731	£95	£165	£400
1732	£80	£150	£350

	F	VF	EF
1735	£95	£165	£350
1737	£95	£165	£350
1739	£95	£165	£350
1740	£95	£165	£360
1743	£95	£165	£400
1746	£95	£165	£325
1760	£95	£165	£395

GEORGE III	F	VF	EF	Unc
1763	*	£75	£275	£375
1766	*	£80	£275	£375
1772	*	£20	£275	£375
1780	*	£80	£275	£375
1784	*	£80	£275	£375
1786	*	£80	£275	£375
1792 wire type	*	£125	£450	£650
1795	*	£60	£225	£325
1800	*	£60	£225	£325
1817-1818	*	£65	£185	£275
1820	*	£65	£185	£275

George III Maundy set, 1818

GEORGE IV			EF	Unc
1822-23	*	*	£165	£325
1824	*	*	£165	£325
1825-30	*	*	£165	£325

WILLIAM IV				
1831	*	*	£175	£350
1831 proof	*	*	*	£500

William IV gold proof Maundy Groat 1831

1831 gold proof	*	*	*	£30000
1832	*	*	£165	£325

				EF	Unc
1833-35	*	*	£165	£300
1836-37	*	*	£170	£325

VICTORIA

	EF	Unc
1838	£145	£300
1839	£140	£285
1839 proof	*	£775
1840	£135	£325
1841	£150	£365
1842	£140	£285
1843-44	£140	£285
1845	£135	£275
1846	£160	£395
1847	£150	£365
1848	£135	£325
1849	£135	£325
1850-51	£135	£325
1852	£135	£325
1853	£150	£350
1853 proof	*	£725
1854-55	£140	£285
1856-59	£125	£250
1860	£130	£235
1861-87	£130	£235
1888 JH	£90	£135
1889 1892	£90	£135
1893 OH	£85	£130
1894-99	£85	£135
1900	£85	£135
1901	£85	£135

EDWARD VIII

	EF	Unc
1902	£75	£110
1902 matt proof	*	£110
1903-08	£75	£110
1909-10	£75	£120

GEORGE V

	EF	Unc
1911	£70	£110
1911 proof	*	£135
1912-36	£80	£110

GEORGE VI

	EF	Unc
1937	£70	£100
1938-52	£70	£120

ELIZABETH II

	EF	Unc
1953	*	£600
1954-69	*	£120
1970-98	*	£120
1999-2000	*	£120
2001-02	*	£120
2002 gold from set	*	£1500
2003-04	*	£120
2005	*	£125
2006	*	£135
2007	*	£135
2008	*	£135
2009	*	£150
2010	*	£200

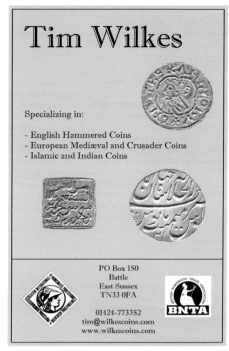
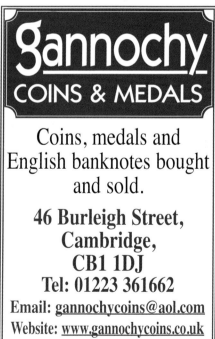
MAUNDY SETS

DECIMAL COINAGE

■ BRITANNIAS

A United Kingdom gold bullion coin, introduced in the autumn of 1987, which contains one ounce of 22ct gold and has a face value of £100. There are also ½ ounce, ¼ ounce and 1/10 ounce versions, with face values of £50, £25 and £10 respectively. The ½ and ¼ oz are issued only in sets. All are legal tender.

The coins bear a portrait of the Queen on the obverse and the figure of Britannia on the reverse.

BV indicates bullion value, at the time of going to press gold is approximately £780 per troy ounce and platinum is approximately £1280 per troy ounce.

1987-2005 1oz, proof	*
1987-2005 1/10 oz, proof	*
1987-2005 ½ oz, proof	*
1987-2005 ¼ oz, proof	*

To commemorate the 10th anniversary of the first Britannia issue, new reverse designs were introduced for the gold coins. A series of four silver coins with denominations from £2 to 20 pence was issued as well. The silver coins were issued only in proof condition in 1997.

1997 1oz, ¼oz and 1/10oz issued individually; all coins issued in 4-coin sets
1997 1oz, ¼ oz silver coins issued individually; all coins issued in 4-coin sets
1998 gold and silver coins issued with new portrait of HM the Queen and first reverse design
2001 new reverse designs introduced

■ FIVE POUNDS

Crown sized.

1990 Queen Mother's 90th birthday, gold, proof	BV
1990 silver, proof	£40
1990 cu-ni, BU	£6
1990 cu-ni, specimen	£7
1993 40th Anniversary of the Coronation, gold, proof	BV
1993 silver, proof	£28
1993 cu-ni, specimen	£8
1993 cu-ni, BU	£5
1993 cu-ni, proof, originally issued in a Royal Mint set	£8
1996 Queen's 70th Birthday, gold, proof	BV
1996 silver, proof	£35
1996 cu-ni, BU	£7
1996 cu-ni, proof, originally issued in a Royal Mint set	£7
1996 cu-ni, specimen	£8
1997 Golden Wedding, gold, proof	BV
1997 silver, proof	£30
1997 cu-ni, BU	£7
1997 cu-ni, proof, originally issued in a Royal Mint set	£7
1997 cu-ni, specimen	£9
1998 Prince Charles 50th Birthday, gold, proof	BV

1998 silver, proof	£50
1998 cu-ni, BU	£7
1998 cu-ni, proof, originally issued in a Royal Mint set	£10
1998 cu-ni, specimen	£8
1999 Diana Memorial, gold, proof	BV
1999 silver, proof	£38
1999 cu-ni, proof, originally issued in a Royal Mint set	£10
1999 cu-ni, BU	£7
1999 cu-ni, specimen	£8
1999 Millennium, gold, proof	BV
1999 silver, proof	£30
1999 cu-ni, BU	£6
1999 cu-ni, specimen	£8
2000 gold, proof	BV
2000 silver with 22 carat gold, proof	£30
2000 cu-ni, BU	£6
2000 cu-ni, specimen	£13
2000 cu-ni, proof, originally issued in a Royal Mint set	£12
2000 cu-ni, specimen, Dome mintmark	£15
2000 silver, proof	£40
2000 Queen Mother commemorative, gold, proof	BV
2000 silver, proof	£35
2000 silver piedfort	£45
2000 cu-ni, BU	£6
2000 cu-ni, proof, originally issued in a Royal Mint set	£7
2001 Victorian Era anniversary, gold, proof	BV
2001 gold, proof with reverse frosting	BV
2001 silver, proof	£35
2001 silver, proof with reverse frosting	£85
2001 cu-ni, BU	£6
2001 cu-ni, proof, originally issued in a Royal Mint set	£10
2001 cu-ni, specimen	£8
2002 Golden Jubilee, gold proof	BV
2002 silver, proof	£35
2002 cu-ni, BU	£5
2002 cu-ni, proof, originally issued in a Royal Mint set	£9
2002 cu-ni, specimen	£8
2002 Queen Mother memorial, gold, proof	BV
2002 silver, proof	£35
2002 cu-ni, BU	£7
2002 cu-ni proof, originally issued in a Royal Mint set	£12
2003 Coronation commemorative, gold proof	BV
2003 silver, proof	£35
2003 cu-ni, BU	£6
2003 cu-ni, proof, originally issued in a Royal Mint set	£8
2003 cu-ni, specimen	£9
2004 Entente Cordiale, gold, proof	BV
2004 platinum, piedfort, proof	BV
2004 silver piedfort, proof	£110
2004 silver, proof	£35
2004 Entente Cordiale, cu-ni, proof	£14
2004 specimen	£10
2004 BU	£5
2005 Trafalgar, gold, proof	BV
2005 silver piedfort, proof	£45
2005 silver, proof	£30
2005 cu-ni, proof, originally issued in a Royal Mint set	£8
2005 specimen	£8
2005 BU	£5
2005 Nelson, gold, proof	BV

2005 platinum, piedfort, proof	BV
2005 silver piedfort, proof	£45
2005 silver, proof	£30
2005 cu-ni, proof, originally issued in a Royal Mint set	£8
2005 BU	£5
2005 specimen	£8
2006 Queen's 80th Birthday, gold, proof	BV
2006 platinum, piedfort, proof	BV
2006 silver piedfort, proof	£45
2006 silver, proof	£30
2006 cu-ni, proof, originally issued in a Royal Mint set	£8
2006 specimen	£8
2006 BU	£5
2007 Diamond Wedding, gold, proof	BV
2007 silver piedfort, proof	£79
2007 silver, proof	£39
2007 cu-ni, proof, originally issued in a Royal Mint set	£12
2008 Elizabeth I, platinum, piedfort, proof	BV
2008 gold, proof	BV
2008 silver piedfort, proof	£80
2008 silver, proof	£39
2008 BU	£5
2009 Henry VIII gold proof	£1100
2009 silver piedfort, proof	£99
2009 silver proof	£54
2009 Countdown to London gold proof	£1100
2009 silver piedfort, proof	£99
2010 Restoration of Monarchy gold proof	£1400
2010 silver proof	£55
2010 Countdown to London silver, piedforf, proof	£99
2010 silver proof	£55
2010 BU	£5

■ TWO POUNDS

1986 Commonwealth Games, proof gold	BV
1986 silver, proof	£25
1986 silver unc	£12
1986 proof, nickel brass, originally issued in a Royal Mint set	£5
1986 specimen	£4
1986 unc	£3
1989 Bill of Rights, silver piedfort, proof, originally issued in a Royal Mint set	£45
1989 silver, proof	£25
1989 proof, nickel brass, originally issued in a Royal Mint set	£7
1989 specimen	£4
1989 unc	£3
1989 Claim of Rights, silver piedfort proof, originally issued in a Royal Mint set	£45
1989 silver, proof	£25
1989 proof, nickel brass, originally issued in a Royal Mint set	£7
1989 specimen	£4
1989 unc	£3
1994 Bank of England, gold, proof	BV
1994 gold 'mule', proof	BV

1994 silver piedfort, proof	£45
1994 silver, proof	£25
1994 proof, nickel brass, originally issued in a Royal Mint set	£5
1994 specimen	£4
1994 in folder, BU	£3
1995 50th Anniversary of end of Second World War, gold, proof	BV
1995 silver piedfort, proof	£45
1995 silver, proof	£25
1995 proof, nickel brass, originally issued in a Royal Mint set	£5
1995 specimen	£4
1995 BU	£3
1995 50th Anniversary of United Nations, gold, proof	BV
1995 silver piedfort, proof	£45
1995 silver, proof	£25
1995 specimen	£4
1995 BU	£3
1996 European Football, gold, proof	BV
1996 silver piedfort, proof	£45
1996 silver, proof	£25
1996 proof, nickel brass, originally issued in a Royal Mint set	£5
1996 specimen	£4
1996 BU	£3
1997 Iron Age, bimetal, gold, proof	BV
1997 silver piedfort, proof	£45
1997 silver, proof	£25
1997 proof, originally issued in a Royal Mint set	£5
1997 specimen	£4
1997 BU	£3
1997 Britannia chariot, proof 1 oz fine silver	£35
1998 bimetal, silver, proof	£27
1998 silver piedfort	£40
1998 proof, originally issued in a Royal Mint set	£6
1998 in folder, BU	£6
1998 Britannia standing, proof, 1 oz fine silver	£15
1998 unc	£10
1999 Rugby World Cup, gold, proof	BV
1999 silver piedfort, proof	£30
1999 silver, proof	£150
1999 proof, originally issued in a Royal Mint set	£5
1999 BU	£3
2000 bimetal, silver, proof, originally issued in a Royal Mint set	£20
2000 proof, originally issued in a Royal Mint set	£5
2000 Britannia standing, unc, 1 oz fine silver	£10
2001 Marconi commemorative, gold, proof	BV
2001 silver piedfort, proof	£35
2001 silver, proof	£25
2001 with reverse frosting, silver, proof	£40
2001 proof, originally issued in a Royal Mint set	£7
2001 specimen	£5
2001 BU	£3
2002 Iron Age, gold proof	BV
2002 Commonwealth Games, gold, proof, four different reverses	*
2002 Commonwealth Games, silver, proof, four different reverses	*

2002 Commonwealth Games, piedfort, four different reverses	*
2002 Commonwealth Games, BU, four different reverses	*
2002 Britannia standing, unc, 1 oz fine silver	£10
2003 DNA gold bi-metal proof	BV
2003 silver piedfort, proof	£40
2003 silver, proof	£20
2003 specimen	£5
2003 proof, originally issued in a Royal Mint set	£6
2003 BU	£3
2003 Britannia helmeted, silver, proof	£25
2003 silver	£12
2004 Locomotive, gold, proof	BV
2004 silver piedfort, proof	£40
2004 silver, proof	£20
2004 BU, silver	£12
2004 proof, originally issued in a Royal Mail set	£6
2004 specimen	£6
2004 BU	£3
2004 Britannia standing, proof, 1 oz fine silver	£25
2004 unc	£15
2005 400th Gunpowder Plot gold, proof	BV
2005 silver piedfort, proof	£50
2005 silver, proof	£30
2005 proof, originally issued in a Royal Mint set	£6
2005 specimen	£5
2005 BU	£3
2005 World War II, gold proof	BV
2005 silver, proof, piedfort	£45
2005 silver, proof	£25
2005 specimen	£5
2005 BU	£3
2005 Britannia seated, silver, proof	£30
2005 silver, unc	£14
2006 Brunel the Man, gold, proof	BV
2006 silver, proof, piedfort	£40
2006 silver, proof	£25
2006 proof, originally issued in a Royal Mint set	£7
2006 specimen	£8
2006 BU	£3
2006 Britannia seated, silver, proof	£30
2007 Abolition of the Slave Trade, gold, proof	BV
2007 silver, proof	£29
2007 Act of Union, silver, proof	£29
2007 Britannia, silver	£17
2008 Olympiad London, gold, proof	BV
2008 silver, proof, piedfort	£49
2008 silver, proof	£30
2008 specimen	£8

■ ONE POUND

1983	£3
1983 specimen	£4
1983 proof, originally issued in a Royal Mint set	£4
1983 silver, proof	£35
1983 silver, proof, piedfort	£125
1984 Scottish reverse	£3

1984 specimen	£4
1984 proof, originally issued in a Royal Mint set	£4
1984 silver, proof	£20
1984 silver, proof, piedfort	£40
1985 new portrait, Welsh reverse	£4
1985 specimen	£4
1985 proof, originally issued in a Royal Mint set	£4
1985 silver, proof	£20
1985 silver, proof, piedfort	£50
1986 Northern Ireland reverse	£5
1986 specimen	£4
1986 proof, originally issued in a Royal Mint set	£4
1986 silver, proof	£20
1986 silver, proof, piedfort	£4
1987 English reverse	£4
1987 specimen	£4
1987 proof, originally issued in a Royal Mint set	£4
1987 silver, proof	£20
1987 silver, proof, piedfort	£45
1988 Royal Arms reverse	£5
1987 specimen	£4
1987 proof, originally issued in a Royal Mint set	£4
1987 silver, proof	£20
1987 silver, proof, piedfort	£45
1989 Scottish reverse as 1984	£4
1987 proof, originally issued in a Royal Mint set	£4
1987 silver, proof	£20
1990 Welsh reverse as 1985	£5
1990 proof, originally issued in a Royal Mint set	£4
1990 silver, proof	£30
1991 Northern Ireland reverse as 1986	£4
1991 proof, originally issued in a Royal Mint set	£4
1991 silver, proof	£25
1992 English reverse as 1987	£4
1987 proof, originally issued in a Royal Mint set	£4
1987 silver, proof	£20
1993 Royal coat of arms reverse as 1983	£3
1993 proof, originally issued in a Royal Mint set	£4
1993 silver, proof	£20
1993 silver, proof, piedfort	£50
1994 Scottish Lion	£4
1994 specimen	£4
1994 proof, originally issued in a Royal Mint set	£5
1984 silver, proof	£20
1994 silver, proof, piedfort	£45
1995 Welsh dragon	£4
1995 specimen, English version	£4
1995 specimen, Welsh version	£7
1995 proof, originally issued in a Royal Mint set	£5
1985 silver, proof	£20
1995 silver, proof, piedfort	£45
1996 Northern Ireland Celtic Ring	£4
1996 specimen	£4
1996 proof, originally issued in a Royal Mint set	£5
1985 silver, proof	£20
1995 silver, proof, piedfort	£40
1997 English Lions	£5
1997 specimen	£4
1997 proof, originally issued in a Royal Mint set	£5
1997 silver, proof	£20

1997 silver, proof, piedfort	£40
1998 Royal coat of arms reverse as 1983	£4
1998 proof, originally issued in a Royal Mint set	£5
1998 silver, proof	£20
1998 silver, proof, piedfort	£35
1999 Scottish Lion reverse as 1984	£3
1999 specimen	£4
1999 proof, originally issued in a Royal Mint set	£5
1999 silver, proof	£20
1999 with reverse frosting	£30
1999 silver, proof, piedfort	£35
2000 Welsh Dragon reverse as 1995	£3
2000 proof, originally issued in a Royal Mint set	£5
2000 silver, proof	£20
2000 silver, proof, with reverse frosting	£30
2000 silver, proof, piedfort	£35
2001 Northern Ireland reverse as 1996	£4
2001 proof, originally issued in a Royal Mint set	£5
2001 silver, proof	£20
2001 silver, proof, with reverse frosting	£45
2001 silver, proof, piedfort	£37
2002 English design, reverse as 1997	£4
2002 gold proof, originally issued in a Royal Mint set	BV
2002 proof, originally issued in a Royal Mint set	£5
2002 silver, proof	£20
2002 silver, proof, with reverse frosting	£40
2002 silver, proof, piedfort	£39
2003 Royal Arms	£45
2003 proof, originally issued in a Royal Mint set	£5
2003 silver, proof	£20
2003 silver, proof, piedfort	£39
2003 Forth Rail Bridge, 'pattern', silver, proof, originally issued in a Royal Mint set	*
2003 gold proof, originally issued in a Royal Mint set	BV
2003 Menai Bridge, 'pattern', silver, proof, originally issued in a Royal Mint set	*
2003 gold proof, originally issued in a Royal Mint set	BV
2003 Egyptian Arch, 'pattern', silver, proof, originally issued in a Royal Mint set	*
2003 gold proof, originally issued in a Royal Mint set	BV
2003 Millennium Bridge, 'pattern', silver, proof, originally issued in a Royal Mint set	*
2003 gold proof, originally issued in a Royal Mint set	BV
2004 Dragon, 'pattern', silver, proof, originally issued in a Royal Mint set	*
2004 gold proof, originally issued in a Royal Mint set	BV
2004 Unicorn, 'pattern', silver, proof, originally issued in a Royal Mint set	*
2004 gold proof, originally issued in a Royal Mint set	BV
2004 Stag, 'pattern', silver, proof, originally issued in a Royal Mint set	*
2004 gold proof, originally issued in a Royal Mint set	BV
2004 Lion, 'pattern', silver, proof, originally issued in a Royal Mint set	*
2004 gold proof, originally issued in a Royal Mint set	BV
2004 Forth Rail Bridge	BV
2004 specimen	£5
2004 proof, originally issued in a Royal Mint set	£5
2004 silver, proof	£20
2004 silver, proof, piedfort	£39

2004 gold, proof	BV
2005 Menai Bridge	£4
2005 specimen	£5
2005 proof, originally issued in a Royal Mint set	£5
2005 silver, proof	£20
2005 silver, proof, piedfort	£39
2005 gold, proof	BV
2006 Egyptian Arch	£4
2006 specimen	£5
2006 proof, originally issued in a Royal Mint set	£7
2006 silver, proof	£25
2006 silver, proof, piedfort	£40
2006 gold, proof	BV
2007 Forth, Menai, Egyptian Arch and Millennium Bridges, gold proof, originally issued in a Royal Mint set	*
2007 silver, proof, originally issued in a Royal Mint set	*
2007 Millennium Bridge, BU	£7
2008 Royal Arms, gold, proof	BV
2008 silver, proof	£30
2009 Shoulders of Giants, proof	£17
2009 BU	£5
2009 Darwin, proof	£23
2009 BU	£5
2009 Burns, proof	£21
2009 BU	£5
2010 Nightingale, proof	£23
2010 BU	£5
2010 Shoulders of Giants, proof	£18
2010 BU	£5

Note that the edge inscriptions on £2 and £1 appear either upright or inverted in relation to the obverse.

■ FIFTY PENCE

1969 unc	£2
1970 unc	£3
1971 proof, originally issued in a Royal Mint set	£3
1972 proof, originally issued in a Royal Mint set	£4
1973 EEC proof, originally issued in a Royal Mint set	£3
1973 silver, proof VIP	ext. rare
1973 unc	£1
1974 proof, originally issued in a Royal Mint set	£3
1975 proof, originally issued in a Royal Mint set	£3
1976 proof, originally issued in a Royal Mint set	£2
1976 unc	£1
1977 proof, originally issued in a Royal Mint set	£2
1977 unc	£1
1978 proof	£2
1978 unc	£1
1979 proof, originally issued in a Royal Mint set	£2
1979 unc	£1
1980 proof, originally issued in a Royal Mint set	£2
1980 unc	£1
1981 proof, originally issued in a Royal Mint set	£2
1981 unc	£1
1982 proof, originally issued in a Royal Mint set	£2
1982 unc	£1
1983 proof, originally issued in a Royal Mint set	£2

1983 unc	£1
1984 proof, originally issued in a Royal Mint set	£2
1984 unc	£3
1985 proof, originally issued in a Royal Mint set	£2
1985 unc	£4
1986 proof, originally issued in a Royal Mint set	£2
1986 unc	£2
1987 proof, originally issued in a Royal Mint set	£3
1987 unc	£2
1988 proof, originally issued in a Royal Mint set	£3
1988 unc	£2
1989 proof, originally issued in a Royal Mint set	£2
1989 unc	£3
1990 proof, originally issued in a Royal Mint set	£4
1990 unc	£3
1991 proof, originally issued in a Royal Mint set	£4
1991 unc	£2
1992 proof	£4
1992 unc	£2
1992 European Community	£5
1992 specimen	£2
1992 proof, originally issued in a Royal Mint set	£7
1992 silver, proof	£20
1992 silver, proof, piedfort	£40
1992 gold, proof	BV
1993 proof	£3
1993 unc	£3
1994 Normandy Landings	£2
1994 specimen	£2
1994 proof, originally issued in a Royal Mint set	£4
1994 silver, proof	£25
1994 silver, proof, piedfort	£40
1994 gold, proof	BV
1995 proof	£3
1995 unc	£2
1996 proof	£3
1996 unc	£2
1996 silver, proof	£15
1997 unc	£2
1997 proof	£3
1997 silver, proof	£2
1997 new size (27.3mm diameter), unc	£2
1997 proof, originally issued in a Royal Mint set	£4
1997 silver, proof	£18
1997 silver, proof, piedfort	£35
1998 proof, originally issued in a Royal Mint set	£2
1998 unc	£1
1998 European Presidency	£2
1998 specimen	£2
1998 silver, proof	£20
1998 silver, proof, piedfort	£40
1998 gold, proof	BV
1998 NHS, unc	£2
1998 proof, originally issued in a Royal Mint set	£2
1998 silver, proof	£25
1998 silver piedfort	£45
1998 gold, proof	BV
1999 proof, originally issued in a Royal Mint set	£2
1999 unc	face
2000 proof, originally issued in a Royal Mint set	£2
2000 unc	face
2000 silver, proof	£15
2000 Library Commemorative, unc	£2
2000 specimen	£5
2000 proof, originally issued in a Royal Mint set	£2
2000 silver, proof	£25
2000 silver, proof, piedfort	£47
2000 gold, proof	BV
2002 gold proof, originally issued in a Royal Mint set	BV
2003 Suffragette, unc	£1
2003 proof, originally issued in a Royal Mint set	£4
2003 specimen	£3
2003 silver, proof	£20
2003 silver, proof, piedfort	£40
2003 gold, proof	BV
2004 Roger Bannister, unc	£1
2004 specimen	£4
2004 proof, originally issued in a Royal Mint set	£4
2004 silver, proof	£20
2004 silver, proof piedfort	£25
2005 Samuel Johnson, unc	£1
2005 proof, originally issued in a Royal Mint set	£4
2005 silver, proof	£4
2005 silver, proof, piedfort	£40
2005 gold proof	BV
2006 Victoria Cross, unc	£1
2006 proof, originally issued in a Royal Mint set	£4
2006 specimen	£3
2006 silver, proof	£20
2006 silver, proof, piedfort	£40
2006 gold, proof	BV
2007 Scouting Centenary, gold, proof	BV
2007 silver, proof	£39
2007 silver piedfort, proof	£79
2008 issued in sets only	*
2009 gold, proof	BV
2009 silver, proof	£40
2009 unc	£1
2010 England, gold, proof	£650
2010 silver piedfort, proof	£54
2010 silver, proof	£32
2010 Northern Ireland, gold, proof	£650
2010 silver piedfort, proof	£54
2010 silver, proof	£32
2010 Shield, silver proof	£29

■ TWENTY-FIVE PENCE (crown)

1972 Silver Wedding	£1
1972 proof, originally issued in a Royal Mint set	£4
1972 silver, proof	£20
1977 Jubilee	£1
1977 proof, originally issued in a Royal Mint set	£4
1977 specimen	£2
1977 silver, proof	£20
1980 Queen Mother 80th Birthday	£1
1980 specimen	£2
1980 silver, proof	£40
1981 Royal Wedding	£1

1981 specimen	£3
1981 silver, proof	£25

■ TWENTY PENCE

1982-1997	face
1982 proof, originally issued in a Royal Mint set	£2
1982 silver, proof, piedfort	£40
1983-1997 proof, originally issued in a Royal Mint set	£3
1998-2008	face
1998-2008 proof, originally issued in a Royal Mint set	£3
2000 silver, proof, originally issued in a Royal Mint set	*
2002 gold proof, originally issued in a Royal Mint set	£250
2006-2010 silver, proof, originally issued in a Royal Mint set	*
2009 error, obverse of 2008, no date	£45

■ TEN PENCE

1968-1981 new pence	face
1972 & 1981 proof, originally issued in a Royal Mint set	£2
1982-1984 Pence, unc & proof, originally issued in a Royal Mint set	£2
1985-1992 unc & proof, originally issued in a Royal Mint set	£2
1992 silver, proof, originally issued in a Royal Mint set	£10
1992-1997 new size: 24.5mm diameter, 1993 & 1994 issued in sets only	face
1992-1997 proof, originally issued in a Royal Mint set	£2
1992 silver, proof	£10
1992 silver, proof, piedfort	£20
1996 silver, proof	£10
1998-2007, 1998, 1999 & 2007 issued in sets only	face
1998-2010 proof, originally issued in a Royal Mint set	£2
2002 gold proof, originally issued in a Royal Mint set	£225
2006-2010 silver, proof, originally issued in a Royal Mint set	*

■ FIVE PENCE

1968-81, 1972-74, 1976 & 1981 issued in sets only	£0.25
1971-1981 proof, originally issued in a Royal Mint set	£1
1982-1984 proof, unc, originally issued in a Royal Mint set	£1
1985-1990, 1985, 1996 & 1990 issued in sets only	face
1985-1990 proof, originally issued in a Royal Mint set	£2
1990-1997	face
1990-1997 proof, originally issued in a Royal Mint set	£2
1990 silver, proof, originally issued in a Royal Mint set	£10
1990 piedfort	£20
1996 silver, proof	£10
1998-2008, 2007-8 issued in sets only	face
1998-2010 proof, originally issued in a Royal Mint set	£3
2000 silver, proof	*
2002 gold proof, originally issued in a Royal Mint set	£175
2006-2010 silver, proof	*

■ TWO PENCE

1971-1981, 1972 & 1974 issued in sets only	face
1971-1981 proof, originally issued in a Royal Mint set	£1
1982-1984 new reverse	face
1983, mule, old reverse issued in sets	ext. rare
1982-1984 proof, originally issued in a Royal Mint set	£1
1985-1992 1992 issued in sets only	face
1985-1992 proof, originally issued in a Royal Mint set	£1
1992-1997	face
1993-1997 proof, originally issued in a Royal Mint set	£1
1996 silver, proof, originally issued in a Royal Mint set	£10
2002 gold proof. originally issued in a Royal Mint set	£250
1998-2010	face
1998-2010 proof, originally issued in a Royal Mint set	£1

■ ONE PENNY

1971-1981, 1972 issued in sets only	face
1971-1981 proof, originally issued in a Royal Mint set	£1
1982-1984 new reverse, proof, unc, originally issued in a Royal Mint set	£1
1985-1992, 1992 issued in sets only	face
1985-1992 proof, originally issued in a Royal Mint set	£1
1992-1997	face
1993-1997 proof, originally issued in a Royal Mint set	£1
1996 silver, proof, originally issued in a Royal Mint set	£10
2002 gold proof, originally issued in a Royal Mint set	£175
1998-2010	face
1998-2010 proof, originally issued in a Royal Mint set	£1

■ HALF PENNY

1971-1981	£0.10
1971-1981 proof, originally issued in a Royal Mint set	£1
1982-1984 new reverse	face
1982-1984 proof, originally issued in a Royal Mint set	£1

DECIMAL COINAGE

PROOF & SPECIMEN SETS

Proof or specimen sets have been issued since 1887 by
the Royal Mint. Before then sets were issued privately by
the engraver.

Some sets are of currency coins, easily distinguishable
from proofs, which have a vastly superior finish. The two
1887 sets frequently come on to the market, hence their
place in this list.

The 1953 'plastic' set, though made up of currency
coins, is official and was issued in a plastic packet, hence
the name. Sets are proof sets unless stated.

GEORGE IV	**FDC**
1826 new issue, £5-farthing (11 coins)	**£35000**
WILLIAM IV	
1831 Coronation, £2-farthing (14 coins)	**£30000**
VICTORIA	
1839 young head, 'Una and the Lion'	
£5, sovereign-farthing (15 coins)	**£52500**
1853 sovereign-half farthing,	
inc Gothic crown (16 coins)	**£32500**
1887 Jubilee head, £5-threepence ('full set': 11 coins)	**£10000**
1887 currency set, unofficial	**£2250**
1887 crown-threepence ('short set': 7 coins)	**£2000**
1887 currency set, unofficial	**£300**
1893 old head, £5-threepence ('full set': 10 coins)	**£11500**
1893 Crown-threepence ('short set': 6 coins)	**£2500**
EDWARD VII	
1902 Coronation, £5-Maundy penny,	
matt proofs (13 coins)	**£3000**
1902 sovereign-Maundy penny, matt proofs (11 coins)	**£1250**
GEORGE V	
1911 Coronation, £5-Maundy penny (12 coins)	**£4650**
1911 sovereign-Maundy penny (10 coins)	**£1500**
1911 halfcrown-Maundy penny (8 coins)	**£675**
1927 new types, crown-threepence (6 coins)	**£475**
GEORGE VI	
1937 Coronation, gold set, £5-half sovereign (4 coins)	**£3850**
1937 silver and bronze set, crown-farthing	
including Maundy money (15 coins)	**£350**
1950 mid-century, halfcrown-farthing (9 coins)	**£150**
1951 Festival of Britain, crown-farthing (10 coins)	**£175**
ELIZABETH II	
1953 Coronation, crown-farthing (10 coins)	**£100**
1953 currency, official, known as the 'plastic' set,	
halfcrown-farthing (9 coins)	**£20**
Specimen decimal set, 1968 10p, 5p;	
1971 2p, 1p, ½p in wallet (5 coins)	**£1**
1970 last £sd coins, (issued 1971-73),	
halfcrown-halfpenny (8 coins)	**£18**
1971 decimal (issued 1973),	
50p, 10p, 5p, 2p, 1p, ½p (6 coins)	**£12**

1972 decimal 50p, Silver Wedding	
25p, 10p, 5p, 2p, 1p, ½p (7 coins)	**£17**
1973-76 decimal, 50p-½p (6 coins)	**£13**
1977 decimal 50p-½p and Jubilee crown (7 coins)	**£13**
1978 decimal, 50p-½p (6 coins)	**£13**
1979 decimal, 50p-½p (6 coins)	**£13**
1980 decimal, 50p-½p (6 coins)	**£13**
1980 gold, £5, £2, sovereign, half sovereign (4 coins)	**£2000**
1981 commemorative, £5, sovereign,	
Royal Wedding silver crown, 50p-½p (9 coins)	**£1200**
1981 commemorative, sovereign and	
Royal Wedding silver crown (2 coins)	**£225**
1982 decimal, 50p-½p (6 coins)	**£13**
1982 gold, £5, £2, sovereign, half sovereign (4 coins)	**£2000**
1982 decimal, 50p-½p including 20p (7 coins)	**£13**
1982 uncirculated decimal,	
50p-½p including 20p (7 coins)	**£6**
1983 gold, £2, sovereign, half sovereign (3 coins)	**£700**
1983 decimal, £1-½p (8 coins)	**£15**
1983 uncirculated decimal, £1-½p (8 coins)	**£13**
1984 gold £5, sovereign, half sovereign (3 coins)	**£2000**
1984 decimal, £1 Scottish rev-½p (8 coins)	**£16**
1984 uncirculated decimal, £1 Scottish rev-½p (8 coins)	**£10**
1985 gold, new portrait, £5, £2,	
sovereign, half sovereign (4 coins)	**£1700**
1985 decimal, £1 Welsh	
rev-1p (7 coins) in deluxe case	**£20**
1985 in standard case	**£13**
1985 uncirculated decimal, £1 Welsh rev-1p (7 coins)	**£10**
1986 gold Commonwealth Games,	
£2, sovereign, half sovereign (3 coins)	**£700**
1986 decimal, Commonwealth Games £2,	
Northern Ireland £1.50-1p	
(8 coins) in deluxe case	**£25**
1986 in standard case	**£19**
1986 uncirculated decimal, in folder	**£10**
1987 gold Britannia, £100-£10 (4 coins)	**£1800**
1987 decimal, £25, £10 (2 coins)	**£275**
1987 gold, £2, sovereign, half sovereign (3 coins)	**£700**
1987 decimal, £1 English rev-1p (7 coins) in deluxe case	**£25**
1987 in standing case	**£17**
1987 uncirculated decimal, 1987, in folder	**£8**
1988 gold Britannia, £100-£10 (4 coins)	**£1800**
1988 £25, £10 (2 coins)	**£275**
1988 £2, sovereign, half sovereign (3 coins)	**£650**
1988 £1 Royal Arms rev-1p (7 coins) in deluxe case	**£24**
1988 in standard case	**£14**
1988 uncirculated decimal, in folder	**£9**
1989 gold Britannia, £100-£10 (4 coins)	**£1800**
1989 £25, £10 (2 coins)	**£275**
1989 gold 500th anniversary of the sovereign,	
£5, £2, sovereign, half sovereign (4 coins)	**£3250**
1989 gold 500th anniversary of the sovereign,	
£2, sovereign, half sovereign (3 coins)	**£1900**
1989 decimal, Bill of Rights £2, Claim of Right	
£2, £1 Scottish rev, 50p-1p (9 coins) in deluxe case	**£35**
1989 in standard case	**£23**
1989 silver, Bill of Rights £2,	
Claim of Right £2 (2 coins)	**£50**
1989 silver piedfort, 1989, £2 as above (2 coins)	**£80**

	FDC
1989 uncirculated, in folder	£12
1989 uncirculated decimal set,	
£1 Scottish rev-1p (7 coins)	£18
1990 gold Britannia, £100-£10 (4 coins)	£1800
1990 gold, £5, £2, sovereign, half sovereign (4 coins)	£2000
1990 £2, sovereign, half sovereign (3 coins)	£650
1990 silver, 5p (large and small size)	£28
1990 decimal, £1 Welsh rev-1p including large	
and small 5p (8 coins) in deluxe case	£30
1990 in standard case	£20
1990 uncirculated decimal, £1 Welsh rev as 1985-1p	
including large and small 5p (8 coins)	£17
1991 gold Britannia, £100-£10 (4 coins)	£1700
1991 gold, £5, £2, sovereign, half sovereign (4 coins)	£2000
1991 £2, sovereign, half sovereign (3 coins)	£700
1991 decimal, £1-1p (7 coins) in deluxe case	£34
1991 in standard case	£25
1991 uncirculated decimal, 1991 (7 coins)	£16
1991 gold Britannia, £100-£10 (4 coins)	£1800
1992 gold, £5, £2, sovereign, half sovereign (4 coins)	£2000
1992 £2, sovereign, half sovereign (3 coins)	£700
1992 silver, ten pence, large and small size	£30
1992 decimal, £1 English rev-1p including	
two 50p, new 10p (9 coins) in deluxe case	£30
1992 in standard case	£26
1992 uncirculated decimal, 1992	£17
1993 gold Britannia, £100-£10 (4 coins)	£1800
1993 gold, £5, £2, sovereign, half sovereign (4 coins)	£2000
1993 £2, sovereign, half sovereign (3 coins)	£700
1993 Coronation Anniversary £5,	
£1-1p (8 coins), deluxe case	£37
1993 in standard case	£30
1993 uncirculated decimal,	
with two 50p, no £5 (8 coins)	£20
1994 gold Britannia, £100-£10 (4 coins)	£1800
1994 gold, £5, £2 Bank of England, sovereign,	
half sovereign (4 coins)	£2000
1994 £2 Bank of England, sovereign,	
half sovereign (3 coins)	£700
1994 decimal, £2 Bank of England, £1 Scottish rev,	
50p D Day-1p (8 coins) in deluxe case	£34
1994 in standard case	£28
1994 uncirculated decimal, 1994	£11
1995 gold Britannia, £100-£10 (4 coins)	£1800
1996 gold, £5, £2 Peace, sovereign,	
half sovereign (4 coins)	£2000
1996 gold, £2 Peace, sovereign,	
half sovereign (3 coins)	£700
1996 decimal, £2 Peace, £1 Welsh	
rev-1p (8 coins), deluxe case	£35
1996 in standard case	£28
1996 uncirculated decimal	£10
1996 gold Britannia, £100-£10 (4 coins)	£1800
1996 gold, £5, £2, sovereign, half sovereign (4 coins)	£2000
1996 gold, £2, sovereign, half sovereign (3 coins)	£700
1996 silver decimal, £1-1p (7 coins)	£85
1996 decimal, £5 60th Birthday, £2 Football,	
£1 Northern Irish rev-1p in deluxe case (9 coins)	£30
1996 in standard case	£28

1997 gold Britannia, £100-£10 (4 coins)	£1800
1996 uncirculated decimal, £2-1p (8 coins)	£8
1997 gold, £5, £2 bimetal, sovereign,	
half sovereign (4 coins)	£2000
1997 £2 bimetal, sovereign, half sovereign (3 coins)	£700
1997 silver Britannia, £2-20p	£100
1997 decimal, fifty pence, large and small size	£55
1997 Golden Wedding £5, £2 bimetal, £1 English rev-1p	
with new 50p in deluxe case	£33
1997 in standard case	£28
1997 uncirculated decimal, £2 bimetal,	
£1 English rev-1p with new 50p (9 coins)	£9
1998 gold Britannia, £100-£10 (4 coins)	£1800
1998 silver Britannia, £2-20p	£100
1998 gold, £5-half sovereign	£2000
1998 £2-half sovereign	£700
1998 decimal, Prince Charles, £5-1p in deluxe case	£35
1998 in standard case	£27
1998 uncirculated, as above, £2-1p (9 coins)	£11
1998 silver, EU and NHS 50p (2 coins)	£40
1999 gold Britannia, £100-£10 (4 coins)	£1800
1999 £5, £2 Rugby World Cup,	
sovereign, half sovereign	£2000
1999 £2 Rugby World Cup,	
sovereign, half sovereign	£700
1999 decimal, Diana £5-1p in deluxe case	£35
1999 in standard case	£28
1999 uncirculated, £2-1p (8 coins)	£11
2000 gold Britannia, £100-£10 (4 coins)	£1800
2000 gold, £5-half sovereign	£2000
2000 £2-half sovereign	£700
2000 decimal, £5-1p Maundy coins (13 coins)	£250
2000 executive (10 coins)	£55
2000 deluxe (10 coins)	£32
2000 standard (10 coins)	£24
2001 gold Britannia, £100-£10 (4 coins)	£1800
2001 gold, £5, £2 Marconi Commemorative,	
sovereign, half sovereign (4 coins)	£2000
2001 £2 Marconi commemorative, sovereign,	
half sovereign (3 coins)	£700
2001 silver Britannia, new reverse designs, £2-20p	£80
2001 decimal, executive (10 coins)	£45
2001 deluxe (10 coins)	£32
2001 gift (10 coins)	£32
2001 standard (10 coins)	£27
2001 uncirculated, as above but no £5 (9 coins)	£12
2002 gold, £5-half sovereign, new reverse design	£2000
2002 £2-half sovereign, new reverse design	£700
2002 Golden Jubilee £5, £2 bimetal, £1 (English rev)-1p	
plus Maundy coins (13 coins)	£4250
2002 Commonwealth Games £2, four reverses: England,	
Northern Ireland, Scotland and Wales	£1800
2002 silver, Commonwealth Games, four reverses:	
£2 England, Northern Ireland, Scotland and Wales	£98
2002 gold Britannia, £100-£10 (4 coins)	£1800
2002 silver piedfort, Commonwealth	
Games £2, four reverses: England,	
Northern Ireland, Scotland and Wales	£195
2002 decimal, Executive, Golden Jubilee £5,	
£2 bimetal, £1 English rev-1p (9 coins)	£58

PROOF & SPECIMEN

BRITISH COINS MARKET VALUES 2011   **151**

	FDC
2002 deluxe (9 coins)	£37
2002 gift (9 coins)	£32
2002 standard (9 coins)	£25
2002 uncirculated, 2002, £2 bimetal, £1 English rev-1p (8 coins)	£14
2002 uncirculated, Commonwealth Games £2, reverses: England, Northern Ireland, Scotland and Wales	£12
2003 gold, £5-half sovereign	£2000
2003 £2 DNA-half sovereign	£775
2003 pattern set gold pounds (4 coins)	£1650
2003 pattern set silver pounds (4 coins)	£80
2003 gold Britannia £100-£10 (4 coins)	£1800
2003 silver Britannia £2-20p	£75
Gold set, mixed dates £100 (4 coins)	£2000
Silver set, mixed dates £2 (4 coins)	£40
Silver set, mixed dates £2 (4 coins)	£40
Silver set, £5 (2 coins) different types	£50
2003 Silver set, £5-50p Coronation-Suffragette (5 coins)	£120
2003 decimal, executive (11 coins)	£55
2003 deluxe (11 coins)	£37
2003 standard (11 coins)	£28
2003 uncirculated (10 coins)	£11
2004 gold £5-half sovereign (4 coins)	£2000
2004 gold, £2-half sovereign (3 coins)	£700
2004 pattern set, gold pounds (4 coins)	£1700
2004 pattern set, silver pounds (4 coins)	£80
2004 silver set, £5-50p Entente Cordiale-Bannister (5 coins)	£125
2004 silver piedfort set, £2-50p Penydarren engine-Bannister (3 coins)	£120
2004 gold Britannia, £100-£10 (4 coins)	£1800
2004 £50-£10	£350
2004 uncirculated set, 'new coin pack' (10 coins)	£9
2004 deluxe (10 coins)	£23
2004 executive (10 coins)	£42
2004 standard (10 coins)	£18
2005 gold, £5-half sovereign (4 coins)	£2000
2005 £2-half sovereign (3 coins)	£700
2005 silver piedfort set, £2-50p Gunpowder Plot-Johnson's Dictionary (4 coins)	£140
2005 silver piedfort set, £5 (2 coins)	£110
2005 decimal, 2005, Executive (12 coins)	£65
2005 deluxe (12 coins)	£40
2005 standard (12 coins)	£30
2005 uncirculated (10 coins)	£12
2005 gold Britannia, £100-£10 (4 coins)	£1800
2005 £50-£10 (3 coins)	£350
2005 silver Britannia, £2-20p (4 coins)	£80
2006 gold, £5-half sovereign (4)	£2000
2006 £2-half sovereign (3 coins)	£700
2006 gold Britannia, £100-£10 (4 coins)	£1800
2006 silver Britannia £2 gold plated, 5 different (5 coins)	£225
2006 gold, Brunel £2 (2 coins)	£900
2006 Victoria Cross 50p (3 coins)	£850
2006 silver, 80th Birthday (13 coins)	£275
2006 silver Britannia (5 coins)	£275

2006 Brunel £2 (2 coins)	£60
2006 silver piedfort, Brunel £2 (2 coins)	£80
2006 silver, 50p, Victoria Cross & Wounded Soldier (2 coins)	£50
2006 silver piedfort, 50 pence (2 coins)	£50
2006 silver piedfort, £5-50p 80th Birthday-Wounded Soldier (6 coins)	£275
2006 executive (13 coins)	£70
2006 deluxe (13 coins)	£45
2006 standard (13 coins)	£35
2007 gold, £5-half sovereign (4 coins)	£1295
2007 £2-half sovereign (3 coins)	£700
2007 'Bridge' series (4 coins)	£1500
2007 sovereign and half sovereign (2 coins)	£375
2007 platinum Britannia, £100-£10 (4 coins)	£BV
2007 silver 'Bridge' series (4 coins)	£115
2007 decimal executive (12 coins)	£79
2007 deluxe (12 coins)	£50
2007 standard (12 coins)	£39
2007 uncirculated (9 coins)	£14
2008 gold Britannia, £100-£10 (4 coins)	£1800
2008 gold, £5-half sovereign (4 coins)	£2000
2008 gold £2-half sovereign (3 coins)	£700
2008 gold, sovereign and half sovereign (2 coins)	£325
2008 platinum Britannia, £100-£10 (4 coins)	BV
2008 platinum Royal Shield (7 coins)	£4500
2008 platinum Emblems of Britain (7 coins)	£4500
2008 platinum Double set (14 coins)	£9000
2008 gold Royal shield (7 coins)	£2500
2008 gold Emblems of Britain (7 coins)	£2500
2008 gold Double set (14 coins)	£5000
2008 silver Britannia, £100-£10 (4 coins)	£1800
2008 silver Piedfort Royal Shield (6 coins)	£249
2008 silver Royal Shields (6 coins)	£149
2008 silver Emblems of Britain (6 coins)	£149
2008 silver Double set (12 coins)	£275
2008 Family (5 coins)	£150
2008 commemorative piedfort (4)	£200
2008 decimal Royal Shields (6 coins)	£2250
2008 decimal executive (11 coins)	£60
2008 deluxe (11 coins)	£40
2008 standard (11 coins)	£30
2008 uncirculated (9 coins)	£15
2008 uncirculated Emblems of Britain (9 coins)	£9
2008 Royal Shields (6 coins)	£30
2008 standard royal shields (6 coins)	£9
2008 double set (12 coins)	£18
2009 gold Britannia, £100-£10 (4 coins)	£18000
2009 gold, £5-half sovereign (4 coins)	£2000
2009 gold £2-half sovereign (3 coins)	£875
2009 silver Britannia, £2-20p	£100
2009 gold, sovereign and half sovereign (2 coins)	£385
2009 silver 50th Anniversary Mini (4 coins)	£150
2009 silver piedfort collection (4 coins)	£225
2009 silver family collection (6 coins)	£150
2009 silver set (12 coins)	£225
2009 decimal executive (12 coins)	£60
2009 deluxe (12 coins)	£40
2009 standard (12 coins)	£32
2009 uncirculated (11 coins)	£16

SCOTTISH COINS

■ MINTS IN OPERATION IN SCOTLAND

= A HOARD

FORRES
INVERNESS
ABERDEEN
MONTROSE
FORFAR
DUNDEE
PERTH H ST ANDREWS
STIRLING
H
LINLITHGOW KINGHORN
DUMBARTON DUNBAR
EDINBURGH BERWICK
RENFREW GLASGOW
KELSO
AYR ROXBURGH BAMBOROUGH
JEDBURGH
H CROSSRAGUEL ABBEY
DUMFRIES
CORBRIDGE
CARLISLE

The mints of the first coinage of Alexander III were the greatest number working together in Scotland, and therefore this area attracts collectors of the different mint issues.

For his reign, we give a price for issues of each mint town, but not for any other reign. From the reign of Mary, all Scottish coins were struck at Edinburgh.

MINT TOWN	KING
Aberdeen	Alexander III, David II, Robert III, James I, II, III,
Ayr	Alexander III
Bamborough	Henry
Berwick	David I, Malcolm IV, William I, Alexander II, III, Robert Bruce, James III
Carlisle	David I, Henry
Corbridge	Henry
Dumbarton	Robert III
Dumfries	Alexander III
Dunbar	William I?, Alexander III

MINT TOWN	KING
Dundee	William I?, Alexander III
Dunfermline	William I
Forfar	Alexander III
Forres	Alexander III
Glasgow	Alexander III
Inverness	Alexander III
Jedburgh	Malcolm IV
Kelso	Alexander II
Kinghorn	Alexander III
Lanark	Alexander III
Linlithgow	James I, II
Montrose	Alexander III
Perth	William I, Alexander III, Robert II-James II
Renfrew	Alexander III
Roxburgh	Alexander III
St Andrews	Alexander III
Stirling	Alexander III, James I, II, Mary Stuart

Prices are for the commonest coins in each case. For further details see *The Scottish Coinage*, by I Stewart (Spink, 1967, reprint 1975) and *Coins of Scotland, Ireland and The Islands*, (Spink 2003).

DAVID I 1124-53

	F	VF
Silver Pennies	£675	£1750

Four different groups; struck at the mints of Berwick, Carlisle, Roxborough and Edinburgh.

HENRY 1136-52

Earl of Huntingdon and Northumberland

Silver Pennies	£1850	£5500

Three types; struck at the mints of Corbridge, Carlisle and Barnborough.

MALCOLM IV 1153-65

Silver Pennies	£4500	£11000

Five types; struck at the mints of Roxburgh and Berwick.

William the Lion Penny, Edinburgh

WILLIAM THE LION 1165-1214

Silver Pennies	£150	£475

Three issues; struck at the mints of Roxburgh, Berwick, Edinburgh, Dun (Dunfermline?), Perth.

ALEXANDER II 1214-49

Silver Pennies	£800	£2450

Mints of Berwick and Roxburgh, varieties of bust

Alexander III first coinage Halfpenny

ALEXANDER III 1249-86

First coinage silver Pennies 1250-80

Aberdeen	£145	£300
Ayr	£225	£465
Berwick	£100	£225
'DUN'	£250	£550
Edinburgh	£145	£300
Forfar	£350	£750
Fres	£300	£800
Glasgow	£200	£450
Inverness	£285	£650
Kinghorn	£375	£950
Lanark	£300	£750

	F	VF
Montrose	£750	£1650
Perth	£100	£225
Renfrew	£525	£1350
Roxburgh	£100	£225
St Andrews	£285	£650
Stirling	£185	£475
'WILANERTER'	£375	£950

Alexander III second coinage Halfpenny

Second coinage c1280

Silver Pennies	£40	£100
Halfpennies	£90	£235
Farthings	£250	£650

Many types and varieties

JOHN BALLIOL 1292-6

First coinage, rough surface issue

Silver Pennies	£130	£365
Halfpennies	£325	£750

Second coinage, smooth surface issue

Silver Pennies	£145	£400
Halfpennies	£200	£575

ROBERT BRUCE 1306-29

Silver Pennies	£650	£1650
Halfpennies	£950	£3500
Farthings		ext. rare

Probably all struck at Berwick.

David II Halfgroat

DAVID II 1329-71

Gold Nobles		ext. rare
Silver Groats	£100	£295
Halfgroats	£110	£325
Pennies	£45	£125
Halfpennies	£375	£950
Farthings	£600	£1350

Three issues, but these denominations were not struck for all issues. Edinburgh and Aberdeen mints.

ROBERT II 1371-90

	F	VF
Silver Groats	£100	£300
Halfgroats	£120	£300
Pennies	£125	£295
Halfpennies	£125	£350

Some varieties. Struck at Dundee, Edinburgh and Perth.

ROBERT III 1390-1406

	F	VF
Gold Lion or Crowns	£1100	£2850
Demy-lions or Halfcrowns	£850	£2250
Silver groats	£95	£250
Halfgroats	£125	£365
Pennies	£300	£675
Halfpennies	£325	£750

Three issues, many varieties. Struck at mints of Edinburgh, Aberdeen, Perth and Dumbarton.

James I Demy

JAMES I 1406-37

	F	VF
Gold Demies	£825	£1850
Half-demies	£1350	£2850
Silver Groats	£150	£400
Billon Pennies	£175	£450
Billon Halfpennies	£375	£925

Mints: Aberdeen, Edinburgh, Inverness, Linlithgow, Perth and Stirling.

JAMES II 1437-60

	F	VF
Gold Demies from	£925	£2000
Lions from	£1350	£3250
Half lions		ext. rare
Silver Groats	£225	£550
Halfgroats	£600	*
Billon Pennies	£200	£525

Two issues, many varieties. Mints: Aberdeen, Edinburgh, Linlithgow, Perth, Roxburgh and Stirling.

ECCLESIASTICAL ISSUES c1452-80

	F	VF
Bishop Kennedy copper Pennies	£90	£275
Copper Farthings	£195	£525

Different types and varieties.

JAMES III 1460-88

		F	VF
Gold Riders	from	£1950	£4250
Half-riders		£2150	£4750
Quarter-riders		£2500	£5750
Unicorns		£1650	£4250
Silver Groats	from	£250	£495

James III Groat

		F	VF
Halfgroats	from	£475	£1200
Pennies	from	£300	£600
Billon Placks	from	£100	£275
Half-Placks	from	£100	£300
Pennies	from	£90	£250
Copper Farthings	from	£275	*

Many varieties. Mints: Aberdeen, Berwick and Edinburgh.

James IV Unicorn

JAMES IV 1488-1513

	F	VF
Gold Unicorns	£1500	£3850
Half-unicorns	£1200	£3250
Lions or Crowns	£1950	£4500
Half-lions	£2250	£6000
Pattern Angel		unique
Silver Groats	£500	£1200
Halfgroats	£575	£1500
Pennies, light coinage	ext. rare	*
Billon Placks	£40	£100
Half-placks	£125	£400
Pennies	£70	£165

Different types and varieties. Mint: Edinburgh.

James V 1540 'Bonnet' piece

SCOTTISH COINS

JAMES V 1513-42

		F	VF
Gold Unicorns		£1950	£4500
Half-unicorns		£2750	£5600
Crowns		£1100	£2500
'Bonnet' pieces or Ducats		£3500	£8000
Two-thirds ducats		£2750	£6250
One-third ducats		£3850	*
Silver Groats	from	£175	£525
One-third groats		£165	£500

James V Groat

	F	VF
Billon Placks	£25	£85
Bawbees	£25	£80
Half-bawbees	£75	£200
Quarter-bawbees		unique

Different issues and varieties. Mint: Edinburgh.

MARY 1542-67

First period 1542-58

	F	VF
Gold Crown	£1850	£4000
Twenty Shillings	£2750	£5500
Lions or Forty-four Shillings	£1500	£3250

Mary three pound piece or ryal

	F	VF
Half-lions or Twenty-two shillings	£1450	£3000
Ryals or Three Pound pieces, 1555, 1557, 1558	£4500	£8500
Half-ryals 1555, 1557, 1558	£5000	£10000
Portrait testoons, 1553	£4000	£8500
Non-portrait Testoons, 1555-58	£275	£750
Half-testoons, 1555-58	£275	£700
Billon Bawbees	£45	£125
Half-bawbees	£65	£175
Pennies, facing bust	£175	£550
No bust 1556	£125	£450
Lions, 1555, 1558	£30	£100
Placks, 1557	£45	£125

	F	VF
Second period, Francis and Mary, 1558-60		
Gold Ducats or Sixty shillings		ext. rare
Non-portrait Testoons, 1558-61	£350	£850
Half-testoons, 1558-60	£275	£625
Twelvepenny groats, Nonsunt, 1558-9	£65	£185
Lions, 1559-60	£30	£95

	F	VF
Third period, widowhood, 1560-5		
Gold Crown 1562		ext. rare
Portrait Testoons, 1561-2	£2250	£5250
Half-testoons, 1561-2	£2500	£6500

	F	VF
Fourth period, Henry and Mary, 1565-7		
Portrait Ryals, 1565		ext.rare
Non-portrait Ryals, 1565-7	£375	£900

Mary and Henry Darnley 1566 Ryal

	F	VF
Two-third ryals, 1565-7	£300	£775
Two-third ryals, undated	£975	£2500
One-third ryals, 1565-6	£325	£850
Testoon, 1565		ext. rare

	F	VF
Fifth period, 2nd widowhood, 1567		
Non-portrait Ryals, 1567	£375	£950
Two-thirds ryal, 1567	£325	£800
One-thirds ryals, 1566-7	£475	£1100

Mints: Edinburgh, Stirling (but only for some bawbees)

JAMES VI
Before English accession 1567-1603
First coinage 1567-71

	F	VF
Ryals 1567-71	£375	£825
Two-third ryals	£325	£775
One-third ryals	£325	£825

Second coinage 1571-80

	F	VF
Gold Twenty Pounds pieces	£25000	£50000
Silver Nobles, 1572-77, 1580	£90	£250
Half nobles	£70	£225

	F	VF
Two merks, 1578-80	£1750	£4500
Merks, 1579-80	£3250	*
Third coinage 1580-81		
Gold Ducats, 1580	£5250	£105000
Sixteen shillings, 1581	£2500	£5250
Eight shillings, 1581	£1500	£3750
Four shillings, 1581	£3500	*
Two shillings, 1581		ext. rare
Fourth coinage 1582-88		
Gold Lion Nobles	£4250	£9500
Two-third lion nobles	£5250	£12000
One-third lion nobles	£4750	£11000
Silver Forty shillings, 1582	£5750	£14500
Thirty shillings, 1582-86	£395	£1150
Twenty shillings, 1582-85	£375	£1250
Ten shillings, 1582-84	£295	£1000

James VI 1582 Ten Shillings

Fifth coinage 1588	F	VF
Gold Thistle nobles	£2500	£5500
Sixth coinage 1591-93		
Gold Hat pieces, 1591-93	£3850	£8750
Silver Balance half-merks, 1591-93	£300	£750
Balance quarter merks, 1591	£475	£1200
Severnth coinage 1594-1601		
Gold Riders	£850	£2250
Half Riders	£875	£1750
Silver Ten Shillings, 1593-95, 1598-1601	£135	£375
Five shillings, 1593-5, 1598-1601	£110	£325

James VI seventh coinage 1593 Five shillings

	F	VF
Thirty-pence pieces 1595-6, 1598-9, 1601	£150	£375
Twelve-pence piece 1594-6	£135	£275

James VI 1603 Sword and Sceptre piece

Eighth coinage 1601-4	F	VF
Gold Sword and Sceptre pieces	£500	£1100
Half sword and sceptre pieces	£425	£975
Silver thistle-merks, 1601-4	£75	£225
Half thistle-merks	£65	£185
Quarter thistle-merks	£60	£175
Eighth thistle-merks, 1601-3	£45	£125
Billon and copper issues		
Billon Placks or Eightpenny groats	£20	£90
Half-placks	£135	£350
Hardheads	£25	£100
Saltire Placks	£200	£495
Copper Twopence 1597	£95	£250
Penny 1597	£600	*
After English accession 1603-25		
Gold Units	£800	£1850
Double Crowns	£1150	£3250
Britain Crowns	£625	£1500
Halfcrowns	£500	£1350
Thistle Crowns	£395	£950
Silver Sixty shillings	£400	£975
Thirty shillings	£125	£325
Twelve shillings	£135	£400
Six shillings	£425	£1100
Two shillings	£40	£110
One shilling	£65	£165
Sixpences	*	*
Copper Twopences	£20	£60
Pennies	£135	£375
CHARLES 1625-49		
First coinage 1625-36		
Gold Units	£1050	£3000
Double Crowns	£1250	£3500
Britain Crowns		ext. rare
Silver Sixty shillings	£825	£2750
Thirty shillings	£150	£450
Twelve shillings	£225	£625
Six shillings	£350	£900
Two shillings	£65	£165
One shilling	£85	£250

SCOTTISH COINS

Second coinage 1636	F	VF
Half-merks	£60	£150
Forty-pence pieces	£50	£135
Twenty-pence pieces	£65	£150

Third coinage 1637-42
Gold Units	£1250	£2750
Half-units	£1250	£2750
Britain Crowns	£1100	£2750
Britain Halfcrowns	£500	£1000
Silver Sixty shillings	£525	£1500
Thirty shillings	£125	£325

Charles I third coinage Briot's issue Twelve shillings

Twelve shillings	£110	£300
Six shillings	£90	£225
Half-merks	£90	£225
Forty-pence piece	£35	£100
Twenty-pence piece	£30	£80
Three shillings	£65	£175
Two shillings	£50	£125
Copper twopences, lion	£20	£50
Pennies	£300	*
Twopences, CR crowned	£15	£35
Twopences, Stirling turners	£15	£35

CHARLES II 1660-85
First coinage
Silver Four merks, 1664 thistle above bust	£850	£1850
1664 thistle below bust	£800	£1650
1665	£1500	*
1670	£900	*
1673	£800	£1750
1674 F below bust	£800	£1800
1675	£800	£1800
Two merks, 1664 thistle above bust	£475	£1300
1664 thistle below bust	£350	£950
1670	£525	£1300
1673	£325	£950
1673 F below bust	£325	£950
1674	£325	£950
1674 F below bust	£325	£950
1675	£325	£950
Merks, 1664	£110	£375
1665	£125	£425
1666	£275	£750

Charles II first coinage 1669 Merk

	F	VF
1668	£225	£575
1669	£80	£300
1670	£80	£300
1671	£80	£300
1672	£90	£325
1673	£80	£300
1674	£150	£475
1674 F below bust	£120	£375
1675 F below bust	£120	£375
1675	£225	£575
Half-merks, 1664	£175	£500
1665	£150	£475
1666	£225	£700
1667	£225	£700
1668	£150	£475
1669	£90	£350
1670	£90	£350
1671	£100	£325
1672	£100	£325
1673	£120	£400
1675 F below bust	£110	£375
1675	£120	£400

Charles II second coinage 1676 Dollar

Second coinage
Silver Dollars, 1676	£425	£1450
1679	£475	£1500
1680	£485	£1750
1681	£485	£1650
1682	£425	£1350
Half-dollars, 1675	£450	£1200
1676	£525	£1600

	F	VF
1681	£450	£1350
Quarter-dollars, 1675	£135	£475
1676	£120	£350
1677	£120	£375
1678	£125	£450
1679	£135	£475
1680	£120	£375
1681	£120	£375
1682	£125	£425
Eighth-dollars, 1676	£85	£300
1677	£85	£300
1678/7	£175	£575
1679	£125	£450
1680	£80	£275
1682	£125	£450
Sixteenth-dollars, 1677	£65	£225
1678/7	£75	£275
1679/7	£100	£375
1680	£75	£275
1681	£70	£275
Copper twopence, CR crowned	£20	£70
Bawbees, 1677-9	£45	£135
Turners, 1677-9	£30	£100

JAMES VII 1685-9

		FDC
Silver sixty shillings, 1688, proof only		£2250
Gold proof only		ext. rare

Struck in 1828, not contemporary.

	F	VF
Silver forty shillings, 1687	£225	£850
1688	£250	£900
Ten shillings, 1687	£135	£475
1688	£175	£650

WILLIAM AND MARY 1689-94

	F	VF
Sixty shillings, 1691	£600	£1650
1692	£600	£1650
Forty shillings, 1689	£250	£850
1690	£250	£695
1691	£200	£595
1692	£175	£550
1693	£175	£550
1694	£250	£695
Twenty shillings, 1693	£375	£1250
1694	£450	£1350
Ten shillings, 1689	*	*
1690	£225	£625
1691	£150	£465
1692	£150	£465
1694	£240	£675
Five shillings, 1691	£175	£425
1694	£150	£350
Copper Bawbees, 1691-4	£50	£140
Bodle, 1691-4	£35	£120

WILLIAM II 1694-1702

	F	VF
Gold Pistole 1701	£3750	£8000
Half-pistole, 1701	£3500	£7000
Silver sixty shillings, 1699	*	*

	F	VF
Forty shillings, 1695	£195	£500
1696	£200	£525
1697	£250	£600
1698	£250	£625
1699	£250	£625
1700	£675	£1750
Twenty shillings, 1695	£225	£625
1696	£195	£525
1697	£325	£875
1698	£175	£500
1699	£375	£950

William III 1696 Ten shillings

	F	VF
Ten shillings, 1695	£125	£325
1696	£125	£325
1697	£150	£350
1698	£165	£425
1699	£175	£475
Five shillings, 1695	£85	£250
1696	£80	£225
1697	£80	£225
1699	£80	£225
1700	£80	£225
1701	£110	£400
1702	£125	£400
Copper Bawbees, 1695-7	£85	£375
Bodles, 1695-7	£50	£160

ANNE 1702-14
Pre-Union 1702-7

	F	VF
Ten shillings, 1705	£150	£400
1706	£150	£400
Five shillings, 1705	£60	£165
1706	£60	£165

JAMES VIII 1688-1766 The Old Pretender

Gold Guinea 1716	FDC	£13500
Silver	FDC	£1350
Bronze	FDC	£1350
Crown 1709		unique
Crown 1716, silver	FDC	£1850
Gold		ext. rare
Bronze		ext. rare

The 1716-dated pieces were struck in 1828 from the original dies.

IRISH COINS

■ HAMMERED ISSUES 995-1661

Most of the Irish coins of this period are in fairly poor condition and it is difficult to find specimens in VF condition upwards.

   For more details see *The Guide Book to the Coinage of Ireland AD 995 to the Present Day* by Anthony Dowle or Spink's *Coins of Scotland, Ireland & the Islands* by Patrick Finn (Spink 2002) and *Irish Coin Values* by Patrick Finn (Spink 1979). Prices are for the commonest coins in each case.

HIBERNO-NORSE

OF DUBLIN 995–1150		F	VF
Silver Pennies, imitative of English coins,			
many types and varieties	from	£375	£700

Hiberno-Norse phase II Penny

Hiberno-Norse phase IV Penny

JOHN AS LORD OF

IRELAND c1185-1199		
Silver Halfpennies, profile portrait	£1950	*
Facing head	£125	£300
Farthings	£400	£1100

Different types, varieties, mints and moneyers.

JOHN DE COURCY LORD

OF ULSTER 1177-1205		
Silver Halfpenny		unique
Farthings	£875	£2500

Different types, varieties, mints and moneyers.

JOHN AS KING OF ENGLAND

AND LORD OF IRELAND c1199-1216

Rex/Triangle types

Silver Pennies	from	£55	£150
Halfpennies		£75	£250
Farthings		£800	£1950

Different types, varieties, mints and moneyers.

HENRY III 1216-1272		F	VF
Silver Pennies, c 1251-1254	from	£55	£150

Dublin only, moneyers DAVI and RICHARD, many varieties.

Edward I Waterford Penny

EDWARD I 1272-1307

Silver Pennies from	£40	£95
Halfpennies	£50	£150

Edward I Farthing Dublin

Farthings	£100	£325

Dublin, Waterford and Cork, many different issues.

EDWARD III 1327-1377

Silver Halfpennies Dublin mint	£6000	*

HENRY VI 1422-1461

Silver Pennies, Dublin mint	ext. rare

Edward IV untitled crown type Groat

EDWARD IV 1461-1483

Silver untitled crown Groats	from	£800	£1850
Pennies		£900	£2500
Titled crown Groats		£1850	£4500
Halfgroats		£2000	*
Pennies		£1500	*
Cross on rose/sun Groats		£2250	£5750
Bust/rose-sun double Groats		£1850	£5500
Groats		£1650	*
Halfgroats		£1500	*
Pennies		£1450	*
'English-style' Groats		£150	£350
Halfgroats		£750	*
Pennies		£60	£150

	F	VF
Halfpennies	£900	*
Bust/rose Groats	£600	£1650
Pennies	£125	£375
Copper crown/cross Farthing	£1000	£3000
Half-farthings	£950	£2500

PATRICIUS/SALVATOR 1463-65

	F	VF
Silver Farthing	£1150	£3250
Three crowns/sun Half-farthings	£1250	£3500

This is an abbreviated listing of the issues of Edward IV which are numerous. There are also many varieties and different mints.

Richard III 'three crowns' Groat

RICHARD III 1483-1485

	F	VF
Silver bust/rose-cross Groats	£1000	£3750
Halfgroats		unique
Pennies		ext. rare
Cross and pellet pennies	£1000	£3000
Three-crown Groats	£675	£1500

Different mints and varieties.

Henry VII early 'three crowns' Groat

HENRY VII 1485-1509
Early issues

	F	VF
Three-crown Groats	£100	£300
Halfgroats	£175	£400
Pennies	£525	£1375
Halfpennies		ext. rare

Henry VII facing bust Groat, Dublin

Later issues

	F	VF
Facing bust Groats	£165	£425
Halfgroats	£600	£1850
Pennies	£800	£2000
Crowned H Pennies	£1000	*

Many varieties. Mints: mainly Dublin, Waterford issues are extremely rare.

LAMBERT SIMNEL, Pretender 1487

	F	VF
Three-crown Groats	£1000	£2750

Different mints and varieties.

HENRY VIII 1509-1547

	F	VF
Silver 'harp' Groats	£65	£175
Halfgroats	£600	£1500

These harped coins carry crowned initials, such as HA (Henry and Anne Boleyn), HI (Henry and Jane Seymour), HK (Henry and Katherine Howard) or HR (Henricus Rex).

Henry VIII posthumous portrait Groat

Posthumous issues

	F	VF
Portrait Groats current for 6 pence	£125	£500
Halfgroats current for 3 pence	£150	£475
Pennies current for 3 halfpence	£400	£1100
Halfpennies current for 3 farthings	£500	£1500

Different busts and mintmarks.

EDWARD VI 1547-1553

	F	VF
Base Shillings 1552 (MDLII)	£825	£2500
Contemporary copy	£50	£225

Mary 1553 Shilling

MARY 1553-1558

	F	VF
Shillings 1553 (MDLIII)	£875	£2500
1554 (MDLIIII)		ext. rare
Groats		ext. rare
Halfgroats		ext. rare
Pennies		ext. rare

Several varieties of the shillings and groats.

PHILIP AND MARY 1554-1558

Base Shillings	£295	£1100
Groats	£100	£400

Several minor varieties.

ELIZABETH I 1558-1603

Base portrait Shillings	£385	£1100
Groats	£110	£475
Fine silver portrait Shillings 1561	£350	£975
Groats	£300	£1000
Base shillings arms-harp	£125	£500
Sixpences	£90	£325
Threepences	£110	£425
Pennies	£30	£100
Halfpennies	£50	£175

JAMES I 1603-1625

Silver shillings	£95	£375
Sixpences	£80	£250

Different issues, busts and mintmarks.

Siege money of the Irish Rebellion 1642-1649

Siege coins are rather irregular in size and shape.

CHARLES I 1625-1649
Kilkenny Money 1642

Copper Halfpennies F	£300	£900
Copper Farthings F	£425	*

Inchiquin Money 1642-1646
The only gold coins struck in Ireland.

Gold Double Pistole		*
Gold Pistole F	£35000	£75000
Silver Crowns	£3000	£7000
Halfcrowns	£2500	£6000
Shillings	£2500	£7000
Ninepences	£5000	*
Sixpences	£4750	*
Groats F	£5000	£13000
Threepences		ext. rare

Three issues and many varieties.

Ormonde Money 1643

Crowns F	£500	£1000
Halfcrowns F	£425	£900
Shillings	£225	£500
Sixpences F	£175	£350
Groats F	£200	£400
Threepences	£135	£300
Halfgroats F	£525	£1250

Many varieties.

Ormonde Money Halfcrown

Ormonde Money Sixpence

	F	VF
Rebel Money 1643		
Crowns	£3850	£9000
Halfcrowns	£4500	£11000

Town Pieces 1645-1647
Bandon

Copper Farthings F	*	*

Kinsale

Copper Farthings F	£500	*

Youghal

Copper Farthings F	£500	£1750
Brass Twopences		ext. rare
Pewter Threepences		ext. rare

Cork

Silver Shillings F	£3850	£7250
Sixpences F	£1100	£2750
Copper Halfpennies	£1500	*
Copper Farthings F	£1350	*
Elizabeth I Shillings countermarked CORKE F		ext. rare

Cork 1647 Sixpence

'Blacksmith's' Money 1649
Based on English Tower Halfcrown.

	F	VF
Halfcrown, varieties	£775	£1850
Dublin Money 1649		
Crowns	£3500	£9500
Halfcrowns	£2750	£8000

■ CHARLES II TO GEORGE IV

All the issues of this series except Bank of Ireland tokens were struck in base metal.

The series features a large number of varieties, but there is space here for only the main types and best-known variants. A number of rare proofs have also been omitted.

Except for the 'gunmoney' of James II, Irish copper coins are hard to find in the top grades, especially the so-called 'Voce Populi' issues and specimens of Wood's coinage.

We have listed some of the 'gunmoney' of James II in only three grades – Fair, Fine and VF. The majority of these hastily produced coins were not well struck and many pieces with little substantial wear are, arguably, not Extremely Fine.

Dating of gunmoney: in the calendar used up to 1723, the legal or civil year started on March 25 in Great Britain and Ireland, so December 1689 came before, not after January, February and March 1689. Coins dated March 1689 and March 1690 were struck in the same month.

CHARLES II	Fair	F	VF	EF
Armstrong issues 1660-1661				
Copper Farthings	£15	£30	£100	*
St Patrick's coinage				
Halfpennies	£875	£2000	*	*
Star in rev legend	£900	*	*	*
Farthings	£125	£400	£950	*
Stars in rev legend	£150	£525	*	*
Cloud around				
St Patrick	£175	£625	*	*
Martlet below king	£150	£525	*	*
Annulet below king	£150	£525	*	*

Charles II St Patrick's Farthing

Regal coinage				
Halfpennies, 1680,				
large letters, small cross	£15	£50	£200	£575
1680 pellets	£15	£50	£200	£575
1681 large letters	£15	£50	£200	£575
1681 small letters	£50	£185	*	*
1682 large letters	£15	£50	£200	£575

	Fair	F	VF	EF
1682 small letters	£15	£50	£200	£575
1683	£15	£50	£200	£575
1684	£25	£95	£350	*

JAMES II
Regular coinage

	Fair	F	VF	EF
Halfpennies, 1685	£20	£65	£225	£600
1686	£20	£65	£225	£600
1687	£125	£450	*	*
1688	£20	£85	£250	*

Emergency coinage, 'Gunmoney'

	Fair	F	VF	EF
Crowns, 1690	£50	£100	£200	£575
1690 horseman, sword to E of REX	£125	£225	£550	£1000

James II 1690 'Gunmoney' Crown

Large Halfcrowns,				
1689 July	£15	£60	£185	*
1689 August	£10	£40	£150	*
1689 September	£8	£35	£100	£400
1689 October	£8	£35	£100	*
1689 November	£10	£40	£125	*
1689 December	£10	£40	£125	*
1689 January	£10	£40	£150	*
1689 February	£8	£35	£125	*
1689 March	£8	£35	£125	*
1690 March	£8	£35	£125	*
1690 April	£8	£35	£125	£400
1690 May	£10	£40	£150	*
Small Halfcrowns,				
1690 April	£20	£75	£275	*
1690 May	£10	£30	£150	£350
1690 June	£10	£35	£185	£500
1690 July	£10	£35	£140	£400
1690 August	£12	£40	£165	£475
1690 September	*	*	*	*
1690 October	£35	£110	£450	*
Large Shillings, 1689 July	£8	£25	£90	£225
1689 August	£6	£20	£70	£200
1689 September	£6	£20	£70	£200
1689 October	£8	£25	£90	£225
1689 November	£6	£20	£70	£200
1689 December	£6	£20	£70	£185
1689 January	£6	£20	£70	£185
1689 February	£6	£20	£70	£185

	Fair	F	VF	EF
1689 March	£7	£20	£70	£200
1690 March	£8	£25	£70	£200
1690 April	£8	£25	£90	£225
Small Shillings,1690 April	£10	£30	£110	£250
1690 May	£7	£20	£80	£225
1690 June	£7	£20	£80	£225
1690 July	*	*	*	*
1690 August	*	*	*	*
1690 September	£20	£135	*	*
Sixpences, 1689 June	£10	£35	£110	£250
1689 July	£8	£30	£100	£200
1689 August	£8	£30	£100	£200
1689 September	£10	£35	£125	£250
1689 October	*	*	*	*
1689 November	£8	£30	£100	£200
1689 December	£8	£30	£100	£200
1689 January	£10	£35	£110	£250
1689 February	£8	£30	£100	£200
1689 March	*	*	*	*
1690 March	*	*	*	*
1690 April	*	*	*	*
1690 May	£15	£45	£140	*
1690 June	*	*	*	*
1690 October	*	*	*	*

Pewter Money

	Fair	F	VF	EF
Crowns	£475	£1750	£4500	*
Groats	£225	£900	£3000	*
Pennies large bust	£300	£700	*	*
Small bust	£325	£750	*	*
Halfpennies large bust	£75	£250	£750	*
Halfpennies small bust	£65	£200	£525	*

Limerick Money Halfpenny

Limerick Money

	Fair	F	VF	EF
Halfpennies	£15	£50	£150	£375
Farthings reversed N	£20	£70	£200	£500
Normal N	£25	£75	£225	*

William and Mary 1693 Halfpenny

	Fair	F	VF	EF
WILLIAM AND MARY				
Halfpennies 1692	£7	£40	£140	*
1693	£7	£40	£140	*
1694	£10	£50	£175	*
WILLIAM III				
Halfpennies 1696 draped bust	£15	£50	£200	*
Halfpennies 1696 crude undraped bust	£40	£175	£525	*
GEORGE I				
Wood's coinage				
Halfpennies 1722 harp left	£12	£50	£200	*
1722 harp right	£8	£25	£125	£450
1723	£6	£20	£70	£325
1723 obv Rs altered Bs	£7	£20	£80	£350
1723 no stop after date	£7	£20	£75	£350
1723/2	£7	£25	£90	£375
1723 star in rev legend	*	*	*	*
1723 no stop before HIBERNIA	£6	£20	£75	£350
1724 head divided rev legend	£7	£25	£110	£500
1724 legend continuous over head	£10	£30	£125	*
Farthings 1722 harp left	£30	£125	£575	*
1723 D: G:	£10	£40	£150	£650
1723 DEI GRATIA	£6	£20	£80	£250
1724	£8	£30	£90	£350
GEORGE II				
Halfpennies 1736	*	£10	£50	£300
1737	*	£10	£50	£300
1738	£1	£12	£60	£375
1741	*	£10	£50	£300
1742	*	£10	£50	£300
1743	£2	£15	£60	£395
1744	£1	£12	£60	£325
1744/3	£2	£15	£60	£375
1746	£1	£12	£60	£375
1747	*	£10	£50	£300
1748	£2	£12	£65	£395
1749	*	£10	£50	£300
1750	*	£10	£45	£275
1751	*	£10	£45	£275
1752	*	£10	£45	£275
1753	*	£12	£50	£275
1755	*	*	*	*
1760	*	£10	£40	£275
Farthings 1737	£1	£12	£65	£300
1738	*	£10	£50	£300
1744	*	£10	£45	£275
1760	*	£8	£40	£250
Voce Populi coinage				
Halfpennies, 1760, Type 1	£35	£150	£425	*
Type 2	£5	£175	£350	*

	Fair	F	VF	EF
Type 3	£75	£175	£400	*
Type 4	£60	£150	£325	*
Type 5	£60	£150	£300	*
Type 6	£60	£150	£300	*
Type 7	£60	£160	£350	£1100
Type 8	£60	£150	£300	*
Type 9	£75	£175	£400	*
Type 9, P before head	£25	£100	£300	£850
Type 9, P under head	£25	£100	£300	£850
Farthings, 1760, Type 1				
loop to truncation	£75	£250	£1250	£3500
Type 2 no loop	*	*	*	*

GEORGE III

London coinage	F	VF	EF	Unc
Halfpennies, 1766	£5	£25	£175	£450
1769	£5	£30	£200	£475
1769 2nd type	£5	£40	£225	£525
1775	£5	£30	£200	£475
1776	£25	£125	£375	*
1781	£5	£20	£160	£450
1782	£5	£20	£160	£400

Soho coinage

		F	VF	EF	Unc
Penny 1805		*	£30	£125	£250
Halfpenny 1805		*	£15	£85	£165
Farthing 1806		*	£12	£50	£120

Bank of Ireland token coinage

	Fair	F	VF	EF
Silver Six shillings 1804	£85	£250	£525	£875

Bank of Ireland token coinage 1804 Six shillings

	Fair	F	VF	EF
Thirty pence 1808	£25	£75	£325	*
Ten pence 1805	£8	£25	£100	£100
Ten pence 1806	£10	£30	£125	£175
Ten pence 1813	£6	£20	£80	£125
Five pence 1805	£6	£20	£80	£125
Five pence 1806	£8	£25	£90	£140

George IV proof penny, 1822

GEORGE IV	Fair	F	VF	EF
Penny 1822	£8	£40	£175	£350
1823	£10	£60	£200	£400
Halfpenny 1822	£5	£15	£110	£200
1823	£5	£15	£125	£225

■ FREE STATE AND REPUBLIC

Proofs exist for nearly all dates of the modern Irish coinage. However, only a few dates have become available to collectors or dealers and apart from the 1928 proofs, are all very rare. They have therefore been omitted from the list.

TEN SHILLINGS	F	VF	EF	Unc
1966	*	£2	£6	£10
1966 proof	*	*	*	£15

HALFCROWNS				
1928	£2	£8	£12	£45
1928 proof	*	*	*	£50
1930	£4	£12	£110	£375
1931	£8	£20	£150	£425
1933	£5	£15	£120	£350
1934	£5	£12	£60	£225
1937	£35	£85	£550	£1350
1938	*	*	*	*
1939	£3	£5	£25	£65
1940	£3	£6	£20	£60
1941	£4	£6	£25	£65
1942	£2	£4	£20	£60
1943	£70	£150	£850	£2500
1951	*	*	£6	£35
1954	*	*	£7	£40
1955	*	*	£5	£20
1959	*	*	£4	£17
1961	*	*	£5	£15
1961 mule normal				
obv/pre-1939 rev	£8	£20	£300	*
1962	*	*	*	£5
1963	*	*	*	£10
1964	*	*	*	£5
1966	*	*	*	£10
1967	*	*	*	£3

FLORINS

	F	VF	EF	Unc
1928	*	£5	£18	£40
1928 proof	*	*	*	£50
1930	£3	£15	£100	£325
1931	£5	£35	£150	£325
1933	£8	£18	£125	£350
1934	£12	£60	£275	£525
1935	£3	£10	£125	£325
1937	£5	£18	£200	£425
1939	£2	£4	£10	£40
1940	£2	£5	£12	£40
1941	£2	£5	£20	£65
1942	£2	£5	£12	£45
1943	£2750	£7000	£12000	*
1951	*	*	£3	£25
1954	*	*	£3	£20
1955	*	*	£3	£20
1959	*	*	£3	£20
1961	*	£3	£6	£40
1962	*	*	£3	£18
1963	*	*	£3	£18
1964	*	*	*	£5
1965	*	*	*	£5
1966	*	*	*	£5
1968	*	*	*	£5
1948	*	£2	£8	£35
1949	*	*	£5	£30
1950	£2	£15	£35	£150
1952	*	*	£4	£20
1953	*	*	£5	£22
1955	*	*	£4	£18
1956	*	*	£3	£12
1958	*	*	£5	£40
1959	*	*	£2	£7
1960	*	*	£2	£7
1961	*	*	£2	£7
1962	*	*	£3	£30
1964	*	*	*	£3
1965	*	*	*	£3
1966	*	*	*	£3
1967	*	*	*	£3
1968	*	*	*	£2
1969	*	*	*	£3

SHILLINGS

	F	VF	EF	Unc
1928	*	£3	£8	£28
1928 proof	*	*	*	£30
1930	£7	£20	£85	£325
1931	£3	£15	£65	£225
1933	£5	£10	£80	£285
1935	£2	£5	£40	£120
1937	£10	£25	£250	£875
1939	*	£3	£8	£35
1940	*	£3	£12	£40
1941	*	£5	£15	£45
1942	*	£5	£8	£28
1951	*	*	£3	£20
1954	*	*	£3	£15
1955	*	*	£3	£18
1959	*	*	£6	£25
1962	*	*	*	£5
1963	*	*	*	£4
1964	*	*	*	£5
1966	*	*	*	£4
1968	*	*	*	£4

SIXPENCES

	F	VF	EF	Unc
1928	*	*	£3	£25
1928 proof	*	*	*	£30
1934	*	*	£12	£65
1935	*	£3	£18	£90
1939	*	*	£5	£35
1940	*	*	£5	£25
1942	*	*	£5	£25
1945	£2	£8	£40	£150
1946	£5	£12	£85	£400
1947	*	£6	£25	£100

THREEPENCES

	F	VF	EF	Unc
1928	*	*	£3	£18
1928 proof	*	*	£3	£25
1933	£2	£5	£60	£250
1934	*	£3	£15	£65
1935	£2	£5	£25	£150
1939	*	£5	£50	£200
1940	*	*	£10	£40
1942	*	*	£5	£35
1943	*	*	£8	£75
1946	*	*	£5	£30
1948	*	£2	£15	£80
1949	*	*	£5	£30
1950	*	*	£2	£6
1953	*	*	£2	£5
1956	*	*	*	£4
1961	*	*	*	£3
1962	*	*	*	£3
1963	*	*	*	£3
1964	*	*	*	£3
1965	*	*	*	£3
1966	*	*	*	£3
1967	*	*	*	*
1968	*	*	*	*

PENNIES

	F	VF	EF	Unc
1928	*	*	£6	£25
1928 proof	*	*	*	£35
1931	*	£2	£25	£80
1933	*	£3	£40	£150
1935	*	*	£15	£45
1937	*	*	£25	£80
1938 (possibly unique)	*	*	*	£20000
1940	*	£15	£90	£400
1941	*	*	£6	£30
1942	*	*	£3	£15
1943	*	*	£5	£20
1946	*	*	£3	£15
1948	*	*	£3	£15

	F	VF	EF	Unc
1949	*	*	£3	£15
1950	*	*	£3	£15
1952	*	*	£2	£7
1962	*	*	£2	£3
1963	*	*	*	£2
1964	*	*	*	£2
1965	*	*	*	£1
1966	*	*	*	£1
1967	*	*	*	£1
1968	*	*	*	£1

HALFPENNIES

	F	VF	EF	Unc
1928	*	*	£4	£20
1928 proof	*	*	*	£25
1933	*	£20	£100	£350
1935	*	£10	£80	£200
1937	*	*	£12	£40
1939	£4	£10	£30	£140
1940	*	£10	£35	£165
1941	*	*	£5	£25
1942	*	*	£2	£20
1943	*	*	£5	£25
1946	*	*	£15	£65
1949	*	*	£3	£18
1953	*	*	*	£4
1964	*	*	*	£2
1965	*	*	*	£2
1966	*	*	*	£2
1967	*	*	*	£1

FARTHINGS

	F	VF	EF	Unc
1928	*	*	£3	£12
1928 proof	*	*	*	£20
1930	*	*	£5	£18
1931	£1	£3	£8	£30
1932	£1	£3	£10	£35
1933	*	£2	£5	£25
1935	*	£5	£12	£45
1936	*	£6	£15	£50
1937	*	£2	£5	£20
1939	*	*	£3	£12
1940	*	£3	£6	£35
1941	*	*	£3	£7
1943	*	*	£3	£7
1944	*	*	£3	£7
1946	*	*	£3	£7
1949	*	*	£5	£10
1953	*	*	£3	£7
1959	*	*	£1	£4
1966	*	*	£2	£6

DECIMAL COINAGE
50p, 10p, 5p, 2p, 1p, ½p, all face value only.

SETS

	F	VF	EF	Unc
1928 in card case	*	*	FDC	£250
1928 in leather case	*	*	FDC	£300
1966 unc set	*	*	*	£10
1971 specimen set in folder	*	*	*	£5
1971 proof set	*	*	*	£9

THE ANGLO-GALLIC SERIES

Anyone interested in studying this series should obtain *The Anglo-Gallic Coins* by E R D Elias, who neatly summarised the series: 'All Kings of England in the period 1154-1453 had interests in France. They were Dukes or Lords of Aquitaine, Counts of Poitou

or Ponthieu, Lords of Issoudun or they were even or pretended to be, Kings of France itself, and, in those various capacities, struck coins.

These coins, together with the French coins of their sons, and of their English vassals, are called Anglo-Gallic coins'.

See our table for the English kings' French titles.

KINGS OF ENGLAND AND FRANCE 1154-1453

ENGLAND	FRANCE
Henry II 1154-89 Duke of Normandy and Count of Anjou, Maine and Touraine. By marrying Eleanor of Aquitaine in 1152, he became Duke of Aquitaine and Count of Poitou. He relinquished Aquitaine and Poitou to his son Richard in 1168. In 1185 he forced Richard to surrender Aquitaine and Poitou to Eleanor who governed between 1199-1204.	**Louis VII 1137-80** **Philip II 1180-1223**
Richard I the Lionheart 1189-99 Formally installed as Duke of Aquitaine and Count of Poitou in 1172.	
John 1199-1216 He lost all parts of the Angevin Empire except Aquitaine and part of Poitou.	
Henry III 1216-72 In 1252 he ceded Aquitaine to his son Edward.	**Louis VIII 1223-26** **Louis IX 1226-70** **Philip III 1270-85**
Edward I 1272-1307 He governed Aquitaine from 1252. In 1279 he became Count of Ponthieu. In 1290 the county went to his son Edward.	**Philip IV 1285-1314**
Edward II 1307-27 He was Count of Ponthieu from 1290. In 1325 he relinquished the county of Ponthieu and the Duchy of Aquitaine to his son Edward.	**Louis X 1314-16** **Philip V 1316-22** **Charles IV 1322-28**
Edward III 1327-77 Count of Ponthieu and Duke of Aquitaine from 1325. He lost Ponthieu in 1337 but it was restored in 1360. In 1340 he assumed the title of King of France, which he abandoned again in 1360. He gave Aquitaine to his son, Edward the Black Prince, (b1330-d1376), who was Prince of Aquitaine 1362-1372, although he actually ruled from 1363-1371. In 1369 Edward III reassumed the title King of France.	**Philip VI 1328-50** **John II 1350-64** **Charles V 1364-80**
Richard II 1377-99 The son of the Black Prince succeeded his grandfather, Edward III, as King of England and Lord of Aquitaine.	**Charles VI 1380-1422**
Henry IV 1399-1413 He adopted the same titles as Richard II.	
Henry V 1413-22 From 1417-1420 he used the title King of the French on his 'Royal' French coins. After the Treaty of Troyes in 1420 he styled himself 'heir of France'.	
Henry VI 1422-61 He inherited the title King of the French from his grandfather Charles VI. He lost actual rule in Northern France in 1450 and in Aquitaine in 1453.	**Charles VII 1422-61**

	F	VF
HENRY II 1152-68		
Denier	£45	£110
Obole	£85	£200
RICHARD THE LIONHEART 1168-99		
Aquitaine		
Denier	£50	£125
Obole	£50	£130
Poitou		
Denier	£40	£90
Obole	£60	£160
Issoudun		
Denier	£225	*
ELEANOR 1199-1204		
Denier	£50	£125
Obole	£265	*
EDWARD I		
During the lifetime of his father 1252-72		
Denier au lion	£30	£80
Obole au lion	£40	£110
After succession to the English throne 1272-1307		
Denier au lion	£70	£200
Obole au lion	£125	*
Denier á la croix longue	£60	£150
Au léopard, first type	£30	£75
Obole au léopard, first type	£45	£120
Denier á la couronne	£225	*
EDWARD II		
Gros Turonus Regem		ext. rare
Maille blanche		ext. rare
Hibernie	£45	£135
EDWARD III		
Gold coins		
Ecu d'or	£1450	£3750
Florin	£3500	£7750
Léopard d'or, 1st issue		ext. rare
2nd issue	£1650	£3950

	F	VF
3rd issue	£1450	£3750
4th issue	£1650	£3950
Guyennois d'or, 1st type	£3500	£7750
2nd type	£1950	£4850
3rd type	£1450	£3750
Silver coins		
Gros aquitainique au léopard	£175	£525
Tournois à la croix mi-longue	£275	£800
À la croix longue	£120	£285
Sterling	£80	£245
Demi-sterling	£125	£385
Gros au léopard passant	£525	*
À la couronne	£125	£385
Au châtel aquitainique	£175	£525
Tournois au léopard au-dessus	£80	£245
À la porte	£80	£245
Aquitainique au léopard au-dessous	£245	*
Blanc au léopard sous couronne	£65	£145
Gros au léopard sous couronne	£185	£550
À la couronne avec léopard	£145	£425
Sterling à la tête barbue	£285	£775
Petit gros de Bordeaux		ext. rare
Gros au lion	£125	£345
Demi-gros au lion	£250	*
Guyennois of argent (sterling)	£95	£235
Gros au buste	£975	*
Demi-gros au buste	£500	£1350
Black coins		
Double à la couronne, 1st type	£95	*
2nd type	£80	£245
3rd type	£150	*
Double au léopard	£65	£165
Sous couronne	£30	£95
Guyennois		ext. rare
Denier au léopard, 2nd type	£30	£95
Obole au léopard, 2nd type		ext. rare
Denier au léopard, 3rd type	£35	£110
4th type	£30	£95
Obole au léopard, 4th type	£35	£110
Denier au lion	£40	£135

Some issues of the 2nd and 3rd type deniers au léopard are very rare to extremely rare and therefore much more valuable.

EDWARD THE BLACK PRINCE 1362-72

Edward III 2nd issue léopard d'or

Edward the Black Prince Chaise d'or of Bordeaux

	F	VF
Gold coins		
Léopard d'or	£1475	£3950
Guyennois d'or	£1850	£4500
Chaise d'or	£1750	£4250
Pavillon d'or 1st issue	£1750	£4250
2nd issue	£1475	£3950
Demi-pavillon d'or	*	*
Hardi d'or	£1375	£3750
Silver coins		
Gros	£750	£1875
Demi-gros	£80	£235
Sterling	£65	£140
Hardi d'argent	£45	£120
Black coins		
Double guyennois	£110	£285
Denier au lion	£50	£135
Denier	£55	£145

RICHARD II 1377-99

	F	VF
Gold coins		
Hardi d'or	£1950	£6000
Demi-hardi d'or		ext. rare
Silver coins		
Double hardi d'argent	£750	£2350
Hardi d'argent	£50	£150
Black coins		
Denier	£80	£240

HENRY IV 1399-1413

	F	VF
Silver coins		
Double hardi d'argent	£500	£1450
Hardi d'argent	£40	£125
Hardi aux genêts	£160	£525
Black coins		
Denier	£50	£140
Aux genêts	£135	£365

HENRY V 1413-22

	F	VF
Gold coins		
Agnel d'or	£4750	£14000
Salut d'or	£5250	£17000
Silver coins		
Florette, 1st issue	£80	£195
2nd issue	£135	£350
3rd issue	£50	£150
4th issue	£70	£175
Guénar	£300	£950
Gros au léopard	£375	*
Black coins		
Mansiois		ext. rare
Niquet	£50	£160
Denier tournois	£70	£175

HENRY VI 1422-53

	F	VF
Gold coins		
Salut d'or	£485	£975
Angelot	£1500	£4650

Henry VI Salut d'or Paris mint

	F	VF
Silver coins		
Grand blanc aux ècus	£60	£185
Petit blanc	£80	£235
Trésin		ext. rare
Black coins		
Denier Paris, 1st issue	£60	£145
2nd issue	£60	£145
Denier tournois	£65	£160
Maille tournois	£65	£160

The prices of the saluts and grands blancs are for mints of Paris, Rouen and Saint Lô; coins of other mints are rare to very rare.

■ PONTHIEU

EDWARD I

	F	VF
Denier	£85	£225
Obole	£75	£195

EDWARD III

	F	VF
Denier	£135	*
Obole	£195	*

■ BERGERAC

HENRY, EARL OF LANCASTER 1347-51

	F	VF
Gros tournois à la croix longue	£750	£1750
À la couronne	£675	*
Au châtel aquitanique	£675	£1750
Tournois au léopard au-dessus	£500	£1100
À la couronne		ext. rare
À fleur-de-lis		ext. rare
Au léopard passant		ext. rare
Double	£1000	*
Denier au léopard	£685	*

HENRY, DUKE OF LANCASTER 1351-61

	F	VF
Gros tournois à la couronne avec léopard	£785	*
Au léopard couchant	£785	*
Sterling à la tête barbue	£650	*
Gros au lion		ext. rare

ISLAND COINAGE

Proofs have been struck for a large number of Channel Islands coins, particularly in the case of Jersey. Except for those included in modern proof sets, most are very rare and in the majority of cases have been omitted from the list.

For further information refer to *The Coins of the British Commonwealth of Nations, Part I, European Territories* by F Pridmore (Spink, 1960).

■ GUERNSEY

	F	VF	EF	BU
TEN SHILLINGS				
1966	*	*	*	£2
THREEPENCE				
1956	*	*	*	£2
1959	*	*	*	£2
1966 proof	*	*	*	£2
EIGHT DOUBLES				
1834	*	£12	£65	£350
1858	*	£12	£65	£350
1864	*	£15	£50	*
1868	*	£10	£50	*
1874	*	£10	£50	*
1885 H	*	*	£15	£70
1889 H	*	*	£15	£65
1893 H	*	*	£15	£65
1902 H	*	*	£15	£45
1903 H	*	*	£15	£45
1910 H	*	*	£15	£45
1911 H	*	£15	£40	£100
1914 H	*	*	£12	£45
1918 H	*	*	£12	£45
1920 H	*	*	£5	£25
1934 H	*	*	£5	£25
1934 H 'burnished flan'	*	*	*	£200
1938 H	*	*	*	£12
1945 H	*	*	*	£10
1947 H	*	*	*	£10
1949 H	*	*	*	£10
1956	*	*	*	£7
1956 proof	*	*	*	£10
1959	*	*	*	£3
1966 proof	*	*	*	£3
FOUR DOUBLES				
1830	*	*	£45	£265
1858	*	*	£50	£300
1864	*	£5	£50	*
1868	*	£5	£50	*
1874	*	*	£50	*
1885 H	*	*	£8	£50
1889 H	*	*	£8	£55
1893 H	*	*	£8	£35
1902 H	*	*	£8	£45
1903 H	*	*	£8	£45

	F	VF	EF	BU
1906 H	*	*	£8	£65
1908 H	*	*	£8	£65
1910 H	*	*	£5	£55
1911 H	*	*	£5	£45
1914 H	*	*	£5	£45
1918 H	*	*	£5	£35
1920 H	*	*	*	£30
1945 H	*	*	*	£15
1949 H	*	*	*	£18
1956	*	*	*	£5
1956 proof	*	*	*	£8
1966 proof	*	*	*	£2
TWO DOUBLES				
1858	*	£30	£125	£375
1868	*	£30	£125	£350
1874	*	£30	£125	£300
1885 H	*	*	£20	£40
1889 H	*	*	£20	£45
1899 H	*	*	£20	£45
1902 H	*	*	£20	£45
1903 H	*	*	£25	£45
1906 H	*	*	£25	£50
1908 H	*	*	£25	£50
1911 H	*	*	£45	£90
1914 H	*	*	£45	£90
1917 H	£25	£50	£150	*
1918 H	*	*	£20	£40
1920 H	*	*	£20	£40
1929 H	*	*	£5	£12
ONE DOUBLE				
1830	*	*	£20	£75
1868	*	£40	£100	£350
1868/30	*	£40	£100	£350
1885 H	*	*	£3	£15
1889 H	*	*	£3	£15
1893 H	*	*	£3	£15
1899 H	*	*	£3	£15
1902 H	*	*	£3	£15
1903 H	*	*	£3	£15
1911 H	*	*	£3	£15
1911 H new type	*	*	£3	£15
1914 H	*	*	£3	£15
1929 H	*	*	£3	£15
1933 H	*	*	£3	£15
1938 H	*	*	£3	£12
SETS				
1956 proof				£35
1966 proof				£8
1971 proof				£8

For coins after 1971 refer to the *Standard Catalogue of World Coins* published by Krause Publications annually.

■ JERSEY

CROWN	F	VF	EF	BU
1966	*	*	*	£4
1966 proof	*	*	*	£8

¼ OF A SHILLING

	F	VF	EF	BU
1957	*	*	*	£6
1960 proof only	*	*	*	£75
1964	*	*	*	£4
1966	*	*	*	£4

1/12 OF A SHILLING

	F	VF	EF	BU
1877 H	*	*	£18	£110
1881	*	*	£15	£75
1888	*	*	£15	£65
1894	*	*	£12	£60
1909	*	*	£15	£85
1911	*	*	£10	£50
1913	*	*	£10	£50
1923	*	*	£10	£40
1923 new type	*	*	£12	£50
1926	*	*	£12	£50
1931	*	*	£5	£25
1933	*	*	£5	£25
1935	*	*	£5	£25
1937	*	*	*	£18
'1945' (George VI)	*	*	£5	£12
'1945' (Elizabeth II)	*	*	*	£8
1946	*	*	*	£12
1947	*	*	*	£12
1957	*	*	*	£5
1960	*	*	*	£5
1964	*	*	*	£4
1966	*	*	*	£3
1966 proof	*	*	*	£7

The date 1945 on 1/12 shillings commemorates the year of liberation from German occupation. The coins were struck in 1949, 1950, 1952 and 1954.

1/13 OF A SHILLING

	F	VF	EF	BU
1841	*	*	£70	£250
1844	*	*	£70	£250
1851	*	*	£77	£250
1858	*	*	£70	£250
1861	*	*	£70	£250
1865 proof only	*	*	*	£750
1866	*	*	£40	£125
1870	*	*	£40	£125
1871	*	*	£40	£125

1/24 OF A SHILLING

	F	VF	EF	BU
1877 proof only	*	*	*	£300
1877 H	*	*	£20	£75
1888	*	*	£15	£45
1894	*	*	£15	£45
1909	*	*	£15	£50
1911	*	*	£12	£40
1913	*	*	£12	£35

	F	VF	EF	BU
1923	*	*	£10	£35
1923 new type	*	*	£10	£35
1926	*	*	£12	£45
1931	*	*	£7	£25
1933	*	*	£7	£20
1935	*	*	£7	£15
1937	*	*	£7	£12
1946	*	*	£7	£12
1947	*	*	£7	£12

1/26 OF A SHILLING

	F	VF	EF	BU
1841	*	*	£50	£200
1844	*	*	£50	£225
1851	*	*	£50	£200
1858	*	*	£50	£200
1861	*	*	£45	£185
1866	*	*	£25	£125
1870	*	*	£25	£125
1871	*	*	£25	£125

1/48 OF A SHILLING

	F	VF	EF	BU
1877 proof	*	*	*	£325
1877 H	*	£25	£95	£200

1/52 OF A SHILLING

	F	VF	EF	BU
1841	*	£40	£175	£425
1841 proof	*	*	*	£650
1861 proof	*	*	*	£750

DECIMAL COINAGE

SETS	BU
1957	£28
1960	£12
1964	£10
1966 four coins proof	£7
1966 two crowns	£8
1972 Silver Wedding five gold, four silver coins	BV
1972 proof	BV
1972 four silver coins	£30

For coins after 1972 refer to the *Standard Catalogue of World Coins* published by Krause Publications annually.

■ ISLE OF MAN

Contemporary forgeries of earlier Isle of Man coins exist.

Copper and Bronze 1709-1839

James Stanley, 10th Earl of Derby, penny, 1709

PENNIES	F	VF	EF	Unc
1709	£60	£250	£425	*
1733	£35	£125	£285	*
1733 proof	*	£250	£475	*

Proof penny in silver, 1733

1733 silver	*	*	£600	*
1758	£20	£70	£275	*
1758 proof	*	*	£650	*
1758 silver	*	*	£1500	*
1786	£10	£40	£200	£400
1786 plain edge proof	*	*	£350	£625
1798	£15	£40	£175	£385
1798 bronzed proof	*	*	£250	£600
1798 AE gilt proof	*	*	£775	£1500
1798 silver proof	*	*	£1650	£2750

1813	£10	£25	£150	£350
1813 bronze proof	*	*	£225	£500
1813 gilt proof	*	*	£600	£1500
1839	*	£15	£75	£250
1839 proof	*	*	*	£750
1841 proof	*	*	*	£1650
1859 proof	*	*	*	£2750

HALFPENNIES

1709	£40	£125	£385	*
1733	£25	£120	£250	£450
1733 proof	*	*	£265	£550
1733 silver	*	*	£500	£750
1758	£20	£50	£200	£550
1758 proof	*	*	*	£850
1786	£10	£50	£165	£275
1786 plain edge proof	*	*	£385	£650
1798	£10	£40	£165	£300

Proof halfpenny, 1798

1798 proof	*	*	£225	£450
1798 silver proof	*	*	£1250	£2000
1798 gilt proof	*	*	*	£925
1813	£8	£30	£125	£250
1813 proof	*	*	£185	£375
1813 gilt proof	*	*	*	£875
1839	*	*	£45	£165
1839 proof	*	*	*	*

FARTHINGS

1839	£10	£25	£45	£125
1839 proof	*	*	*	£450
1841 proof only	*	*	*	£1150
1860 proof only	*	*	*	£2850
1864 proof only	*	*	*	£3850

BRITISH PAPER MONEY

Notes signed by the current Chief Cashier, Andrew Bailey, are generally available at a little above face.

Notes prior to his tenure tend to increase in value, especially the very early notes.

Condition is the most important factor in banknote pricing although it is possible to collect an attractive selection in lower grades; some notes are never seen in better than Very Fine.

We have not listed banknotes prior to 1914 as these are scarce and are generally only available in grades up to Very Fine.

Serial numbers with the prefix 'No' are referred to as 'dot' if 'No' is followed by a full stop and 'dash' if followed by a dash.

Reference numbers are according to Vincent Duggleby's *English Paper Money*. The 7th edition (Pam West, 2006) is a must for the collector.

■ TREASURY NOTES

JOHN BRADBURY

			EF	Unc
First issue				
T8	10s	Red on white, six digits	£550	£950
T9	10s	Prefix 'No'	£375	£700
T10	10s	Red on white, five digits	£750	£1250
T1	£1	Black on white, prefix large letters A, B or C	£1200	£2350
T2	£1	No full stop after serial letter	£1700	£3600
T3	£1	Six digits	£600	£950
T4	£1	Large serial number, 'dot' and five digits	£750	£1500
T5	£1	Large serial number, 'dash' and five digits	£800	£1450
T6	£1	Letter, letter, number, number	£750	£1400
T7	£1	Small typeface serial number	*	£5500
Second issue				
T12	10s	Red on white, five digits	£225	£450
T13	10s	Six digits	£300	£600
T11	£1	Black on white	£250	£475
T15	10s	Arabic overprint	£800	£1500
T14	£1	Arabic overprint	£3000	£6000
Third issue				
T16	£1	Green and brown on white	£90	£180
T17	10s	Black serial no with 'dot'	£350	£600
T18	10s	Black serial no with 'dash'	£450	£750
T19	10s	Red serial no with 'dot'	£900	*
T20	10s	Red serial no with 'dash'	£250	£500

NORMAN FENWICK WARREN FISHER

			EF	Unc
First issue, overall watermark				
T25	10s	Green and brown on white, 'dot'	£170	£340
T26	10s	'Dash'	£170	£340
T24	£1	Green and brown on white	£70	£140
Second issue, boxed watermark				
T30	10s	Green and brown on white	£140	£250
T31	£1	'Dot'	£65	£140
T32	£1	Square 'dot'	£180	£330
Third issue, Northern Ireland				
T33	10s	Green and brown on white	£130	£260
T34	£1	'Dot'	£70	£160
T35	£1	Square 'dot'	£220	£350

Unissued notes prepared during World War I

Bradbury				
T21	5s	Deep violet and green on white		*
T22	2s 6d	Olive-green and chocolate on white	from	£7000
T23	1s	Green and brown on white	from	£7500
Warren Fisher				
T27	5s	Violet and green on white	from	£5000
T28	2s 6d	Olive-green and chocolate on white	from	£5000
T29	1s	Green and brown on white	from	£5000

■ BANK OF ENGLAND NOTES

			EF	Unc
CYRIL PATRICK MAHON 1925-29				
B210	10s	Red-brown	£70	£120
B212	£1	Green	£50	£95
B215	£5	Black and white	£320	£540
BASIL GAGE CATTERNS 1929-34				
B223	10s	Red-brown	£40	£80
B225	£1	Green, prefix: letters, number, number	£40	£100
B226	£1	Prefix: number, number, letter	£65	£150
B228	£5	Black on white	£250	£480
KENNETH OSWALD PEPPIATT 1934-49				
B236	10s	Red-brown, prefix: number, number, letter 1st period	£30	£65
B251	10s	Mauve, 2nd period	£25	£50
B256	10s	Red-brown, prefix: number, number, letter, 3rd period	£60	£140
B262	10s	Metal filament, 4th period	£30	£55
B238	£1	Green, prefix: number, number, letter, 1st issue	£20	£45
B249	£1	Blue (shades), 2nd issue	£8	£16
B258	£1	Green, prefix: letter, number, number, letter, 3rd issue	£20	£40
B260	£1	Metal filament, 4th issue	£12	£20
B241	£5	Black on white, one straight edge, three deckled	£130	£320
B255	£5	Straight edges, metal filament, thick paper	£130	£240
B264	£5	Straight edges, metal filament, thin paper	£130	£240

B253	5s	Olive-green on pale pink background	from	£6300
B254	2s 6d	Black on pale blue background	from	£6300

PERCIVAL SPENCER BEALE 1949-55

			EF	Unc
B265	10s	Red-brown, prefix: number, number, letter	£70	£130
B266	10s	Prefix: letter, number, number, letter	£25	£60
B268	£1	Green	£8	£15
B270	£5	Black on white	£140	£220

LESLIE KENNETH O'BRIEN 1955-62

B271	10s	Red-brown, prefix: letter, number, number, letter	£15	£35
B272	10s	Replacement	£90	£200
B286	10s	Red-brown, Queen's portrait	£4	£8
B273	£1	Green	£12	£18
B281	£1	Prefix: letter, number, number, Queen's portrait	£3	£6
B282	£1	Prefix: number, number, letter	£3	£6
B283	£1	Variety letter 'R' (research) on reverse	£350	£600
B284	£1	Prefix: letter number, number, letter	£15	£30
B275	£5	Black on white	£120	£230
B277	£5	Blue, pale green and orange, solid symbols	£35	£80
B280	£5	Symbols for £5 white	£35	£80

JASPER QUINTUS HOLLOM 1962-66

B294	10s	Red-brown, prefix: number, number, letter	£4	£8
B295	10s	Red-brown, prefix: number, number, letter	£4	£8
B288	£1	Green	£4	£6
B292	£1	Green, letter 'G' (Goebel machine) reverse	£6	£14
B297	£5	Blue	£22	£40
B299	£10	Multicoloured brown	£28	£50

JOHN STANDISH FFORDE 1966-70

B309	10s	Red-brown, prefix: number, number, letter	£4	£8
B310	10s	Prefix: letter, number, number, letter	£4	£8
B311	10s	Prefix: letter, number, number	£8	£15
B301	£1	Green	£4	£12
B303	£1	'G' variety	£6	£12
B312	£5	Blue, prefix: letter, number, number	£18	£35
B314	£5	Prefix: number, number, letter	£18	£35
B316	£10	Multicoloured brown	£24	£50
B318	£20	Multicoloured purple	£160	£340

JOHN BRANGWYN PAGE 1970-80

B322	£1	Green, prefix: letter, letter,		

		number, number	£3	£6
B324	£5	Blue	£24	£50
B332	£5	Multicoloured, prefix: letter, number, number, 1st series	£14	£34
B334	£5	L on reverse, signifies lithographic printing	£12	£30
B326	£10	Multicoloured	£24	£55
B330	£10	Prefix: letter, number, number	£20	£40
B328	£20	Multicoloured purple	£40	£80

DAVID HENRY FITZROY SOMERSET 1980-88

B341	£1	Green	£3	£6
B343	£5	Multicoloured, prefix: letter, letter, number, number	£10	£25
B346	£10	Multicoloured, prefix: letter, letter, number, number	£32	£70
B350	£20	Multicoloured purple	£50	£100
B352	£50	Olive green, brown, grey	£70	£140

GEORGE MALCOLM GILL 1988-91

B353	£5	Blue	£10	£25
B357	£5	Multicoloured, Series E	£10	£20
B354	£10	Brown	£18	£35
B355	£20	Multicoloured purple	£50	£100
B358	£20	Multicoloured purple	£35	£80
B356	£50	Olive green, brown, grey	£80	£160

GRAHAM EDWARD ALFRED KENTFIELD 1991-1998

B362	£5	Multicoloured blue	£8	£22
B363	£5	Multicoloured letter, letter, number, number	£8	£22
B364	£5	Multicoloured blue	£12	£20
B360	£10	Multicoloured brown	£25	£60
B361	£50	Olive green, brown, grey	£80	£140
B366	£10	Multicoloured brown	£14	£32
B369	£10	Multicoloured brown	£12	£28
B371	£20	Multicoloured purple	£30	£80
B374	£20	Multicoloured purple	£35	£75
B377	£50	Red	£70	£120

MERLYN VIVIENNE LOWTHER 1999-2004

B380	£5	Multicoloured blue	£6	£12
B393	£5	Multicoloured blue	£6	£10
B395	£5	Multicoloured blue	£6	£8
B382	£10	Multicoloured brown	£14	£23
B388	£10	Multicoloured And 'Co'	£12	£20
B390	£10	Multicoloured The 'Co'	£12	£20
B384	£20	Multicoloured purple	£40	£90
B385	£50	Red	£60	£95
B386	£20	Multicoloured purple	£24	£36

ANDREW JOHN BAILEY 2004-

B398	£5	Multicoloured blue	face	£8
B400	£10	Multicoloured brown	face	£15
B402	£20	Multicoloured purple	face	£28
B405	£20	Adam Smith reverse	face	face
B404	£50	Red	face	face

A new £50 will be issued at the end of 2010 featuring James Watt and Mathew Boulton.

BRITISH STAMP
MARKET VALUES 2011
The essential guide to 170 years of GB stamps

NEW EDITION!

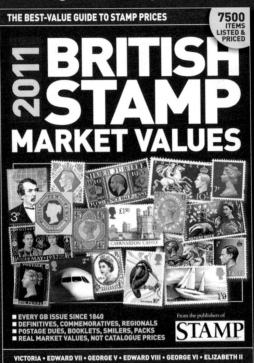

Find out what your collection is really worth

- Newly updated market prices for all GB stamps since 1840
- A uniquely independent value assessment, not a dealer's catalogue
- Collecting and market advice for novice and experienced philatelists
- Written and compiled by the team who bring you Stamp Magazine

CAN YOU AFFORD TO
BE WITHOUT IT?

from the publishers of

STAMP
MAGAZINE

AVAILABLE FROM ALL GOOD BOOKSHOPS
Order online at www.aarons-books.co.uk
Order by phone on 01562 69296
Order by mail from Black Books, PO Box 3875, Kidderminster DY10 2WL.
Price £10.99. Postage and packing is free!

Stamp Magazine

The world's most entertaining and informative magazine for stamp collectors

Every issue includes:

- All the latest news from the world of philately
- In-depth features on classic rarities
- Advice on buying from dealers and on eBay
- The most spectacular pieces sold at auction
- Full details of the newest issues
- Detailed analysis of a popular collecting theme
- Postal history and modern first day covers
- Your questions answered by our experts

Available from newsagents, or visit www.stampmagazine.co.uk